CHAMPIONS

CHAMPIONS
Lou Holtz's Fighting Irish

Updated Edition

by BILL BILINSKI
With a Foreword and Afterword
by Lou Holtz

Diamond Communications, Inc.
South Bend, Indiana

1990

CHAMPIONS
Copyright © 1989, 1990 by Diamond Communications, Inc.

Manufactured in the United States of America

DIAMOND COMMUNICATIONS, INC.
POST OFFICE BOX 88
SOUTH BEND, IN 46624
(219) 287–5008
FAX: (219) 287–5025

Library of Congress Cataloging-in-Publication Data

Bilinski, Bill, 1957–
    Champions : Lou Holtz's fighting Irish / by Bill
  Bilinski : with a foreword and afterword by Lou Holtz. —
Updated ed.
          p.   cm.
      ISBN 0–912083–43–3 : $10.95
      1. Holtz, Lou.   2. Football—United States—Coaches—
Biography.   3. University of Notre Dame—Football.
I. Title.
GV939.H59B55   1990
796.332′092—dc20   90–33900
  [B]   CIP

*To Jolene, my beautiful co-pilot, and
Mom and Dad, the world's best navigators*

Contents

PART THREE: DEFENDING CHAMPIONS— The 1989 Season

Foreword

A lot of things have to combine for a team to win the national championship. Some are obvious: hard work, discipline, dedication, teamwork, skill in the fundamentals. Others are more subtle: the emergence of leaders, finding ways to win even when that day's performance is not as crisp as it should be, the growth of chemistry and confidence, escaping serious injuries, the surprise of young players growing into roles with ability and enthusiasm. And some are intangibles, but no less real—things like spirit, tradition, and the will to win.

Bill Bilinski's book takes the reader from the Miami game in 1985 through the Fiesta Bowl of 1988. Bill is an ideal guide, and a talented writer. . . . As football reporter and assistant sports editor of the *South Bend Tribune*, he has covered not just the games, but the practices and the Notre Dame scene on a daily basis for the last four years. He knows the university, the coaches, and the players and he knows the game of football.

As Bill shows so well, we had a lot of things to do in taking over the program at Notre Dame. When Father Joyce called to offer me the job (and this was before I even knew it was open), he summed it up this way: We run an honest program according to not only the letter but the spirit of the law; you will have nothing to do with admissions; academic demands always come before football; we do not do redshirting per se; you play a very difficult schedule; we have no athletic dorm or training table; and the demands on your time will be unbelievable. Would you like the job?

I didn't feel commissioned to win a national championship; just to build the best football team we could have within the framework and guidelines of the University of Notre Dame. Clearly we had to begin by developing a number of things immediately: we needed more team speed, discipline, and caring; we needed good recruiting and to stress the fundamentals. In the first two years we made progress. But I certainly didn't go into 1988 thinking we'd win the national championship.

One of the things that makes Bill Bilinski's book such an accurate account of what happened is that he wasn't just up in the press box on Saturdays, he was watching our practices and he saw all of the ups and downs firsthand. He saw the unbelievable job our assistant coaches did. Coaching is nothing more than teaching and explaining what you want done and how to do it and then helping the players execute it well. Bill also does a great job of capturing the leadership of our players, their determination, their commitment, and their willingness to accept whatever role was in the interest of the team. Bill is right in singling out the practice on August 29 as the one that exemplified how much this team wanted to excel. From the opening game on, we kept improving. There is such a thin difference between winning and losing at this level of college football that you have to be your best week in and week out. We didn't let the pressure of being on top of the polls get to us.

I am often asked whether there is a special spirit at Notre Dame. In 1936 a judge ruled that there is a Santa Claus and a spirit of Christmas. The spirit of Notre

Dame is the same kind of thing. The minute you make up your mind to believe in it you feel it. As George Connor said, "When you put your uniform on you can feel it and you play for it." I told the squad before the Miami game that if they believed in the coaches, believed in each other, and believed in the Notre Dame spirit, that spirit would carry us through. The rest, as they say, is history.

Bill Bilinski's fine book really captures the magic of an unbelievable season. All Notre Dame fans will enjoy it.

Lou Holtz
Notre Dame
February 1989

Preface

To begin to put this project in focus, I started at the end. Only a few hours after Notre Dame's victory over West Virginia in the Fiesta Bowl, tailback Mark Green was wondering aloud what "all the doubters are thinking now."

I don't know about the rest, Mark, but this one was allowed the opportunity to put the thoughts in print.

On paper in September, there wasn't enough evidence to logically pronounce Notre Dame a contender for a national championship. As I've been reminded on more than one occasion by Lou Holtz—and certainly by his football team in the '88 season—the game of football is not played on paper.

But that's what makes this story more special—amazing in some respects. It's not about tradition and living up to it; it's about creating it. It's also about the formula put in place by Holtz only three years ago, the price paid by some, and the pieces that eventually dropped into place.

The goal of the book is to examine more than the games; it is to explore the retooling of the program, the gradual change in attitude, and the character that made it click. There were few stars, but numerous heroes. It was a team that could balance the fun of the game with the seriousness of the business, and the book is meant to show both sides.

There was so much healthy sports drama. You will read how the coaches saw it develop, how the players lived it, and how others observed it.

I am indebted to many for the final product of *Champions*. In the spring before the championship season, defensive coordinator Barry Alvarez emphasized how enthusiasm can compensate for experience. I hope Jill Langford of Diamond Communications and Jim Langford, director of Notre Dame Press, feel that way. I thank them for the opportunity, their direction, and constant encouragement along the way.

I also am especially grateful to the following: *South Bend Tribune* Sports Editor Bill Moor for his positive influence and valuable input; Lou Holtz and members of his exceptional coaching staff for generosity with their time and true professionalism; John Heisler, who heads the top sports information department in the country, for his valuable assistance; and the players for their openness—and for making it possible.

Bill Bilinski
February 1989

Part One

THE RETURN TO GLORY

"Fiesta" Means "Celebration"

At around 4:15 P.M. on Sunday, January 1, 1989, Notre Dame's football team assembled in a large room of the Sheraton Hotel in Scottsdale, Arizona.

It wasn't feeding time.

In less than 24 hours the Fighting Irish would perform in the biggest game of their lives, the most important football game Notre Dame had played in 11 years, and it was time to apply the game face. Lou Holtz was Mr. Makeup.

He already had pushed, yanked, and dragged a team ahead of its time to an unlikely spot, one step away from a national title. Now it was time to apply the final emotional coat.

Routine is a big part of Holtz's style. With the Fiesta Bowl matchup against West Virginia on Monday, that Sunday was more like a Friday in relation to game week. So Holtz had his players meet in a large room, as he did the day before every game.

Holtz ordered his players to lie back and relax. Then he spoke to them about being positive, about dreaming big things and big plays.

"He'll come in and say, 'You're completely relaxed

and nothing's on your mind but positive thoughts,'" explained senior tailback and tri-captain Mark Green. "He'll talk about the game and thinking through your assignment. You actually think about running through them and having success on every play. . . .

"I consider it part of the program and part of the preparation."

"He kind of puts you in a trance," observed offensive guard Tim Grunhard.

Four months earlier it would have taken an extremely wild imagination to envision Notre Dame playing for a national title. Who would have believed that, predicted it or bet on it? (Mentally blind Notre Dame fanatics who are out of touch with reality, anyway, don't count). "About 400 things have to happen . . . ," Holtz had said back in August.

Amazingly, most of them did; going into the Fiesta Bowl they were only a few short of completing the list and Holtz was just one game from equaling a ritual particular to some great Irish coaches—Knute Rockne, Frank Leahy, Ara Parseghian, and Dan Devine won national titles in their third season.

But even as the Irish lined up for the kickoff the doubts hung around like a low cloud. "I just don't feel very good about this one," reported one sportswriter who had covered the Irish all along the way.

Maybe he had good reason. West Virginia was loaded with talent and size, with a considerable edge in experience as well. No one had contained the Mountaineers' high-powered offense and their blossoming Heisman Trophy candidate at quarterback, Major Harris. They had those 25 fifth-year seniors for a mountain of stability and muscle all over the field—one-third of them bench-pressed 400 pounds or better. Let's see, Notre Dame had three of the former and five of the latter. The Irish had earned their Fiesta Bowl invitation, but did they really belong? Is this where the dream season ended?

West Virginia was like a team groomed for this big payday. Notre Dame was Cinderella trying to beat a 12 o'clock deadline. Of course, no one more than Holtz liked to further that notion. He built the Mountaineers into, well, mountains.

The man likes his underdog role. It's what he was born to, where he has resided most of his life, and where he is comfortable. It's psychological tag. Keep players, coaches, and everyone else involved with the program reaching. It is difficult to define where his sincere fear or respect leaves off and the mental twist begins, but from week to week it worked. Holtz said it was a matter of stating facts, not a snow job. But the fact remains, it always came out top heavy for the opposition. If he can make a country believe that his team's climb is always uphill, as he did for the most part, imagine what he can do with a football team. Holtz seems to be at his best working from that angle. He's had a lot of practice—at William and Mary, North Carolina State, Arkansas, and Minnesota. When it's "us against the world," there are side effects—second efforts, closeness, internal support. And if Notre Dame had anything that stood out in '88, it was a specially developed, durable chemistry.

"I think our players will find that the journey's more enjoyable than the destination," Holtz offered following a good practice late in the season. It was like building a puzzle. The challenge, proving themselves while proving others wrong, was as exhilarating as the view from the top.

Anyway, by game time, the Irish tended to think of themselves as underdogs with something to prove.

"We know we're the underdogs," Grunhard announced.

"I was watching ESPN," Green said, "and everybody they had on was picking West Virginia. We thought, 'We still aren't getting the respect we deserve!' It was a big deal to a lot of guys."

Following the victory over Southern California at the

close of the regular season, strong safety George Streeter remarked, "When we come into the locker room (after a game) we wonder what they're going to say now."

They were a perfect 11–0, had won 1-point and 2-point games, sidestepped three of the top 10 teams in the country along the way, and were ranked No. 1 to the Mountaineers' No. 3, but still felt the world was selling them short. Can Holtz sell or what?

He does that almost as well as he worries. Almost.

When the Irish returned for their first practice two weeks after the season-ending victory over Southern Cal, Holtz was barking and got dramatic.

"It would be a shock to me," he said, "if Tim Grunhard plays." He was frustrated that one mild injury was causing one of his top offensive linemen to take a day off. It didn't help his mood that the other starting guard, Tim Ryan, was out with a virus and quarterback Tony Rice was very erratic. He was walking on eggshells with his fullbacks—one with a tender ankle, another with a bruised knee, and a third with a sore shoulder.

"If you don't practice, you don't get any better," he moaned. "You digress. We're worse off in the offensive line than we were going into the (season-opening) Michigan game."

It seemed like a lot of fuss to make three weeks before the Fiesta Bowl kickoff, but there was the grim reminder of Notre Dame's performance in the Cotton Bowl a year earlier when Texas A & M ran away, 35–10. Holtz has specific daily goals in his head—he is very goal-guided—and if his club falls short, he's no fun to be around.

He appeared more edgy than the previous year, but this was a different team and he was playing for No. 1 for the first time.

There also was the academic schedule. He couldn't practice as much as he wanted (What coach does?) and it was another week before exams would be over and he could have his players for his own. At that point, he started doubling up practices.

Peace of mind didn't improve until the last couple of practice days before he sent his players home for Christmas. His intensity was rubbing off. A couple of scuffles broke out in an afternoon scrimmage in the mud. His club was getting antsy to play. A good sign.

When they regrouped in Arizona the day after Christmas, it was mostly business as usual. They put in a couple of long days of contact, one in which Holtz even sent No. 1 against No. 1, before pulling back.

From Holtz's manner it was obvious he was starting to feel better. "Tony Rice has been throwing very well," he said at a mid-week press conference. He still talked more often about the Mountaineers.

"Nobody has stopped Major Harris. . . . West Virginia is the kind of team that can embarrass anybody. . . . There's no way we can possibly score a lot of points on West Virginia."

West Virginia coach Don Nehlen was caught between Holtz singing his club's praises and Jimmy Johnson yapping that his Miami club should be No. 1 if Notre Dame fell.

"Half the people in the country don't think we should be here and Lou thinks we're so good we shouldn't even play it," Nehlen joked at one press conference. He just didn't think there was much difference between the two teams.

Containing Major Harris—which no one had done, Holtz reminded—was a primary concern. When the Irish won the coin flip, they kicked off anyway and put it in his hands.

On the first series of the game, the Irish hurt him. Inside linebacker Michael Stonebreaker tripped him up and tackle Jeff Alm landed on him, putting a crease in Harris' left shoulder. The damage was minor—he was able to keep playing—but devastating to WVU.

It hindered Harris, who typically had a hand in more than half of the Mountaineers' offense. Nehlen had to do an about face with the game plan. "If he wasn't hurt we probably would have run 10 to 12 more option plays," Nehlen mentioned.

Harris wasn't the only injured Mountaineer; the offense lost guard John Stroia to a concussion and tailback Undra Johnson to a knee injury.

Now the Irish could stack up against the run. Harris was forced into passing situations and the Irish could tee off. It took a quarter for WVU to get its bearings and even manage a first down. By that time the Irish had put 16 points on the board. In five first-half possessions they had scored four times for a 23–6 lead.

There was only one short Mountaineer uprising in the second half. After West Virginia scored to pull within 26–13, Tony Rice made his only mistake of the day, throwing an interception late in the third quarter to give WVU momentum and the ball at the Notre Dame 26.

"Our motto all year was 'Don't flinch,'" said Holtz afterward.

This was prime time. It was a chance for Notre Dame's defense to put it away. In contrast to what might have been the case a few seasons before, the defense smelled opportunity rather than disaster. That's the way the Irish had conditioned themselves to look at it, the way a few of them probably even dreamed about it in the think-session the day before in the hotel.

West Virginia thought the tide had changed, that it was charging. Notre Dame was thinking championship ring. Stop the Mountaineers cold from the 26 and hear the air whistle out of the West Virginia balloons.

On first down Harris was thrown for a 2-yard loss by fifth-year senior, defensive end Darrell "Flash" Gordon, who had fought his way back into a starting role for the Fiesta Bowl.

Then, after throwing an incompletion, Harris dropped back again and was on the run from ends Frank Stams and Arnold Ale. It was Stams who got to him first and wrapped him up along with the game's defensive MVP honor. Stams was another one of those dark horses who came into his own as a senior. One of Holtz's first moves when he took over the program was to move Stams from fullback to defense. In three years Stams had become a first-team All-American.

From first down at the 26 to fourth down at the 40, the Mountaineers came up empty and had to punt. It was the beginning of the end when the Irish offense grabbed the momentum and ran.

Rice led a seven-play, 80-yard touchdown drive, hitting tight end Frank Jacobs on a jump pass from three yards out for the score. Rice then capped off a career day—seven completions for 213 yards and two touchdowns, 75 yards rushing—with a 2-point conversion run. The once-maligned Rice, who started the season five for 21, rose to all the big occasions, but never more artfully than in the Fiesta Bowl. He was named Most Valuable Player going away on a day when he was considered the "other" quarterback.

The Irish reserves closed it out—it was a semi-rout at 34–21—and the celebration was on, marking Notre Dame's first national title since 1977.

For a couple of years Holtz had related how strongly he believes in a weight program—"If we win a big game, I'd like to think our players are strong enough to carry me off the field"—and now was the moment of truth. Holtz got more of a post-game liftoff than carry-off. That about fit in with a magical year. Nothing too pretty.

Only a year earlier, Notre Dame had left the Cotton Bowl a 25-point loser with more questions than answers in its future. Two weeks after the Fiesta Bowl, the Irish were standing on the lawn of the White House Rose Garden, getting a handshake from President Ronald Reagan, "The Gipper" of movie fame.

"I noticed Coach Holtz said Rockne would be proud of this team and I'm sure he would be," said Reagan two days before he was to leave office. "Right now I can't help but think that somewhere, far away, there's a fellow with a big grin and a whole lot of pride in his school who might be thinking to himself, 'Maybe you won another one for the Gipper.'"

They won another one because of their resolve, not because of the Irish luck and ghosts in their corner. It certainly was no gift. West Virginia followed Michigan, Miami, and USC as the fourth Top 10 team to fall to the Irish.

"I thought those three teams were as fine a football team as any we played in any year," Holtz said. "I thought those were some of the best teams ever."

Only against West Virginia had the Irish been favored. The Tuesday following the Fiesta Bowl they were officially crowned national champions.

"There was not that excitement in the locker room after the game," Holtz said. "I think they sort of expected to win and it was sort of a relief when they did."

"We've just had so many big games," Grunhard said of the celebration.

In three years Notre Dame had gone from 5–6, its second consecutive losing season, to 12–0 and its eighth official national championship, more than any other school. It was a glorious start to its second century of football.

Said Holtz, "Now that it's over, I can say they were outstanding competitors. A team that won 12 games—what more could you ask?" Indeed.

For at least a few months, Irish fans would be sated.

But they were heard to say, "Lou, what took you so long?"

Remember the Hurricane of '85?

In November of 1985 Notre Dame closed out its season at a warm-weather site, as it usually does, and closed the book on the tenure of head coach Gerry Faust.

Well, let's be more specific: The book was slammed shut.

This was no emotional farewell, no going-away gift for a departing coach—unless you consider it a gag gift. It was one final stinging slap in the face to pronounce Notre Dame's program officially out of its league.

The Irish were a mess and mopped up by Miami, 58–7, in a piece of surgery that forever branded Jimmy Johnson as a bully, at least in the eyes of a Notre Dame faithful who had had their fill.

A few days earlier, the loyal but unsuccessful servant Faust had accepted his fate and resigned before the axe fell. The mark he left would be forever linked to Miami's mauling. All Faust won over at the end was the sympathy vote. He was the nice guy with no answers for a program that had slipped under his five-year rule to 30-26-1.

Because of his pronounced love for Notre Dame, his absolutely unbridled enthusiasm, and the national acclaim he had brought to Moeller High School in Cincinnati, Faust had been a sentimental favorite when he was hired in 1981 to replace Dan Devine. Notre Dame officials, particularly Rev. Edmund Joyce, who then served as executive vice-president, also had been impressed with the players Faust had sent on to Notre Dame from Moeller. College experience was all Faust was missing. Notre Dame took four out of five and took a big chance.

It was not a chance the Notre Dame powers cared to take the next time.

In his five years the Irish got to only two bowls, neither played on January 1, with a highwater mark of 7–5 in 1983 and '84. But Faust, for a brief moment in 1981, captured the imagination of the country when a team captained by Bob Crable and Phil Carter toppled Louisiana State, 27–9, in Faust's first game at Notre Dame. The Irish climbed to No. 1 and Irish fans were making room in their hearts for another coaching legend. It was back down to earth the following week with a 25–7 thumping at the hands of Michigan, then the start of a recurring nightmare—no comebacks and a lot of excuses. It started with a 1-point loss to Purdue and followed with a 6-point loss to Florida State, 7-point defeat to Southern California and 3-point loss to Penn State. After Miami applied the finishing touches, 37–15, the Irish were 5–6. They'd be in the same hole four years later.

Whoever stepped into Faust's shoes would have his hands full. In Miami on November 30, 1985, in Faust's last trip to the sidelines for Notre Dame, the Irish were dead on arrival and the Hurricanes truly enjoyed the burial.

Faust braved it, accepted it, as his team did. "The game kind of mushroomed," (like the cloud of a nuclear bomb) he said that day. "They started rolling and just kept going. When you lose, it really doesn't matter what the score is. The score doesn't make much difference."

It did that day. It was an indictment against the Irish for how far they had fallen. The Hurricanes didn't mind playing the heckler at all. Defensive back Bennie Blades high-fived a teammate before reaching the end zone on an interception return. Others just pointed fingers and accused the Irish of tossing in the towel and it was difficult to argue, though the Irish at least did do that very well that day.

"Everybody tried to cover it up, but underneath we still had the pressure and the tension," cornerback Mike Haywood said after the game. "There was so much tension, no one had a good week of practice.

"We just never were emotionally into it and once we realized we had a game . . ." he added. "For four years our seniors developed a closeness with the coaches. Coach (Andy) Christoff (defensive coordinator) is more like a friend. It hurts us just as much as it does them when we know they're losing their jobs. It was a real emotional week. Guys came up to me and told me they just couldn't get into it."

"There is no doubt in my mind," quarterback Steve Beuerlein said, "we didn't quit."

It probably hit home hardest with the seniors who were leaving with Faust. "More than anything I wanted to win this one for Coach Faust," said defensive tackle Eric Dorsey, who would become a first-round draft pick of the New York Giants. "I hated to see him leave like that."

"He deserved a win for all the work he's put into the program," added Notre Dame's leading rusher, Allen Pinkett. There was little chance. At that stage confidence was running thin and the direction was at a dead end. Even if the Irish meant well, they didn't have the means.

Miami passed at will and until the final gun. Backup quarterbacks need their work, too, Johnson said. There was a blocked punt recovered in the end zone in the fourth quarter when Johnson claimed that only two men rushed. Notre Dame's special team fiascos had been common enough to make that believable.

That reverse with 1:10 left in the game, though, left a taste that would last like a stale beer. It has yet to be expunged. Miami, and Johnson particularly, took a lot of heat for the nationally televised execution, but the sentiment was clear.

"I don't like all that tradition stuff," Miami's tailback Melvin Bratton remarked then. "I don't like Notre Dame. I hate them."

The feeling seemed to be mutual. Dorsey sent a message by giving quarterback Vinny Testaverde a solid shove long after the whistle had blown following his 1-yard bootleg run for a touchdown in the fourth quarter (Yes, Testaverde was still in). "I'm a sore loser," Dorsey announced. "I didn't care whether the play was dead or not. We got embarrassed . . . If I was on Miami's team and I had the decision to make, I'd tell them to run it up. I don't like Miami and I'm sure they don't like us."

Haywood added, "They're front-runners without class. When they got on top they just tried to score as many points as they could no matter what happened."

Bad Blood, Part I. The honest feelings came pouring out and touched off an intense rivalry. Something big, if not always good, was started that day between the two programs. But massacres sometimes make for good messages and Notre Dame learned it had a long way to go in temperament and talent to touch Miami.

Johnson praised Faust after he had razed Faust and the sincerity of it all was questioned.

"I feel for the man," Johnson said afterward. "I have sympathy. I have a lot of respect for Gerry Faust but we could not let that affect our preparation. We had no control over their emotions. We had to go out and play our game."

On his way to the press conference, Johnson had received word of the criticism aired by CBS-TV's Brent Musburger and analyst Ara Parseghian, the Notre Dame coaching legend. "How many times have they [Notre Dame] done that in the past?" Johnson grumbled.

When all the criticism of the Hurricanes was measured, Notre Dame was pierced by some valid points.

"What is this?" questioned *Miami Herald* Sports Editor Edwin Pope. "Notre Dame or Little Sisters of the Poor?" (It is just as well he didn't answer his own question.)

"Phooey on Notre Dame," he continued.

"Phooey on all those dear Celtic hearts bleeding from coast to coast for the Fighting Irish. . . . Notre Dame was scooping up the cream of America's crop for nearly four decades before the UM even threw up its original Cardboard College.

"And now sympathy stricken souls who have been looking down their noses at Miami throughout modern history want us to feel sorry for Notre Dame not being able to hold up its end."

A direct hit.

The feud was on and Notre Dame's tradition was history. It looked good on the mantel piece but didn't mean much on Saturdays, not to teams with confidence in themselves and the game plan. The Irish had hit rock bottom because they had run out of both.

The game was changing and the Irish weren't. Notre Dame was getting lapped in overall team speed and it was taking its toll. Air Force, with mandatory size restrictions, gave Faust's teams fits and won the last four meetings. Factor in other problems, such as misuse of timeouts and special team confusion, and losses started to add up. Notre Dame finished 5–6 in '85 and Gerry Faust bowed out without a party.

If anyone would have told Pinkett at the start of that year that the Irish would finish with a losing record, "I would have told them they were crazy," he said, following the loss to Miami. "We had 97 percent attendance in the weight room all winter, we had a really good spring, and the guys worked hard all summer and came back stronger and faster."

Things just didn't fall into place.

South Bend Tribune Sports Editor Bill Moor presented a few thoughts on why the well-intentioned Faust strug-led at Notre Dame. He mentioned Faust's handling of the coaching staff and also his inability to change his approach to players older than his Moeller athletes.

"According to too many of his past players," wrote Moor, "he treated them more like boys than young men — and was far too critical after losses."

He was, in some players' terms, more father figure than boss and the relationship didn't work.

In contrast, Lou Holtz doesn't try to play best friend to his players. "It's never been important to him," said Holtz's wife Beth. "He needs their respect. That's been a part of his plan over the years and I know he wouldn't deviate from it . . ."

One of Faust's former players, Tony Hunter, said, "When things were bad at Moeller, he'd say things to players, but there was a limit to how far he went. At Notre Dame, he went over the limit when the tension mounted."

Unlike what Holtz did with some of Faust's recruits, Faust was never able to make the players he inherited from Dan Devine's successful tenure feel comfortable.

"I was under the impression that to a large extent we (Devine recruits) were at fault," said defensive back Dave Duerson, who went on to become an All-Pro with the Chicago Bears.

"Motivation was sadly lacking," senior strong safety George Streeter told Ken Murray of the *Baltimore Evening Sun.* "Guys felt they were helpless. I'd hear a senior say the system is messed up. I'm not sure if it was because of the system or the pressure on him to win. But guys felt like it was a no-win situation. There was a lack of trust in the coaching staff."

Devoted to his job, Faust never lacked effort, only the tools, in a job considered the most pressurized in college football.

It was difficult to imagine then (although maybe not

too unlikely for Notre Dame fans who seem to consider championship football teams to be a birthright) that in three years it would be Notre Dame nosing in and stopping Miami from a second straight national title. Some will call that justice.

Miracle is more like it.

Imagine Lou Holtz watching on television as his future team was skinned in Miami. He would be left to pick up the pieces.

"I prefer to look at the positives," Holtz said afterward. "We do have to improve in a lot of areas and I think it could be a rallying cause. 'Remember the Alamo' is one cause."

Two days after the debacle in Miami, Holtz met his players for the first time. They were dragging, too casual for Holtz's liking, and he brought them to attention with a spicy speech.

"The players sat anywhere they wanted in meetings under Coach Faust," George Streeter recalled. "We were slouched in our seats, legs over the backs of chairs. It showed a lack of respect.

"Coach Holtz comes in and says, 'First of all, I want you to sit up straight at attention and look at my eyes.' Just like that, 100 players sit up at attention and look at this guy right away."

They must have thought they had just joined the army when Holtz told them what was in store for them, including the 6 A.M. winter conditioning program. He reemphasized the chain of command and who pulled it. He also circulated a lengthy questionnaire to get a feel for what he had to work with in the seasons ahead.

"I only found one misspelled word and no grammatical errors," cracked Holtz. "I did not run across an athlete who was not happy that he came to Notre Dame."

He did find out that there were more quarterbacks than defensive linemen on scholarship at the time. He rolled up the sleeves and went to work.

"One of the first things he did was pass out T-shirts

that said 'TEAM' with 'me' in small letters underneath it," remembered linebacker Wes Pritchett. "We had much better unity than before he got here."

Miami had laid bare every weakness the Irish had defensively and that concerned Holtz more than any other single problem. Foge Fazio, the former Pittsburgh head coach, joined the staff as defensive coordinator and Holtz endeared himself to the community by bringing back Joe Yonto—one of the valuable assistants and local favorites from the Parseghian-Devine era—after he had been placed on desk duty when Faust took over.

Next step: Pick a quarterback.

It was a particularly anxious time for Steve Beuerlein. He had heard of Holtz and his reputation for using quarterbacks who could move. Beuerlein was more likely to anchor himself into the pocket. But he gave it his best shot. He shed some pounds, worked with a running coach, then found out Holtz would go with his strength. The Irish had some good receivers like Tim Brown, Milt Jackson, and Alvin Miller on the perimeter and Beuerlein had a good arm. He also had the right temperament to hold up to Holtz and hold off a challenge that spring and pre-season from Terry Andrysiak.

The Irish also didn't have much returning in the way of a backfield with heir-apparent Hiawatha Francisco and backup Alonzo Jefferson recovering from injuries. Holtz moved Mark Green from flanker to tailback and made one of his two projected fullback recruits a tailback for support. Holtz felt it would be easier for Anthony Johnson to adjust to Notre Dame and college life since he was from South Bend and Johnson became a major contributor at tailback, a starter from the fourth through 10th games. Holtz kept California native Braxston Banks at fullback where he could play a reserve role to Pernell Taylor and Tom Monahan.

In Holtz's first game with the Irish, they fell by a point, 24–23, to Michigan when a controversial call went against them. It started a season of near misses when they lost five games to good teams by a total of 14 points, including a 5-point loss to eventual champion Penn State.

The last of the gut-twisters came at LSU in the 10th game of the season. They lost by two points, 21–19, because they shot themselves in the foot—once they came up empty on first and goal from the 2. Another time fate intervened with a roundhouse. Before the end of the first half, John Carney nailed a 49-yard field goal, but it was nullified by a LSU penalty before the snap. "Isn't that crazy?" said Holtz, who knew what crazy felt like at that point. When his team had come up short again he didn't know what to say. "You've got to be kidding," he mumbled. . . . "Unbelievable," he added. . . . Then "This is getting ridiculous."

Where was all that Irish luck Notre Dame teams were supposed to have and about which Holtz had heard so much?

"It will be there," he said with a half-smile. "When that sucker finally comes around, it will be unbelievable."

The Irish were just learning to walk again, but the old habits died hard and they kept tripping over them. In the close calls there was no confidence on which to rely.

"Confidence comes from execution," Holtz said, "execution comes from good practices, good practices come from concentration, and concentration comes from a cause."

Confidence took time to create and the Irish hadn't had enough of it. Going into that final game, all four Irish victories had been blowouts—over Purdue, Air Force, Navy, and Southern Methodist. The tough losses came against Michigan, Michigan State, Pitt, Alabama, Penn State, and LSU. "There was some talent there," said Fazio after the year. "If we would have had them a little longer . . ."

One early victory might have turned things around, but for the first time since 1888 Notre Dame would suffer consecutive losing seasons. They had been good enough to give themselves a chance in the final minute against everybody, except Alabama as Cornelius Bennett and company rocked them, 28–10.

Then came a shock. Three hundred and sixty-four days AM (after Miami), the Irish went to Southern Cal with nothing on the line and a losing season locked up. It was only after they fell 17 points down that they learned how far they had come. It could have been a blowout for Southern Cal. Instead it was a rebirth for Notre Dame.

John Carney's field goal with no time left capped an 18-point fourth quarter and clinched a 38–37 victory to set off a wild celebration. It also planted a seed.

"I don't know what it is about this team," Beuerlein said, "but it refused to roll over and play dead. We've never given up. We knew that would finally pay off."

Both teams made it worth the price of admission, providing one of the all-time classics in the lengthy series. The Irish had fallen behind, 20–9, at halftime when Don Shafer booted a 60-yard field goal as time ran out. There was no indication the Irish could stop the USC offensive front. The gap grew to 30–12 at one point when a USC drive was kept alive by a personal foul—roughing the kicker by Skip Holtz, the coach's son, on a Trojan punt.

The Irish defensive front was ailing, with Wally Kleine hanging on despite a badly bruised shoulder, and both Mike Griffin and Tom Gorman forced to the sidelines by injuries. With the Trojans running at will on the small Notre Dame reserves, 290-pound offensive lineman Marty Lippincott was sent in to help stop the flow. Among the many big plays was an Irish defensive stand in the fourth quarter on fourth and less than a yard from the Irish 5. Quarterback Rodney Peete sneaked and the ailing Kleine made a quick stop. But it still appeared that he had it. The officials said no. It was cause for celebration in itself—Irish breaks have been rare in the LA Coliseum.

"I not only thought I had made the first down," Peete

said, "but I also thought I made it by about a yard and a half. Then an official marked it as losing yardage. It was a very bad call, the worst I've ever seen. They didn't even measure it. Then I lost my cool."

Peete's unsportsmanlike conduct gave the Irish 15 yards and initiated an 80-yard drive, sparked by Beuerlein's 49-yard pass to Tim Brown, and climaxed with his toss to fellow-Californian Braxston Banks for the final five yards. Another big play followed when tight end Andy Heck, then carrying 235 pounds instead of the 270-plus he did as a senior tackle, caught a Beuerlein pass and fought off two USC defenders to reach the end zone for the 2-point conversion.

The Irish still were down by two with 4:24 to play, but the Trojans had to punt it away in three plays after Mike Kovaleski made the critical third-down, short-yardage stop. Tim Brown made the last part easy, returning a punt 56 yards to the USC 16. The Irish kept it on the ground from there, getting it all the way to the 1. They let the clock wind down and just got to the officials in time, getting the timeout with two seconds to play.

First Notre Dame called the timeout, then USC called a timeout. When it was time to play, CBS was still on a commercial break and missed the kick. Carney didn't. He had had an extra point blocked earlier, but he hit the 19-yarder high and clean. The picture of seniors Beuerlein and Carney embracing and the Irish coaching staff racing out on the field to join in the celebration was worth a few thousand words.

Carney had had a brilliant career with a record-setting 21 field goals, but had missed against Michigan and Pittsburgh, both 1-point losses earlier that year.

Beuerlein's career nearly ended on the sidelines when Holtz yanked him after Louis Brock intercepted a pass and returned it 58 yards for a touchdown. Beuerlein, who had thrown 119 passes without an interception in one stretch, got a second chance and threw for 254 yards and four touchdowns, an Irish record.

"We've beaten them (USC) four times and that's something no one can ever take away from us," Beuerlein said. "This eases a lot of pain."

"When it started to get bad, we started playing for pride," said linebacker Dave Butler, playing his last game. "We were digging in and digging in and then we thought 'Hey, we've got a chance.'

"It's going to help (the program) a lot. They're going to go from here. I've already invited everybody to my first tailgate party next year."

Mark Green, getting his fourth start of the year at tailback, responded with 119 yards in 24 carries and earned Holtz's respect. The job would be his the following fall, with Anthony Johnson going back to fullback.

"We've been so frustrated," Holtz said. "Every time we'd get close, somebody would kick sand in our face. . . .

"I can't think of a finer way to end the season. We could have easily been 10–1, but overall we played better than I had any right to expect. Our players never quit."

Beuerlein, Notre Dame's all-time passing leader, had come into his own as a senior under Holtz's drilling and varied offense, and Tim Brown made his play for the following pre-season's Heisman hype with 252 all-purpose yards (89 receiving, 10 rushing, 97 kickoff returns, 56 punt returns) against USC. It was another 5–6 season, but there was renewed hope and something on which to build. Holtz could make an offense sing—he coaxed an impressive 411.6 yards a game from the Irish offense that first year—but defensively, he needed more speed.

And even though the overall play was encouraging, the program's second straight losing season raised some doubts about a full and complete recovery in the near future. If a Holtz-coached team finished 5–6 . . .

The schedule made it look improbable if not impossible. The four previous champions—Penn State, Oklahoma, Brigham Young, and Miami—had had accommodating schedules with some lightweight opponents spaced around some of the heavyweights. Notre Dame played two of the academy teams every season, but even they were beginning to get a lot of mileage from new coaches and wishbone offenses to become competitive. Annually, the Irish played three straight Big Ten teams, independents like Pitt, Miami, and Penn State, and a Pac-10 power like USC. There was no time to heal or look ahead.

There was another lingering question—had Notre Dame's policy of not allowing wholesale redshirting caught up with them? Most of the Irish opponents could afford to take the bulk of an incoming freshman class, put it in the weight room, and watch it grow. Except for special cases, the Irish allow their athletes just four years to practice instead of five. For an offensive lineman, a year can make a big difference.

"Eleven times a year—12 times hopefully—I wish we redshirted," Holtz said. "But it doesn't blend in with Notre Dame's philosophy or its purpose.

"People have five classes and they mature and grow and develop," he added, explaining the advantages. "We have four classes. You need three classes to win; and when people redshirt, they have five classes to draw three."

The hurdles didn't change. But Holtz was able to change the effect.

With the limitations, Notre Dame must grab its fair share of the small number of ready-made recruits who can come in and play. Without an extra season to build a player, ND has less margin for error. Given the reputation, Holtz's machine, and his gift of gab, the Irish should continue to hold their own in the recruiting race.

"There are a lot of differences, but I find it workable," Holtz said. "I could be tongue-tied and still recruit at Notre Dame."

Along the way, Holtz had to learn to accept the fact that his football team wasn't always his football team.

"At other places I've coached, the players were like in-dentured servants. Here I have them for three hours a day or whatever and that's it. The players belong to the university. There is an image and philosophy that Notre Dame has and the football team has to reflect that philosophy."

In his second season at Notre Dame, Holtz's system began to take hold. He had to replace a quarterback during his second spring practice and Terry Andrysiak had the inside track after battling Beuerlein for a couple of seasons. Defensive linemen Wally Kleine and Robert Banks left a couple of holes with their graduation and the search for someone to replace John Carney began immediately. Their strength, just about all of it, was in the offensive line with four fifth-year seniors, including captains Chuck Lanza at center and Byron Spruell at tackle.

In the opener at Michigan, placekicker Ted Gradel hit a 44-yard field goal to alleviate one concern and Andrysiak was superb, connecting on 11 of 15 for 137 yards and one touchdown to Tim Brown. The catch was for the highlight films and kicked off his bid for a Heisman Trophy. In the first quarter Notre Dame faced a second and goal situation from the 11. Andrysiak got plenty of time and floated a pass toward Brown. It probably was not a wise decision but the confidence Andrysiak had in Brown was showing. Brown's athletic ability took over. He was well covered in the corner of the end zone, but outjumped Erik Campbell, and Allen Bishop then held on as he was sliding out of bounds.

"I didn't know there was a guy behind me," Brown said after the game. "After I found that out, I couldn't believe he threw it." Brown later got used to it. Defensively, the Irish gave up a lot of yards, but recovered three fumbles and picked off four passes in a 26–7 victory. They had erased the flavor of the previous year's 1-point loss and handed a Bo Schembechler team its first opening-season loss at home.

"I don't know what would have happened had we not won this game," said Holtz. "The ante they've put up since last season and then through pre-season practice was very steep."

Tim Brown reached the summit the following week against Michigan State, when he returned consecutive Spartan punts for touchdowns in a 31–8 Notre Dame blowout against a team that would go on to win the Big Ten and Rose Bowl. Hello Heisman! Defensively, the Irish were better, limiting the MSU rushing attack to under 100 yards while recovering four turnovers.

After a victory over Purdue, the turnovers didn't come as easily in the rain at Pittsburgh and neither did tackling Craig "Ironhead" Heyward. He rushed for 132 yards and two touchdowns as Pitt put 27 points on the board before the Irish scored. Andrysiak went down with a broken collarbone just before the end of the first half and, suddenly, the offense was in the hands of sophomore Tony Rice. He almost engineered a miracle. The Irish came back to within 30–22 and recovered an onside kick with a minute to go. They ran out of downs at the Pitt 42. It was another indication, similar to the victory at USC, that the Irish would no longer be cashing in the chips when they were down. In the hole, 27–0, at the half without their starting quarterback, they still managed to give the Panthers a scare. "Three scores and a big play from our defense," said Holtz, "I thought we could come back." His confidence was rubbing off.

The Irish went on a streak, almost coasting through five straight, including victories over USC and Alabama. Two regular-season games to go and they could still harbor hopes of a national title. They went up in smoke at frigid Penn State when some critical mistakes and Blair Thomas got the best of them in a 21–20 loss. Just before the end of the half, Notre Dame got the ball to the Penn State 3-yard line when Holtz inserted freshman backup quarterback Kent Graham. He tried to flip to tight end Andy Heck and the pass was intercepted. Rice had yet to show much touch so Holtz went with the 6-5 Graham, who had been most efficient at running the play in practice. Considering the numbing weather conditions, it seemed an odd move; but even after the error, Holtz defended it as the right play and the right player.

The Irish did make a run, scoring with 31 seconds to go, but they had to win to keep their dreams alive and attempted a 2-point conversion. Rice was shut down on a rollout and the Notre Dame party was over. Penn State caught the Irish defense on a very bad day, and Thomas rushed for 214 yards in 35 carries. Notre Dame's lack of depth defensively may have caught up with it. Inside linebackers Wes Pritchett and Ned Bolcar, for example, were going most of the way and were ailing enough late in the season that they were held back in several practices.

In the following season, when Michael Stonebreaker joined the middle linebacking corps, Pritchett acknowledged, "I think it will be an advantage for us to have Ned, Mike, and myself at the linebacker spots. Ned and I went all the way almost every week. By the end of the year, you start to feel it. You don't realize the toll it takes, but looking back it took something out of us to be on the field that much."

After the loss to Penn State, an excruciating defeat considering the stakes going into the game, Notre Dame officials and Holtz had to grin and bear it—or at least try—while they accepted a bid to meet Texas A & M in the Cotton Bowl. It was the first major bowl bid for the Irish since Dan Devine took his last team to the Sugar Bowl in 1980 to face Georgia. The Irish were in no mood to celebrate. It was almost as if the season ended that day.

A week later it was back to Miami for another stroll down misery lane with the country's best team. The wear and tear emotionally, as much as physically, was showing. The Irish were in no condition for a payback and swallowed a bitter pill, 24–0. A collapse in the Cotton Bowl to Texas A & M, 35–10, wrapped up a disappointing finish to a once promising season.

"There are a lot of questions at Notre Dame right now," Holtz remarked the day after, "but I feel there are some answers here too.

"A team can take disappointing losses like these last three and bounce back higher."

Funny you should say that, Lou.

"A Rockne Sort of Guy"
—*Gene Corrigan on Lou Holtz*

Fourth down, 8-yard line, six points down, 10 seconds to play. You make the call. Sprintout? Sweep? Option? Tight-end drag?

Try a fullback dive. Lou Holtz made the call 14 years ago when he was head coach at North Carolina State and his club was trying to rally against Virginia.

Touchdown!

The moment stuck with then-Virginia Athletic Director Gene Corrigan, who would eventually come to Notre Dame to replace the legendary Ed "Moose" Krause as AD. As much as it hurt his team, Corrigan couldn't help but admire the decision.

"Their fullback was in the end zone before our guys knew what happened. I thought 'What a gutty play,'" recalled Corrigan, now commissioner of the Atlantic Coast Conference. "A guy's got to have a lot of confidence in himself to make a call like that."

There's always that element of surprise surrounding Lou Holtz, whether it's in what he says, his personnel decisions, or his play selection. The impression Holtz made that day at Virginia remained in the back of Corrigan's mind, though it wasn't Corrigan's first encounter with Holtz. Corrigan had known Holtz when he was head coach at William and Mary and had even recommended him for the post at NC State.

"Lou always had a way of moving the football and scoring points and the guy is just very bright," Corrigan added.

When Gerry Faust resigned after five years as Notre Dame's head football coach, Corrigan knew whom he wanted. Then-Executive Vice-President Rev. Edmund Joyce, who had known Holtz through NCAA committee work, agreed he was the right man. He was Catholic, had no skeletons, and his most celebrated coaching victory—a 31–6 victory over Oklahoma in the Orange Bowl while he was at Arkansas—came after he had suspended three of his top players.

His flashy personality (how many football coaches are magicians?), considered by some to be a bit out of character for Notre Dame, didn't deter Corrigan. "Hey, Lou's a Rockne sort of guy," Corrigan said then. "He's glib, he's clever, and he knows how to motivate."

Also, to an extent, the flashiness of a Holtz team begins and ends with his personality. His small-town roots and ideals have stuck. Notre Dame does not wear names on the back of the jerseys—that's another Holtz nudge to promote the team element—and Holtz didn't keep any green dye in his back pocket to spring any surprises on his players. In fact, before the Miami game, he was getting asked so often about the gimmicks he had planned to heighten the emotion of his club that he announced four days before the game that his club would not be turning to green on Saturday. There was no special Fiesta Bowl insignia attached to Irish blue jerseys in Tempe. It was meant, in part, as a reminder that it was just another football game. "We've tried to look at it that way all year," Holtz explained then. "If you keep thinking that you want something so bad, you tend to get tight, you get nervous, and you become afraid of failure."

Holtz plus a fundamental approach? Doesn't seem to add up, does it? Holtz, the enigma.

Before anyone was hired to replace Faust, Corrigan sought the advice of former Irish coaching great, Ara Parseghian. He emphasized to Corrigan that his own 14 years of head coaching experience prior to coming to Notre Dame had been vital to surviving the pressures. Holtz, who had 16 years at four different institutions behind him, in contrast to Faust who had none, had a good idea about the pressures. Ara gave Holtz a strong vote of confidence.

"Nobody is neutral about Notre Dame," Holtz said. "Either they love the place or they have a tendency to feel that Notre Dame is too lucky, or they get too much publicity, or they're overrated. You have those two factions."

And the coach goes about his business in the eye of the storm.

"No. 1, which we thought was important, is that we could get him," said Corrigan of selecting Holtz. "He wanted the job."

Holtz said he had always wanted the job. He went to St. Aloysius Grade School, was taught by the sisters of Notre Dame, and grew up with the Notre Dame Victory March pounding in his head. He didn't get sick of it. "Those were my formative years and those were the years when Notre Dame never lost a game."

"Where do you go from here?" Holtz repeated a question one day. "As my mother said, 'From Notre Dame, you go directly to heaven.'"

His fervor for Notre Dame was pretty clear and two days after Faust resigned, Holtz was introduced as Notre Dame's 25th head coach. At the time, Holtz had been in the process of resurrecting Minnesota from the pits: The Gophers were wallowing in a 17-game Big Ten losing streak when he stepped in. He created instant life, stopped the bleeding and, in his second season there, Minnesota was on its way to the Independence Bowl. It's a good thing. Holtz had an escape clause written into his contract with Minnesota that, if Notre Dame called, he would be available. He later acknowledged that it was contingent on the Gophers being invited to a bowl game.

"In that short time Lou energized the state of Minnesota," remarked Harvey Mackay, former president of the University of Minnesota, upon Holtz's departure. "We're saddened that he's leaving but if we had it to do all over again, we would have taken him even if it was just for one year. He laid a solid foundation. . . . The people of Minnesota can't be upset with him because he was up front and honest with us. He never tried to hide anything."

Frank Broyles, athletic director at Arkansas, said upon Holtz's hiring by ND: "Through the years he's had a drive to achieve higher goals. He's never satisfied."

Most coaches are dealt reclamation projects when they're hired. That is generally why they are hired. Holtz got an early lesson on that fact. After a particularly successful season at North Carolina State (he went to four straight bowls while there), he went to his boss (former Athletic Director Willis Casey) to see about a raise for himself and the staff. He mentioned the tickets sold, the games won, the bowl appearance. "He told me that's what I was hired to do," Holtz recalled. End of conversation.

Notre Dame was not scared off by Holtz's number of coaching stops. The record spoke for itself—19 years, five teams, 14 bowls. Every college team he took over was in a bowl game by the second season, including a William and Mary team that went to the Tangerine Bowl with a losing record because of its conference play.

Holtz's pro experience, on the other hand, was less than memorable and closer to miserable—less than one full season and a 3–10 record with the New York Jets. He admitted the mistake, bowed out, and went off to Arkansas. For a guy who thrives on control and close touch with his program, the pro style wasn't his cup of tea.

In a *Los Angeles Times* article, he relived the rude awakening:

"One of the first things I wanted to do when I took the Jets job was to talk to (Joe) Namath. I called the Jets' office and asked a secretary for Joe's phone number. I was told no one had it, that it was classified information. She suggested I call Joe's lawyer, Jimmy Walsh. I called him and asked for Joe's number. He said he couldn't give it to me. I said, 'Oh?'

"He told me if I wanted to talk to him, I should leave my number and if Joe could get back to me, he would."

That must have created some combustion. You might say Holtz was a little more comfortable with the levels of authority and order in the college game. What else could you expect from someone who numbered Woody Hayes among a list of impressive role models? He handled the defensive backs at Ohio State when they won a national championship in 1968.

"I hate losing," Holtz said. "You let it ruin your day, you let it ruin your week. You can't sleep, you can't eat. I hate to lose. . . . Oh, I hate to lose."

At anything. In his first spring at Notre Dame he was a member of a Bookstore Basketball team, the campus-wide outdoor tournament staged each year, such a large part of university activities it even cuts into football practice time. Well, Holtz hadn't touched a basketball in some time, so he took off for a few minutes, got a ball from the equipment manager, and put in some practice time.

Holtz hates to lose so much that putting in 12-hour-plus days are more the rule than the exception. When he was asked about the feeling on campus during the week of the Miami game, he said he was the worst person to ask. He didn't run into many people by arriving at the office before daylight, heading to the practice field, then going back to the office, and leaving well after dark. His secretary will vouch for the hours.

Born in Follansbee, West Virginia, on January 6, 1937,

and reared in East Liverpool, Ohio, Holtz had a mind made for football and a body that could get lost in a crowd of two. His weight in season will dip below 150 pounds and the post-season banquet circuit doesn't add much. Little about him physically announces that he is a football coach.

"We're continually stressing to our players that they've got to become stronger. But I tell them not to use my physique as a guide," he quips.

Size didn't keep Holtz from playing—or at least trying—at East Liverpool and then at Kent State, where he earned a letter as a center-linebacker. To continue to play a game—a violent game—in which he was physically overmatched says a good deal about his inherent mental toughness. He was locked into a role in the background and still kept plugging away. It is an axiom that non-stars tend to make the better coaches, in part because they understand what it means to have nothing come easily.

"I just think you have to have the ability to get off the ground, brush yourself off, and not wallow in self-pity—and look at where you're at," Holtz says.

"Show me anyone who's successful and I'll show you someone who has overcome adversity."

Most of the time it seems like Holtz laughed his way through it. He probably knocked down a lot of barriers with his humor and it has been a constant companion for a long time. He has a number of theories on why it developed. He'll attribute part of it to an insecurity from being small and a poor athlete and student. Maybe another portion of it grew out of the times—the end of World War II and the generally good outlook on life people had at that time. He mentions being the middle child and using humor to attract attention. There also was the influence of his uncle, Lou Tychonoveich, 10 years older, who befriended him. Some of Uncle Lou's wit rubbed off on his nephew.

Looking back Holtz said he was dull and never had a

date in high school, but one of his early nicknames was "Sunshine," so some of those lines just have to come naturally. Everybody remembers someone from school who just had a knack for getting a laugh. Holtz probably did. And still does. It served him well when he was trying to drum up fan support at William and Mary, North Carolina State, and Minnesota.

No chapter on Holtz should go without mention of one of his better lines. After Arkansas had clinched a bid in the Orange Bowl, Holtz was asked what he thought about the students throwing oranges on the field. "I'm glad we're not going to the Gator Bowl," he answered.

Maybe one more. The best way to stop Rodney Peete: "Graduation."

Humor is energy, sometimes a lifeline, and for Holtz it helped pump some pizazz into areas where the product of football wasn't selling. Humor also is in demand on the banquet circuit. A speaker can motivate all he wants, but a little laugh makes the whole thing go down easier. A man who has his own motivational tape and can sell it to companies for more than $500 should know. But as well as Holtz can draw a smile, he can also let out a good laugh—at himself.

You've heard the one about Lou Holtz, head coach at Notre Dame: "I'm 5-feet-10 inches, weigh 152 pounds, speak with a lisp, and appear afflicted with a combination of scurvy and beriberi." Add a hint of drawl, hands in the pocket, and a shrug of the shoulders and that line could set anybody up.

His self-deprecating humor in regard to his playing career enlivened a press conference before the Fiesta Bowl. West Virginia coach Don Nehlen quarterbacked three of Doyt Perry's great Bowling Green teams in the late 1950s and Holtz said he had a chance to meet Nehlen then, for the first time, "because he ran out of bounds at the bench where I was sitting." Holtz could not have been the bad athlete he makes himself out to be. Bad athletes don't play college football. Holtz also played a little baseball and shoots a fair game of golf.

Holtz went to Iowa to get his master's degree in arts and education and served as the freshman coach. He was an assistant for eight years, at William and Mary, Connecticut, South Carolina, and Ohio State. He was the hustler he demands in his own assistants now. He came under the influence of such respected coaches as Forest Evashevski, Paul Dietzel, Rick Forzano, and Hayes.

And he became driven by his own personal goals.

At the age of 28, he was hired at South Carolina by Marvin Bass and, one month later, Bass was on his way to the Canadian Football League. Holtz was unemployed. Tough times. Adversity. Out of work and with his wife expecting their third child, Holtz hit a crossroads. He picked up a pen and paper and started fiddling, dreaming big things and listing things he wanted to accomplish, and things he just wanted to do for the fun of it. It was Holtz's release and became his focus. He had 107 down on paper when his wife suggested making it 108 — "Why not add getting a job."

Paul Dietzel, the new head coach at South Carolina, covered No. 108, but Holtz had to accept a pay cut. He stuck it out and in two years was coaching the defensive backs for national champion Ohio State.

By now, Holtz has checked off over 80 of his goals, including meeting the president at the White House, appearing on the Tonight Show, playing on the world's 50 greatest golf courses, and, in January after winning the title, touring the submarine USS Cincinnati. Last summer he crossed out a tough one with a hole-in-one. Winning a national championship looked easy next to that one.

Holtz would have made a good reporter. He has never been afraid to ask questions. When he was just getting started in the business, he went to then-Texas coach Darrell Royal to ask him a few questions. Once he got into his office he unraveled a list of 80 questions. Royal had to cancel a golf game, but Holtz had something to add to his foundation. Many of Royal's points in organization and approach were made part of his philosophy.

"One thing that helps Lou is that he's a listener," Frank Broyles has said. "When there's something to be learned, he's not afraid to sit back and take it in. The resources he has are always on the upgrade, you'll never catch him sliding back a step. . . .

"Why did he succeed? He knows how to manage people just like in any other business. How does he manage people? It comes down to motivation. He's got that special touch."

"I ask everybody questions," Holtz says. "I never learned anything by talking."

When he was recruiting Lindsay Knapp, an offensive lineman out of Deerfield, Illinois, Holtz said he asked Knapp's coach, Paul Adams, what it was that made his high school teams so successful. He told Holtz, "We don't get bored watching the same play over and over." Holtz thought that fit. Holtz, innovative and unpredictable with his offense, believes there's nothing better for a team than practice and repetition. He felt one of the most important factors in the improvement of Tony Rice as a passer over the year was in simplifying the system — breaking the passing game down to a few chosen plays, then working them to death.

Holtz will tap anyone's brain. His ego doesn't appear ever to get in the way of asking for advice or ideas. Before the Irish were to depart for Southern Cal to face the No. 2 team in the country in the 11th game of the 1988 season, Holtz put in a phone call to Miami coach Jimmy Johnson, whose team had fallen out of the country's top spot when Notre Dame handed the Hurricanes a 31–30 defeat in October. Now it was November and Miami had just gone on the road to crush LSU, 44–3. When Holtz wanted to get a few ideas about winning on the road, he put aside the intensity of a rivalry that had developed with Miami and dialed Jimmy Johnson, whose teams did it better than any club in college football. Over a five-year stretch, Miami had gone 24–2 in regular-season games away from the Orange Bowl.

Johnson shared some thoughts: "Basically, it's a matter of the players developing so much pride in showing opposing crowds what they can do. . . . You know, Lou, a lot of teams can play at home. A team's own crowd bails it out of a lot of psychological letdowns. But you don't have that on the road, and an average team exaggerates its letdowns. So it takes a team that's strong mentally to overcome it, to turn it back around."

No one knows how much it helped, but the Irish took control of USC from the start in the 27–10 victory. Everyone figured that must have been a pretty tough phone call to make. Asked about it, Holtz didn't think it was a big deal. "I talk to a lot of coaches," he said.

Coaches are not an easy breed to decipher and Holtz falls right in line, maybe at the front of it. He admits to being a very private person, also one who is "very complex"—maybe because of all of the weapons he has at his disposal. One minute you call him a disciplinarian, the next you're calling him a father figure. As quickly as his temper can multiply the tension on a practice field, his sense of humor can cut through and dissolve it. There were signs of that every day during his first season at Notre Dame when he was breaking in Steve Beuerlein, then a senior. Holtz likes his quarterbacks to be able to move and Beuerlein, though he improved in the season under Holtz, just wasn't going to win a lot of dance contests. He had a great arm and wound up as Notre Dame's all-time passing leader, but it took some time getting down the occasional option Holtz wanted to run. After being verbally ripped for days for a wrong read, or just a slow one, Beuerlein finally got it just right. Perfect. Holtz feigned a fainting spell and lay sprawled on his back on the turf, arms out from his side. Beuer-lein, angry and frustrated a minute earlier, was wearing a grin from ear to ear.

"He was very tough on me in the practices," Beuerlein agreed. "But just when things would get pretty tense between us, he had a one liner at just the right moment to take the heat off the situation."

Holtz can be tough on everyone on a football field. In trying to trim the number of penalties—"I've never been anywhere else where we had more than the opposition," he noted—he has brought in officials to his practices. When he gets going, he'll even argue with them on a call they make there. Most people would consider that intense.

Holtz hasn't grown any bigger or stronger since his football-playing days, but he still likes to mix it up on the field. He believes in visual aids—with him as the aid. He broke a finger a couple of years ago while catching a punt in practice and he'll run an end's route or throw a pass to make his point. He's very fussy about the execution, a perfectionist. "You don't need big plays to win," he will tell his players often. "You need to eliminate the bad ones." He figures a player gets himself into the deepest trouble when he's trying to do too much. He can do without the heroes and stars. Give him the guy that understands his responsibilities and executes then watch things fall into place.

One of the things Gerry Faust expected—something a number of coaches expect—was for his players to run on to the practice field and run off the practice field. Holtz looks at it differently. They can't talk very well when they're huffing and puffing. He wants his club shuffling out together, talking, getting to know one another just a little better. It's not a major point of his coaching style, just a little detail that might add an ounce or two of morale and unity to the club. Besides, the players might as well conserve the energy for the field. They usually need it.

Holtz sets a rapid pace. He said the only time he'll make use of a coaching tower is to jump off. A golf cart, where he can store his pipe and tobacco, is about his only concession to making it easier to oversee the whole operation. But once practice starts he's seldom on it. For the most part, he stays with the offense and leaves the defense to his coordinator. Holtz is the team's offensive coordinator. Tuesdays and Wednesdays are the hard contact days and Holtz is, as former assistant Bill Mallory (now Indiana head coach) says, "a fiery kind of guy." He's into it, yelling, yanking, going nose-to-nose, throwing an occasional cap. "His voice really carries," said Tony Rice. "He can really scare you." By the end of game week the intensity diminishes and generally there's a noticeably lighter mood by Thursday.

Holtz can bring a player down to his size with a few explosive words and expression. A couple of years ago, when Mark Green was struggling to adjust to a new position, Holtz barked, "Son, you're a great athlete, but you're no tailback. You're probably the worst excuse for a tailback I've ever seen in my life." Holtz has a sense of what buttons to push. Green was hurt—and determined to change his mind. He obviously did.

Free safety Corny Southall said, "He's the greatest leader I've ever met."

"I'm a teacher," said Holtz. "I love to be an active coach and instruct the players. But I wish I were more patient. If I were murdered as soon as practice were over, there would be so many suspects among the players they wouldn't even try to investigate."

Holtz's impatience can flare up, as it did coming off the field against Miami. Interviewed on national television amidst the post-game confusion on the field, Holtz barked at the wild students around him to back off and quiet down. Then he calmly credited the Notre Dame spirit with the victory. There also can be a very patient side. In the second game of his first season at Notre Dame, the Irish were in East Lansing against Michigan

State and suffered their second straight loss by less than a touchdown (20–15). The Irish still had a chance late in the game when an interception stopped them cold. It was a damp but warm day and the post-game press conference was held in a make-shift press room, a small, dingy room under Spartan Stadium. With reporters and cameras jammed shoulder to shoulder in stifling conditions, Holtz fought his way through to a chair against a wall in the back of the room. He had little voice left at the time and the Spartan band came through the tunnel just as he was beginning the conference. He couldn't be heard over the band, so he waited. And waited. The reporters were more restless and they hadn't suffered a second straight heartbreaker. When the band finally got through, the conference continued and Holtz stayed until the last difficult question had been asked.

"He's such a great teacher," Athletic Director Dick Rosenthal said. "He very purposefully is a teacher to his players and his position coaches. That's his job. But for all of us who come in contact with him, he's constantly a teacher to the rest of us. The way he handles himself, the standards he sets for himself, his incisiveness, and ability to analyze a given situation. . . . And to me and all the rest of us he's very even-keeled."

"The guy is just very bright," said Corrigan. "He knows football on both sides of the ball."

One of Holtz's greatest strengths is his work on the sidelines on game day. Michigan coach Bo Schembechler said simply, "He knows how to line 'em up." In Holtz's short tenure at Notre Dame, the Irish have not lost a game in which they were leading going into the fourth quarter.

Before the Fiesta Bowl, former coach Dan Devine, who guided the Irish to the '77 national championship, said, "A team has to have the ability to hit the field razor-sharp and Coach Holtz has the ability to do that as well as any coach I know."

Not bad for a guy who says he finished 234th in a class of 278.

"We realized once Coach Holtz got here that we'd have opportunities to win a national championship," remarked Heisman Trophy winner Tim Brown. "He told us if we'd do what he asked, things would work out."

Holtz first met his Notre Dame players two days after the 58–7 debacle in Miami. Tailback and tri-captain Mark Green remembers the moment Holtz walked in and how the players were not even sure of his identity. "Everybody was looking and wondering 'Is that him? Is that him?' We didn't know what to expect. When he spoke he didn't sound anything like he looked."

Then the new coach introduced them to a six-week winter conditioning program that started at 6:15 A.M. To get an idea of what they were asked to do before breakfast, the players referred to the daily affairs as "Puke-fests." Misery loves company. They started to develop a bond through the intense work. The players hated every minute and admitted it may have brought them a little closer together. "They thought the sessions were hard because we told them they were hard," Holtz said. "They probably wouldn't think that much of it now. We didn't get 'em up that early to punish them. It was because of recruiting. It was so we could give our coaching staff a chance to meet them before they went on the road."

One of the areas he pushed hard to develop in that first off-season was his team's quickness. Then he sent his coaches out on the recruiting trail to find more. Bear Bryant used to say, "Luck follows speed," and Holtz said, "I want some of that luck to follow me." In three years, the mission was accomplished. The speed in the Irish defense overwhelmed West Virginia. The Irish roster in the 12–0 run featured 26 players who ran 4.6 or better in the 40-yard dash. But just as important was the general foot speed of a player such as 280-pound defensive tackle George Williams, who runs it in 5.0.

"You see those signs 'Speed Kills' and I always thought that kind of fit," Holtz mentioned.

How long Holtz will last at Notre Dame is difficult to say. Parseghian says the pressure really thickens after you win the title. And certainly, in years to come, the expectations will be greater than ever because of the experience and the talent in stock. Holtz took a team to a national championship, often starting three freshmen and only six seniors.

"When they (students) pay tuition here, they believe it entitles them to one national championship in four years," jokes Holtz. More often, when the horses are in place. But when Holtz was trying to play down the importance of the Fiesta Bowl, he said, "The real pressure is when you have to win to keep your job." At Notre Dame you have to win often. It's not in the contract. It's in the tradition.

Holtz says Notre Dame has changed him some, made him a little more serious. If he has a timetable, or particular goal, it isn't clear.

Being remembered "as a dumb coach who was the luckiest guy to ever win three national championships" would suit him just fine. "'He was dumb, but that little sucker was sure lucky. Can you believe he won three national championships?' That's how I'd like to be remembered." That would mean at least a couple more years of work.

During the season Holtz's weight dropped into the 140s, but he's accustomed to dropping a few pounds in the season. He's allergic to a lot of foods and, with his hectic schedule during the season, his eating habits don't keep pace. There may have been a couple more pounds lost in nervous sweat with a first-time lunge for the brass ring, but other than that the wear and tear didn't show.

His wife Beth acknowledges, "Ever since we came to Notre Dame, there have been more demands on Lou's time. Yet, somehow he's more relaxed. . . . He's not striving anymore for where he wants to be. He's there."

"I won't be at Notre Dame for 11 years unless they bury me there," he said at one time late in the season. But he also said he gets "burnt up, not burnt out," and can't imagine coaching anywhere else.

Neither can Notre Dame alums, now that they have another coaching icon to add to their illustrious lineup.

It was indeed, as a banner pronounced at the Fiesta Bowl, *"A Happy Lou Year."*

Spring Fever

When Lou Holtz blew the whistle in the middle of one of his spring scrimmages in 1988, he had three orders: "I want Mark Green at cornerback, (Pat) Terrell at free safety, and Braxston (Banks) at strong safety." The command came right out of the blue and must have bewildered the three involved, considering they had been working with the first string offense all spring. Holtz should don a lab coat during spring practice for all his experimentation. In this particular scrimmage, which was designed to evaluate individual personnel, Holtz wanted the three on film as a keepsake. It was the first and last time Green and Banks would change positions. It was the start of a new position for Terrell. That's the way spring practices go with Holtz. He'll make double-figure position switches by the day, some of which don't seem to last much longer than that.

After an 8–4 season and three straight losses to end it, it took only a couple of months for Notre Dame's football team to recharge the batteries. Toward the end of March, Lou Holtz had the third edition of his Fighting Irish in pads for spring practice and, before the first day was over, he had to pull their plug. They had the motor running hard before they were even warmed up and Holtz wanted them to cool it. Ninety minutes or so into the practice held in the indoor facility, Holtz blew the whistle and called his team to the 50-yard line where he lectured them on the value of easing back into the physical part of the game.

"We just wanted some 'thud' work and it turned into a full-scale scrimmage," Holtz said of the first day of practice in Notre Dame's indoor facility. "When you're concerned about numbers and you're working against each other every day, if you don't work intelligently you're going to have problems."

In his heart he knew it was a good sign. With a team and a program that needed all the work it could get, it would help if they were hungry. That was a good omen. But on day one there also was bad news. Nose tackle Chris Zorich, a 6-1, 260-pounder whom everyone was anxious to see, injured a knee and limped to the sidelines, where he spent the rest of the spring. He had not played at all as a freshman, but his prep team play and off-season conditioning evaluation made him the heir-apparent to Mike Griffin at the position. He had come to Notre Dame as a linebacker from Chicago Vocational, which had produced a linebacker by the name of Dick Butkus, and he was a product of a tough South Chicago neighborhood. Chicago Vocational does not hone many students for college. "I was taking sheet metal and auto mechanics courses when I found out that Notre Dame was interested in me," said Zorich, who has worked hard to overcome a stutter. "So, in my senior year, I had to take four extra courses. I had two history classes, an English class, and an extra math class. I started school at 8 o'clock and finished at 3:30, with no lunch hour. Then I went to football practice."

Zorich had always struggled to keep his weight down at linebacker. He came to Notre Dame overweight and crash-dieted to cut his weight to 225. The diet didn't last. The coaching staff took a look at him at nose in an early-season practice in his freshman season and decided he was a natural for the position. The kid, who used to get mugged and beat up simply walking home from school, was no one to mess with. The staff was impressed with his aggressiveness during his freshman year as he went head-to-head daily with one of the country's top centers, 6-2, 270-pound Chuck Lanza. "We got into a couple of skirmishes," Zorich related. "We exchanged words a few times and threw each other around a little." That was just in practice.

Now, thanks to his knee injury in spring, Zorich would have to wait until pre-season practice in August to prove himself again. It wouldn't take long. It was generally understood the spot would be his to lose — and he sparkled when given the opportunity. With a bench press of 450 pounds and biceps like balloons, he was Notre Dame's strongest player. Even better, he clicked off a 40-yard sprint time of under 4.7 — he was pass-rush material. He was also mean, spit-fire mean, at least on the field.

He got into a minor scrape during the Stanford game and said, "They were talking some garbage. But that just fires me up more. It's always a straight-up dogfight in there. The best man wins."

Zorich grew up fighting, clawing, and scratching to survive on the streets of Chicago and those habits surfaced on the football field. He seems to leave it there. Considered a calm, friendly sort off the field by his teammates, his roommate Kent Graham told Mike Boaz of the *Evansville Courier*, "When he gets in uniform, he just goes nuts. He screams and yells constantly. He taunts you and points his finger at you and tries to grind you into the dirt.

"I tried to punch him out last year during practice. Then off come the pads and he's back to being a Cosby Kid. It's weird."

He was wonderful for the Irish, respectful of the seniors, but generating some youthful enthusiasm they needed. Against Michigan and its seasoned offensive front, Zorich had 10 tackles and followed it up with nine against Michigan State. He was on his way. In his first season, he impressed enough people to be named honorable mention All-America.

A year earlier no one on the Irish defensive front had finished higher than sixth in tackles. Zorich would finish third with 74 and three fumble recoveries. He is dedicated to his weightlifting regimen and determined to succeed. Stardom is waiting—and playing nose is more fun than he ever could have first anticipated. "There are so many guys you can smash. Everywhere you go, bang, bang, bang, that's my idea of fun."

Fun to Lou Holtz is spring practice. If the NCAA ever did away with it, as is regularly proposed, Holtz would be the unhappiest man in the world. He'd probably look for a junior high team that needed help and volunteer his services. It's when he can just play coach without worrying about a schedule, a game plan, or daily press conferences. It's when he can afford to spend a little time with the defensive backs, or maybe the linemen, instead of having his time consumed by trying to develop his quarterbacks.

"I believe spring practice is the best part of coaching," he has said. "If we had no spring practice, there would not be enough time early in the fall to work on developing and improving players. Nor would there be time to experiment with position changes."

Before the spring session of the national championship season, he mentioned again, "This is the time of year you can afford to give everybody an equal opportunity. That's not something you can do in the fall. This could be one of the most interesting springs I've ever been involved in."

It wound up as one of his most challenging. Of the 11 offensive starters against Texas A & M in the Cotton Bowl, seven had graduated and two of the four returning were in new positions. That grew to three out of four for a while when guard Tim Grunhard was moved to center.

From the fans' standpoint, the biggest question was who would step in for Heisman Trophy winner Tim Brown. His position had been flanker, but he had done just about everything offensively and on special teams for the previous two seasons. The first time Holtz got a look at Tim Brown was in spring practice and that's where he started devising all those plans to use his 4.3 speed and great hands. Holtz made him do everything—run deep, run out of the backfield, run back kickoffs, run back punts—and squeezed all the mileage he could from his assets. He made him into a star and first-round draft selection by the Los Angeles Raiders. It was the first evidence, at least for Irish followers, of Holtz's knack for making the most of a player's special skills. Brown would be greatly missed offensively—it would take three players to replace him—for what he did with the ball and what he meant as a decoy. "I can't imagine," said Holtz, "that there's anyone else who can have such a major effect on a football game in as many ways as Tim Brown can."

It was time to begin looking for others. Mark Green got the first call to step in for Brown at flanker. He was a logical choice because they had a pair of tailbacks—Tony Brooks and Ricky Watters—waiting in the wings, seemingly ready to blossom after each rushed for more than 250 yards as freshmen. And Green had some experience on the perimeter. He had played at flanker in his first season at Notre Dame under Gerry Faust, seeing action in 10 games. Holtz had to move him to tailback, out of necessity, in his sophomore year at Notre Dame, and, in two years there, he had served the Irish well. He had gained a little weight, become a little stronger, maintained his speed, and grabbed hold of the position. He had quietly become a fine tailback. When Holtz said they needed him at flanker, Green didn't even wince. No problem.

"It really doesn't matter to me," he said. "I'll play flanker, I'll play tailback, I'll play anywhere."

No one in the Irish camp could replace Brown's impact—that kind of talent is rare—but Green could supply what the Irish needed. He had good speed, was the most coachable of the Irish players, and had a good track record for catching passes, with 47 career receptions going into his final season. And when Holtz wanted to apply a little wishbone, he had a natural three-horse backfield. Except maybe for a few more pounds, Green had been everything Holtz could have hoped for in a tailback. Only twice in the previous two years did Holtz allow the 181-pound Green to carry more than 20 times in a game. Brooks, at 215, and Watters, at 200, had the size Green didn't. It didn't seem to matter. As a junior, Green averaged 5.9 yards a carry, had proven himself durable, and, most importantly, reliable with the football under his arm. His 861 rushing yards was the 11th best season total in Irish history. As he closed out his career at Notre Dame as captain, he was willing to make the switch and give up the football.

Green always had been a model citizen and had to grow up in a hurry after making the difficult decision to leave the West Coast, Riverside, California, for the Midwest. His mother, who had shared in his college decision and encouraged him to choose Notre Dame, died during the second semester of his freshman year. Green hung tough.

"I wanted to go home and be closer to my family," he said. "But my mom and I had sat up so many long nights. When I looked back, I knew I had to stay with it."

"His personality is always the same," Holtz said. "He's usually got a smile on his face and he's kind of bubbly.

"I've watched him grow and develop as a football player, as a running back, but not as a person. He came here a great person."

Because Green could have starred in a lot of positions, he was seldom given his just due as a tailback, where he had 24 straight starts. In high school he had 21 career interceptions and was pegged by many universities as a defensive back. He did not select Notre Dame because of a guarantee to keep him on offense. It just felt right to him — just as it felt right to do what he was asked and move to flanker without a fuss, regardless of whether he had become quite attached to his role as a Notre Dame tailback.

"I thought that move to flanker was more of an experiment, just to see how the chemistry of that worked with the team," Green noted.

Something didn't click and the problem was more at tailback than at flanker. Brooks and Watters were chewed on regularly as Holtz tried to push them to the next level. After a three-week look, he wanted Green back in the backfield. In his mind, neither Brooks nor Watters was ready for the full-time responsibility. "With two freshmen (sophomores-to-be in the fall) at tailback, we felt we needed a little bit more leadership there," Holtz explained.

"There's nobody I'd rather talk about than Mark Green," Holtz said later. "We felt we had to leave him in at tailback because of his leadership, his toughness, his ability to protect the football, everything. He is just an excellent football player — but his greatest talents lie within him."

Green had another great senior season at tailback, rushing for 707 yards, with 15 pass receptions and seven touchdowns, second on the club. He played hard when he was nicked up, didn't miss a practice, and went all the way at tailback against Southern California. With 2,038 yards in three seasons, he ranks eighth on Notre Dame's all-time rushing list, one yard short of Neil Worden's total and 302 yards off fifth-place George Gipp's total. And Worden had 476 attempts to Green's 395. Suffice it to say that Green made his presence felt.

With the jam-up at tailback, Holtz tested another option and tried Watters at flanker. "Ricky's got natural catching ability," receivers coach Pete Cordelli said then. "He has a knack of finding the ball, finding the open area, and making the catch."

Watters showed some promise in his first scrimmage, then more in the spring Blue-Gold game, after doing some soul-searching and accepting Holtz's request to move. It was a difficult decision for someone who took great pride in his abilities as a tailback.

"He does some things at wide receiver that seem to just come naturally to him," Holtz acknowledged. "He has a way of coming down with the ball." Watters wound up as the leading receiver in the championship season with 16 catches for 343 yards, but he went through a couple of periods when he got lost in the run-oriented offense. He missed having the ball in his hands regularly. He found it difficult to get in sync with the game without carrying the ball often. When he did touch it, he tried too hard to make something big happen. Only mistakes started to happen. He was frustrated and his running skills seemed to deteriorate. He managed only 76 yards in 33 carries and was uncomfortable and unhappy. On special teams, he had played both hero and goat regularly, returning two punts for touchdowns, while flubbing a couple of others. Against Rice he fumbled both a punt and a handoff.

"He (Holtz) thought maybe I was putting myself before the team," Watters said of a fumbled punt against Air Force. "But nothing is further from the truth." During the Rice game, Holtz told Watters he would return to tailback, but the 6-3, 200-pounder actually worked at both positions and basically played out the season at flanker. "It was some time after the second fumble when he told me I'm going to be a tailback," Watters related. "That's my natural position and Coach Holtz knows that. I'll do what's best for the team. If he wants me there (flanker), I'll be there, but I know next year I'll be back at tailback.

"At the bottom of my heart, I'm a tailback," he said.

After the Fiesta Bowl, Holtz announced Watters would be returning to tailback, filling the shoes of Green, who was graduating.

But as the spring closed out, it appeared Holtz had something special going with his new alignment. Watters scored twice in the spring game, once on a 9-yard reception and the second on a 3-yard run, and Green rushed for a game-high 70 yards, with Brooks adding 68.

Notre Dame's offensive line must have been glad it was over. It had been a long, bumpy road and they had been the fall guys.

They were starting over. Four of the five starters from the 8–4 season were fifth-year seniors, sending everything up for grabs. One of Holtz's first moves was to switch senior captain Andy Heck from tight end to tackle and junior Dean Brown from guard to tackle. Heck won the job hands down and Brown got a little competition early from Marty Lippincott, but was never seriously challenged after that. The other three spots became a three-ring circus.

Two sophomores, Mike Heldt and Tim Ryan, were battling it out at center when Holtz threw his hands up during a scrimmage in the Stadium. "I've got one center that can't snap and another that can't block!" So he called on Mr. Fixit, Tim Grunhard, the junior who had once played at tackle and started at guard, to take over at center. Grunhard, a rough-and-tumble, 279-pound Chicago product whom Holtz praised as the ultimate overachiever, would start somewhere.

"Gruney," Holtz said, "would have fit in real well back in the days when you didn't have a facemask and you'd just fold up your helmet and put it in your pocket." At the time the Irish needed a few Grunhard clones. He had tinkered with the center slot for a short time as a sophomore when Chuck Lanza was ailing and had served as the club's long snapper (he was credited with eight tackles on punts in his sophomore season). Freshman guard Winston Sandri was showing a lot of promise and

Holtz had the experienced Jeff Pearson for the other guard slot—when the junior wasn't injured. As it turned out, it was just as well Pearson didn't get in much playing time because he left school in the summer, "for personal reasons," Notre Dame officials and Holtz announced. Pearson had been involved in disciplinary action before and rumors circulated that Notre Dame initiated his departure.

Before the spring was out, Grunhard went back to guard as Heldt, all of 18 years old, settled down and into the center slot.

When the 6-4, 255-pound Heldt first arrived at Notre Dame, he was dispatched to the defensive line. That's where the former state champion heavyweight wrestler (25–0 record as a senior) created the most interest coming out of high school in Tampa, Florida. "I wasn't doing much on defense," Heldt admitted. "I couldn't find the ball. I didn't sense where the ball was going. On defense you have to know who has the ball. I found myself always tackling the lead back who didn't have the ball." The Irish staff took care of that problem. They made him a center and let the official hand him the ball. That erased one problem, but there were others.

With Pearson's departure, the other guard spot was left up in the air over the summer. Could it be Ryan Mihalko, a former fullback? Sandri? He started the opener against Michigan, but the eventual winner, former linebacker Tim Ryan, didn't even surface as a candidate until August.

"Right now, everybody's just learning how to walk," guards-centers coach Tony Yelovich said. "Then we'll take the second step. They have to learn together and breathe together."

With all the indecision over the offensive front, and the Irish staff still searching for a flock of new receivers to replace Brown's 39-catch total, the offense never hit much of a rhythm during the spring. The quarterbacks really suffered. But the choice of who would take over the offense was fairly simple. When Holtz talked about the timing of his quarterbacks, he didn't mean with the receivers: He went with the guy best equipped for self-preservation. "Tony (Rice) is the only one who has any sense of timing when it comes to avoiding the blitz." Hardly encouraging when you have to base a quarterback decision on who best avoids the rush. There were other reasons, of course, for selecting Rice, but at the time the offense needed someone who could buy time and occasionally turn trouble into positive yardage.

"We wouldn't sell many tickets if they like to see a lot of offense," Holtz lamented. Now if they enjoy a day at the Forum . . .

Considering the humble beginnings, the rushing average of 256.7 yards a game becomes all the more impressive. The total was four yards a game better than a year earlier when the Irish had four fifth-year seniors in the front line. That was one for the books. No one figured they would top the previous year's total. There were several reasons why they did: At the top of the list is Rice and his expert handling of the option; the other backs ran hard and were as good as the pre-season publicity made them out to be; Holtz's system was setting in and the line simply played better as a group than anyone could have expected. Credit Heck with setting a grand example and also the pace. Remarkably, after one season in the position, he was named first-team All-American.

The offensive frustration in the spring can be traced back to one other problem: "Defensively, we do seem to be closing up the holes a little bit quicker than we used to," Holtz observed.

The key missing element the previous two years was foot speed and it finally filtered into the Irish defensive system. Junior middle linebacker Michael Stonebreaker had run a 4.65 40-yard sprint and returned to the Irish from a year of academic ineligibility with 10 more pounds on his frame.

"It was really hard (sitting out)," said Stonebreaker. "More than anything I wanted to be out there. But I was able to sit back and watch (Saturday games). I learned more about linebacker and what I can do coming into games.

"I was able to just watch the linebackers and the way you can read an offense," he added. "I was reading them a lot quicker."

When linebacker Ned Bolcar missed most of the spring with an ankle injury, Stonebreaker took over his "eagle" spot and never let go. On the outside it was seasoned Darrell Gordon and blossoming Andre Jones on one side and Frank Stams coming into his own on the other.

"I thought Frank had a great spring," defensive coordinator Barry Alvarez had said, reflecting on the start of Stams' All-American year, "and I was hoping he could carry it over into the season. He just really looked good. Our new coaches like John Palermo (defensive line) and Chuck Heater (secondary), they'd been around other kids before, one of the first things they talked about was how impressed they were with him and just how physical he was. They were impressed with how hard he played and I think he improved technique-wise all year."

No one would have guessed All-American status was in Stams' future. He had been around for five years, his first two as a fullback. He was good enough to start 11 games as a sophomore but carried it only four times a game and for only a 3.7 average. In Holtz's first spring he broke a bone in his lower leg during a March scrimmage. If not for the break, he may never have been moved to defensive end, or at least have the extra year to grow into the position. The next season was wiped out by one leg injury after another, which he attributed to trying to return too quickly. But that gave him another season of eligibility. As a junior, he played in 11 games, but never started and was credited with one sack and 14 tackles. Then came the spring of his final season and he was suddenly running over everybody.

"I've had experience all around," he said, "on special teams, on defense, and on offense. If it's one thing I can get through to the guys it's to be physical. If you're playing a physical game at least you've got a chance." He was fifth on the team in tackles, had caused three fumbles and recovered two, and led the team in sacks with nine for 76 yards. The Irish voted him their Lineman of the Year.

Stams wasn't the only player to come into his own last spring. The defensive front that started in the Cotton Bowl was gone—lone returner John Foley was out for the year with a nerve injury—and the new blood was getting tested. George Williams, nicknamed "Big Boo" with his 6-3 framed by his 282 to 290 pounds, saw action in six games as a rookie and emerged as No. 1 at nose in Zorich's absence. His body was built for tackle and he eventually wound up there in the fall. When Williams was recruited out of Willingboro, New Jersey, with experience on both sides of the line, he had a resumé that made him one of the top 100 prospects in the country and enough excess baggage to have trouble with some doorways. He came in at a very soft 297, unprepared for the heat of pre-season camp. "I hadn't done anything during the summer (after his senior year in high school). I didn't think I had to. I guess I was kind of big-headed. In high school you're bigger than everyone else and it's easier.

"The weight hurt my quickness, but my stamina more than anything. I'd go five plays and be dead tired." When his freshman season ended, Williams started running hard and left behind 23 pounds. When he reported for spring practice, he whittled his 40-yard time down to 4.9.

"There's a lot of pressure, not only on the field, but also in the classroom," he said. "And you have to perform every day because there's somebody right behind you. What you do in practice you do in a game. I had to learn how to practice." He had it down pat by the end of the spring session.

Junior Jeff Alm, a one-time outside linebacker, moved in immediately at one tackle slot and was superb, earning the club's Most Improved Defensive Lineman honor.

Alm was coming of age and the potential was starting to show. It coincided with added weight and better health. Alm had always been given high marks for potential. As a freshman, a short time after getting moved from outside linebacker to tackle, he found himself in the big time, going against Pittsburgh's mammoth offensive front. It was not the right time. He wasn't even supposed to play that day because a bout with the flu that week had taken 10 important pounds from him. When an injury felled Robert Banks, Alm, weighing then a thin 228, got the premature call.

"I got slaughtered," he said, remembering that day. He also got hurt. A neck injury knocked him out for the following three games and haunted him again the following spring after two and a half practices. He came back to play in nine games as a sophomore, and in 31 minutes of playing time, registered nine tackles. Alm came back in the spring of '88 ready to go, much stronger, and heavier at 250 pounds. He put the injury jinx behind him and got better with every practice. He became a dominant member of the front during spring drills and it carried over.

His 6-6 frame and athletic ability caused the kind of problems for opposing quarterbacks that the coaching staff had hoped it would. Oddly enough, with three interceptions in the championship season, Alm shared the team lead with strong safety George Streeter and Pat Terrell. He got his third interception in the 10th game of the year against Penn State after defensive end Arnold Ale tipped a pass. "I don't know about good hands," Alm laughed, "I couldn't catch it when I was a tight end in high school."

Tom Gorman rounded out the front three coming out of camp, but an injury in the pre-season curbed his practice time and eventually cost him his job as he moved to offensive guard. The players started talking about Gorman being "Wally Pipped," the man who took a day off and never returned to the lineup because of a player named Lou Gehrig.

For the third straight season, there was a punter to find. It was a three-legged race down to the wire. Sean Connor gave up his senior year of basketball to give it a try and had the size (6-7) and leg strength over the others. He boomed a couple of 50-plus yarders during spring drills and was listed at the top of the depth chart going into August practice. Jim Sexton, a sophomore walk-on from South Bend, and Pete Hartweger, a senior walk-on from Maryland, also applied. Recruiting coordinator Vinny Cerrato handled the punters until it was time to hit the road. Late in August, he wasn't expressing too much confidence. Who was the punter? "We might not punt," he responded. Eventually, Sexton's consistency, good hands, and quick release won out, and he punted 38 times for a 38.7 average with a long punt of 53 yards. Hartweger got in four punts and Connor two. Holtz would have liked a better average, but at least there were no disasters.

Coming out of spring camp, Holtz was only certain of a couple of things: One, that the defense had been improved in its overall speed and they might even generate a pass rush; two, that the depth would make things very competitive come August.

In between were a couple of miserable months.

It started with the loss to academic trouble of Pierre Martin and Bobby Carpenter, the two top receivers coming out of camp. They were neck-and-neck at split end coming out of spring practice, then gone by the fall, leaving the job to seniors Steve Alaniz and whatever freshmen could help. Before their departure, receivers coach Pete Cordelli said of the recruiting class, "We're excited about the guys coming in. Again we're going to have some competition there. It's going to be a fun, fun situation." By August it would be a desperate situation, but with the maturity of freshman Raghib Ismail and the Irish more dependent on the run than the pass, they were able to get by at split end.

After the news of Martin and Carpenter, Holtz got another headache when he was informed of Pearson's situation. A lot of spring work was going down the tubes. Holtz also had to worry about Tony Rice's academic progress in summer school. Unless Rice performed well, Holtz would have a quarterback derby in August.

But the worst was yet to come. Crisis followed turmoil.

Allegations by a former academic advisor at Minnesota charged that Holtz, while head coach at Minnesota in 1984–85, had given money to a player through him. The advisor, Leroy Gardner, charged that Holtz instructed him to give money to a player and Luther Darville, director of the Office of Minority Student Affairs, alleged Holtz was aware of an illegal distribution of funds.

Holtz denied the charges. "What can I say, other than I didn't do anything."

Then, a former running back, Pudgy Abercrombie, charged in a newspaper story that he had received cash and travel accommodations from an assistant coach, Jim Strong, who joined Holtz at Notre Dame in 1987. Strong issued a denial, supported by a polygraph test that he requested, and Abercrombie later denied making the accusations.

"I used to enjoy bantering with the writers and broadcasters a lot, especially before the season," Holtz said. "It was a lot of fun. Now, I dread it because I know those questions are coming.

"I don't like having to watch every word, every statement I make and whom I make it to," Holtz said of the questions. "But it makes me a little upset when it's made to look like I'm not being honest and truthful, when I am. I do not lie."

At the pre-season media day in August, Holtz said he would make his last statement on the subject until the season was over. "It's terribly unfair for this to be hurting kids (Notre Dame) who have nothing to do with Minnesota. Terribly unfair. I can't prepare my football team correctly with all this swirling about." It was never brought up again, seemingly forgotten overnight, as the flow of reports disappeared from the papers.

Holtz received complete support from the university and no evidence of truth was ever brought forth in support of the allegations.

It was not exactly the most ideal condition to begin preparation for a national championship season.

"We didn't think much about that stuff," said Mark Green. "We didn't think any of that would be true."

"He Leads, We Follow"
—*Ricky Watters on Tony Rice*

"I'll tell you this, Tony Rice is definitely a quarterback."
No one had prompted Lou Holtz to make that comment as he walked off the field after the first pre-season practice in August of '87. The Notre Dame head coach stated it as fact, without solicitation, as if there had been some doubt in his mind and everyone else's. Then, maybe he was just breaking in a line he'd have to use over and over and over . . . Get the question out of the way in a hurry. It seemed like an odd remark at the time, though. There didn't seem to be much doubt with Irish fans anxious to see Rice perform. His high school stats had everybody drooling.

Rice had thrown for 40 touchdowns and accumulated over 7,000 yards as a four-year starter at a small school, Woodruff High in Woodruff, South Carolina. He was a Parade All-American, he was South Carolina's Player of the Year, he was co-MVP in the state's Shrine Bowl, he scored 460 career points . . .

Holtz had been around long enough to know that doesn't always translate into college stardom. What about the level of competition? What about the adjustment to college life? Late in his high school career, not even

Rice was certain of the road he wanted to take. "At that time, you're tired of school," he said. "You think 'four more years.' I guess I hated to think about starting over."

He started over *without* football. A casualty of Proposition 48, Rice didn't get to set foot on the field during his freshman year at Notre Dame. Now, as Holtz was looking at him for the first time as a sophomore, he didn't know exactly what to expect. Holtz had never seen him on the football field. He knew he had an athlete, but did he have a quarterback? Holtz, who takes personal responsibility for the carving of his quarterbacks, has his own idea of what he's looking for. He had to see Rice throw. He looked gangly and wild but there was no doubt about the strength of his arm. (One of the first things you notice about Rice when you meet him is the size of his hands. He drapes a football.) Holtz had to see him move. Rice was raw, but there was a deep well of natural talent from which to draw. Holtz liked the way he carried himself on the field, the way he worked with the rest of the players. A couple practices were enough to tell him he had a quarterback.

It would take some time, however, before everyone was finally convinced.

At 6-1, 198 pounds, and a four-year letter-winner in basketball in high school, Rice would have made a great wide receiver, flanker, or defensive back. But what a waste. At any other position he couldn't take control and mold a team's mood. As Rice emerged as Notre Dame's quarterback, that stood out as his greatest quality.

"What you don't appreciate about Tony Rice unless you're there at practice is that he has great command of the huddle, the players have great respect for him, and he's an excellent competitor," Holtz remarked early in the season. "The team just functions very well when he's in there."

At Notre Dame there is always a quarterback question when it comes to its fans. Funny how the No. 2 man always seems to be the right quarterback until he

becomes No. 1. It happened with Blair Kiel and Steve
Beuerlein, then Beuerlein and Terry Andrysiak, then
Andrysiak and Rice, then Rice and Kent Graham. If the
Irish are using a mobile, sprint-out type quarterback,
they want to see the classic pocket passer. If the Irish
are using the conventional QB, they want to see the guy
who can move. No quarterback wins Fighting Irish fans
over until he wins it all.

Rice also had myths to dispel in many minds, though
neither he nor Holtz thought much about it. Rice was
only the second black quarterback to start for Notre
Dame and the image of black quarterbacks as great athletes, not great quarterbacks, remains. Holtz, who had
had black quarterbacks before, could have cared less. To
explain how Rice looked at it, his quarterback model in
high school was white left-handed Jim Zorn, then playing at Seattle.

Think back on the quarterbacks of previous championship teams at Notre Dame in the past two decades
or so and you recall the grace and finesse of Joe Mon-
tana, Tom Clements, Terry Hanratty, and John Huarte.
The style of Tony Rice was all his own and different
from that bunch. They were Corvettes, sleek, smooth,
and creative. Rice was a souped-up jalopy, fast and strong
but with an awkward look. "I know it may look sloppy,"
Rice once acknowledged. That didn't matter. What he
had in common with the rest was that he could push
a team.

Losing a full season hurts any player, but it's particularly true for a quarterback and especially so for the
quarterback learning to weather Holtz's high-pressure
system. In football years Rice was just a sophomore when
he returned in August, coming off his first spring practice in the program. He was a pup with a lot of training
ahead.

But patience doesn't grow in abundance at Notre Dame
and two games into the 1988 season, Irish fandom was
restless. Letters poured into the football office, notify-

ing Holtz that his team couldn't win with Rice at quarterback. Of course, Holtz was squirming a little, too. But his confidence was growing and he wanted it to show. "Tony can have a great game or a poor game, but I think by the end of the year he'll be an excellent quarterback."

In the 19–17 victory over Michigan, Rice completed three passes in 12 attempts for 40 yards with an interception. At Michigan State the following week the passing game went from bad to worse when Rice was two of nine with an interception. But the Irish escaped with a 20–3 victory. Two weeks, five completions, two interceptions and Holtz said he never before had a passing game look so inept in consecutive weeks. Yes, Rice was struggling but his receiving corps wasn't so hot either. It would have taken an accountant armed with a calculator to total up the passes dropped in practice. On most days the receivers were bad. On others they were terrible. They were not exactly instilling confidence in the Irish quarterbacks.

Assistant coach Pete Cordelli was earning his money, molding two converted tailbacks (Raghib Ismail and Ricky Watters) and one converted strong safety (Pat Eilers) into wide receivers. They were all good athletes, but with a lot to learn about routes and reads. There were no holdovers from the previous season at the wideout slots and while they were getting their feet wet, Rice was in hot water.

From a seat in the stands or in front of the television set, all anyone saw was Rice's passes falling incomplete. For all they knew the quarterback who completed under 43 percent of his passes the previous season hadn't changed much. In fact, Rice had. His passes were sharp and on the money from Monday through Thursday. His confidence level remained high, though with Rice it's hard to notice. There's not much swagger to him, if any at all. He feels and plays like a kid. Notre Dame Stadium might just as well be a big sandlot. Sometimes his love of the game reduces even the toughest situation into basic feelings.

Against Pittsburgh in the fifth game of the season, the score was tied at 17 in the third quarter when Holtz held a conference with Rice. The kid quarterback looked his coach in the eyes, put on a smile, and let the emotions hang out: "Boy, this is fun, isn't it, Coach? This is a heckuva game." Talk about disarming. Nothing like a kid to put a game in perspective.

"I've never seen anybody who hates to see a game over as much as Tony Rice," Holtz added later when recalling the incident.

But after the Michigan State game all Holtz could do was worry and wonder how far Rice could take the offense with just his legs and the option attack. Holtz, the offensive coordinator, knew that, without a respectable passing attack, he was in for a struggle and eventually serious trouble. One dimensional teams don't beat the likes of Miami and Southern California. Holtz wanted at least a hint of balance, an attack that could keep a defense honest and play catchup. The Irish needed a short, safe passing game. Rice needed to find a softer touch.

Like a manager trying to help a hitter out of a deep slump, Holtz kept his mind open about unsolicited advice. When a fan wrote to suggest Rice take up dart throwing, Holtz figured there was nothing to lose. Rice got a dartboard, put it on his dorm-room wall, and started flicking about 100 a day at it. How much it helped is debatable and Rice admitted it to be "a little overblown," but the tide changed the next week in a home game against Purdue.

Rice got to throw six times and completed four for 85 yards and two TDs. The four completions started a string of 10 straight that continued the following week against Stanford to tie an Irish record. Against Stanford he was 11 of 14 for 129 yards and the pass that would have established a Notre Dame record was completed 65 yards downfield to Raghib Ismail—but out of bounds. In one stretch Rice completed 23 of 34.

Still, everybody wanted to know how Notre Dame was going to go all the way with a quarterback who couldn't pass. Rice felt he could get the job done, though he wasn't getting the chance to prove that part of his game since he was averaging only 13 passes a game. He didn't complain.

"I'm just trying to do what's asked," he said. "If we throw 10 passes or we don't throw any, it doesn't matter. I'm not worried. I just feel a lot more comfortable with the situation."

With a quarterback who can be so deadly with his legs, Holtz has a tendency to get a little nervous when everything starts to click for him in the passing game. "I've found they'll run—until the first sign of something going wrong and then all of sudden they want to start throwing. . . . [After they have some success] They're not too sure they want to run anymore."

Whatever Rice does in his senior season, his mark will always be as a running quarterback (his 775 yards led the Irish and set a school record for quarterbacks), but what made him Holtz's quarterback was his competitiveness and fire. He is described by most—and, most importantly of all, by Holtz—as a winner. "I just love competing," he says.

Back on October 10, 1987, a nervous Rice inherited a 27–0 halftime deficit at Pittsburgh after Terry Andrysiak exited with a snapped collar bone. On his first snap of the second half, he was looking for the 25-second clock and lined up under the guard. Fullback Anthony Johnson had to tell him to scoot over. Then he got the Irish going in the right direction, nearly pulling out a lost cause.

"It was obvious to me that this wasn't your average individual," Holtz said. "He just had something about moving the football team. His confidence in his teammates is unbelievable. And they believe in him. He has learned to handle all the pressure."

Mostly, Rice ignored it.

He showed a great ability to do that in his freshman year at Notre Dame when he couldn't play. "I went to the pep rally before the Michigan game my freshman year," he recalled. "Everybody was cheering. Somebody said, 'What's your name?' When I told them, they said, 'Oh, you're the guy who can't play because of Proposition 48.' It hurt. It took a while to get comfortable with that."

But in the same way that Rice was to show a knack for turning a bad play into a good one, Rice looked at the bright side and made the most of a difficult situation. "It was frustrating, but it made me realize there's more to life than football. I enjoyed the year off (from the game). I met a lot of people that first year I probably never would have met if I'd been busy playing football from the beginning."

Only five games into his career at Notre Dame, he was under intense fire at Pitt. On-the-job training. He winged it. "At halftime of the Pitt game I really didn't know what I was doing," he acknowledged.

That day Rice ran for 76 yards and threw for 125 with only five completions. He earned starts in six of the final eight games and the Irish won four, including wins over Southern Cal and Alabama. Holtz didn't ask much of him in the passing department. He threw only five times in his first start against Air Force the following week, completing one for 10 yards. But he carried for 70 yards and scored two touchdowns, and ran the team well. He had been running the option since seventh grade and it showed. It was one-dimensional, but for the time being it was working. As far as his handle on Holtz's system, he was still a rookie. Against Miami's impressive defense he managed only 14 yards on 10 carries. He also hit only seven of 19 passes for 84 yards with an interception in the 24–0 loss.

That's when Holtz started thinking about bringing Andrysiak back for the Cotton Bowl. Rice got in when the game was already decided in favor of Texas A & M. He threw three times without a completion and with one interception. His season totals showed four interceptions to one touchdown and a 42.7 completion rate. That final printout wasn't making anyone believe a national championship quarterback was ready to put it all together. Least of all, Coach Holtz.

"We know we can't win unless we throw the ball," Holtz said. "I know that and you (media) know that, but our players don't know that. He (Rice) knows we can't win being one-dimensional."

Holtz declared the job open at the start of spring practice. Rice had to battle Kent Graham, a 6-5 freshman with a style in direct contrast to his own. Graham, from Wheaton, Illinois, was named High School National Quarterback of the Year by the Washington, D.C., Touchdown Club. He had both a soft touch and strong arm. He could feather the dump or heave it long. But even his linemen would give him a good run for the money in a 40-yard race. At nearly 230 pounds, Graham wasn't going to do much with the option and it didn't help him that the Irish were rebuilding both their receiving corps and an offensive line. His style depended on good hands and strong pass blocking. In the spring game, throwing from his heels and on the run, he completed two of seven passes and had two intercepted. In limited action Graham as a freshman had completed 16 of 24 with a touchdown, but he had four interceptions, and that was with an experienced set of hands on the other end. As Rice's backup, he threw only 26 passes in 1988, completing 17 with a couple of interceptions. Through two years in a bit part, Graham completed an impressive 66 percent of his passes, but he also was throwing an interception about once in every eight passes. What made his situation tougher was his predictability. If he was inserted into a game for Rice, everybody in the place, including the opposition, knew the ball was going into the air.

Another quarterback making a play for the starting role in 1988 was senior Steve Belles, a hard-nosed, 6-4, 211-pound competitor who had thrown a total of three passes the previous two seasons. Not as fast as Rice, Belles was a stronger runner and his equal as a scrambler. In spring scrimmages he could look like a fullback bouncing off tacklers. (That was one of the reasons Holtz later used him as a tailback and on special teams.) Belles actually had a pretty good day in the annual Blue-Gold spring game, directing a couple of long scoring drives. It earned him the No. 2 slot for a while, until Holtz devised other ways of using him.

Rice had the inside track going into the spring and did just enough to keep it, though it was difficult to assess his progress. To anyone with good vision, he was struggling, erratic on the intermediate passes, while showing little touch on the dumps. To Holtz, Rice was moving ahead.

In one of the late spring scrimmages he completed only six of 20 passes for 99 yards and he lost 16 yards on nine rushes. "I know you're going to quote stats and say, 'Gee, he only completed 22 percent (actually 30 percent),'" Holtz said afterward. "But I can't believe that Tony can throw any better than he did today." He was trying to say Tony looked good while the receivers didn't.

Rice went into the annual Blue-Gold Game as No. 1 and completed only six of 19 with two interceptions—he still left as No. 1.

"There were times when he showed a great release and great timing," said Holtz of Rice's spring passing effort. "They stand out in my mind because they are exceptions." He was only half-kidding. There was nothing funny about the scare Rice gave him in the summer.

It was another big test for Rice.

Academically, Notre Dame would be a big challenge
for Rice. That was understood from the day the university discovered he had failed to reach the NCAA's Proposition 48 entrance requirements. Rice's high school
grades were good enough to qualify for Notre Dame, but
the entrance exam scores sent up the warning signal
that it would be a struggle for him. The first year Proposition 48 went into effect, Rice and linebacker John
Foley failed to qualify. That didn't thrill Notre Dame officials, who take great pride and care in protecting the
academic image of the university. They have been the
last Proposition 48 casualties on Notre Dame's football team. After that first trial year, Notre Dame has
required all its athletes to meet the NCAA's entrance
standards before being accepted. Had Rice or Foley graduated from high school a year later, they never would
have been admitted to Notre Dame.

But in the summer after his sophomore year, Rice
would face an uphill climb in the classroom. He had remained eligible as a freshman without football, but when
the time-demands as a sophomore were added to the
mix, his grade point average slipped. So much so, in
fact, that he had to take three courses in summer school
and score a B or better in each to be eligible. Rice put
down the football, took up the textbooks, and made it
with two A's and a B. Another clutch performance.

Waiting the last few days for the results created more
turmoil for the Irish when a local television station
reported that Rice had not made the grade and would
be ineligible. Rice, who had returned home to South
Carolina following the summer classes, was tracked
down by members of the media to get his response. At
the time he was certain he would be eligible, but his
family, particularly, was concerned over the report. It
was another headache he really didn't need. A few days
later the university confirmed that the report was false
and that Rice would be eligible. For Rice it was another

clue to the scrutiny he would receive in the limelight as Notre Dame's quarterback. When the matter was settled, he responded calmly to the media error, letting the storm dissolve instead of venting any frustration.

Getting behind in class was more than a close call. He counted it as a special lesson in itself. "I don't think I was applying myself," he said afterward. "If you don't make it, it's because you don't want to. There are so many people here who helped me. I'm competing in both the classroom and on the football field. I've grown up a lot. I'm not the playful little Tony all the time anymore."

But he *is* on the football field—all the time. In fact, "playful" perfectly describes his approach.

First of all, it's the style that is natural to Rice that flows from his personality. If he played hard-ass leader, he'd have a difficult time pulling it off. He'd be acting. Rice can take charge with a smile better than a bark.

The rest of the offense responded to that. They respected it. This was a group of young overachievers that needed a cool hand more than a heavy boot. They were all playing for keeps, but Rice helped keep it fun.

"His personality is like none I've ever met—he's the nicest person," said offensive guard Tim Ryan. "And, the way he comes through at times and has so much fun. There are other times when Coach Holtz is chewing on us and he just looks at us, smiles, and tells us to relax. With that kind of personality, he's a natural.

"He's always slapping you on the butt when you get yelled at and telling everybody to smile. I mean, you *know* he's a quarterback."

When the club returned from the Navy game a sloppy 22–7 winner, they were in for a good chewing out by Holtz. Rice wasn't among them. He had thrown for 95 yards, run for 88, and generally kept the mistakes in-check. He stood up and took the blame anyway, feeling he should have done more to keep the offense on a better psychological track.

"He said it was his fault because he didn't keep the team loose and his attitude wasn't what it should have been," recalled Ryan.

"When I'm on the field I want to have fun no matter what," Rice said. "If something goes wrong on a play, I want to have that smile and say, 'Don't worry, we'll get it right next time.'

"I didn't really take control out there (against Navy) on offense. In the huddle, I'm always smiling, trying to pick my teammates up," explained Rice. "In that situation I really didn't show that kind of attitude. It was like 'We're going to win this game no matter what.'"

Offensive lineman Tim Grunhard admitted. "He's our backbone."

"He has begun to reach his potential," Holtz noted. "He's not what you'd call an outstanding quarterback— yet—but there's something about him that gravitates people to him—on and off the field."

Ironically, Rice emerged as the offensive star and the club's Most Valuable Player at the end of a season which opened with him as its biggest question mark. With so many tools, a growing maturity, and a sense of the system, he could simply dominate a game. Ask Stanford. The Cardinal simply couldn't stay up with him nor anticipate his next move.

On a day when he hit 11 of 14 passes with one touchdown, he rushed for 107 yards and two touchdowns. Rice was taking hold.

"I thought Tony, for the first time, executed in a ball game the way he has in practice," Holtz said, following the game.

"He's always had a take-charge attitude," flanker Ricky Watters told Ken Murray of the *Baltimore Evening Sun*. "He's like a general. He leads, we follow. He always comes up with big plays when we need them."

Like against Miami. Rice needs a big day and completes eight of 16 passes for a then-career best 195 yards. At Southern Cal, the Irish are without their leading rusher in Tony Books and top receiver in Watters, so Rice takes matters into his own hands and breaks off a 65-yard touchdown run. Against West Virginia in the Fiesta Bowl, he rises to the occasion, throwing for a career-best 213 yards with two TDs on only seven completions and runs for 75 yards in 13 carries.

"He knows the game plan inside and out," tailback and captain Mark Green said of Rice before the Fiesta Bowl. "He has improved a lot. You can see it out there. I think a heck of a lot has to do with him just knowing what he's doing. I'm sure for him he just feels more comfortable with his timing and where the receivers are."

But going into the 12th game of the season, Holtz still felt his team was too one-dimensional and in a lot of trouble against West Virginia if they got behind. Smooth? "When I look at our film our offense wouldn't make a highlight film," Holtz said, "unless it was for somebody else's defense."

"I don't care what the critics say or what he (Holtz) says," Rice responded in a friendly tone. "I know what I can do and I'll have fun doing it. If he (Holtz) says we don't have a passing game, I'm not going to argue with him. I think I'm a fair passing quarterback and I think I can get the job done. I just love to compete and I love winning."

Partially responsible for the turnaround in Rice was getting the receivers in sync. On the perimeter, they were all new. There were a couple of major freshmen acquisitions who were still adjusting to college life, let alone to Rice's passes.

The Irish needed some receivers, fast, so they took the fastest player they could find. Raghib Ismail (call him "Rocket") was a standout halfback in high school with world-class quickness. During freshmen workouts, before the varsity arrived, he was sitting around with a couple of linebackers and offensive linemen when recruiting coordinator Vinny Cerrator started dropping hints that the Irish were in desperate need of help at wide receiver. Ismail looked around and figured he was it. From day one, he was running deep patterns, streak after streak. He must have felt he was back running track. At 5-10, 175 pounds, Ismail was a smaller target than Tim Brown but he would become as good a deep threat. "We've been going deep and deep so often that a lot of defensive backs are playing 15 yards off me," he said only three games into the season.

Ismail, running on 4.28 40 speed, got behind a lot of teams. He beat Purdue for 54 yards and a touchdown, he caught a 57-yarder on Miami, a 67-yarder against Penn State, and 55-yarder against USC. It took a lot of work. He was used to taking handoffs at Meyers High School in Wilkes-Barre, Pennsylvania, where he rushed for just under 4,500 yards in his career. It took a lot of pass patterns to get him comfortable catching it on the run, but he had the maturity and work ethic to make big strides. "They always say you have to have a good base and the high school I graduated from was disciplined about our behavior—about our actions in public, and about how you carry yourself—that it should be second nature." Holtz paid him a grand compliment. He said he didn't act like a freshman.

Because he was always a deep threat, Rocket was a great decoy, driving off defensive backs, and he became quite competent as a blocker on the outside. But his speed got him on the field in a hurry and he put it to good use elsewhere, blocking a punt against Michigan State and returning two kickoffs for touchdowns against Rice to equal an NCAA record. His 36.1-yard average on kickoff returns led the nation. He had only 13 receptions, but they went for 360 yards, a 27.7-yard average with three touchdowns. Rice and Ismail became quite efficient.

Derek Brown was the other freshman to become a primary Rice target. The Irish had lured the 6-7, 235-pound Parade Prep Player from his home state of Florida and put him to work with sophomore Frank Jacobs at tight end. Great hands and maneuverability—he played a lot of soccer as a youngster—Brown also held his own as a blocker, a must for him to have a job with the Irish, who threw only 16 passes a game. Of his 14 receptions for 220 yards, the first two went for touchdowns and he finished with three in all.

"He's one of those rare individuals who came in here with a great reputation which, I personally feel, was underestimated," Holtz said. "I think he's better than we thought he was going to be and I thought he was going to be awfully good. He's a great athlete, he's a better-than-average blocker, he has tremendous hands, [don't stop now, Coach Holtz], he runs very good routes, he loves the game, he's unselfish, he has a great deal of self-pride, and he will be the difference in an awful lot of games before he leaves here."

When Brown and Ismail grew in the system, Rice's statistics got well.

He finished the year completing a shade under 52 percent of his passes and made the cover of *Sports Illustrated* for the third time after the bowl beauty. "He competed against three of the top five Heisman candidates (Rodney Peete, Steve Walsh, Major Harris) and all he does is win," Holtz noted. "I told him (after the Fiesta Bowl) you're not going to be in the background anymore. You'll be the hunted, not the hunter."

That will be a new experience and one in which Rice will feel less comfortable. Before he went on to overshadow West Virginia's nationally-acclaimed Major Harris, he said, "I'm not looking to get that much credit. I really like being in the background. It makes me work harder. I'm not trying to prove anything to anyone but myself.

"I'm not complaining," he added. "I can't compare myself to him [Harris]. I'm bowlegged."

Rice fit in well with the pressure of the big moment. He laughed it off. He could never have lasted otherwise. Every practice day is a war of nerves—Holtz vs. quarterback. The 152-pound Holtz doesn't instruct, he dissects.

He goes nose-to-nose with his quarterbacks, chiding, riding, even literally on occasion.

At a practice in '87, Rice was tackled from behind in the backfield by a guy he never saw coming—Holtz. Rice had made a wrong read and Holtz climbed on top of him screaming, "Who were you reading? Who were you reading?" Before Rice could gather his senses and blurt out an answer, the scene got the better of Holtz and he started laughing. Imagine Rice going back to the dorm and telling his buddies it had been a rough day: "He was on my back all day."

A couple of mistakes in a row is usually more than Holtz can handle. In comes the backup until he screws up or Holtz cools down and feels a lesson is learned. Notre Dame's three quarterbacks under Holtz—Steve Beuerlein, Terry Andrysiak, and Rice—agreed that games were a piece of cake because Holtz can't get to them in the huddle. That, of course, is Holtz's reasoning. Make them stand up to him and face the music in practice. If they respond, they will when the clock's ticking down and the game's up for grabs.

"Push 'em to the edge and make sure they don't jump." It's like breaking a wild colt, then crossing the fingers in the hope you don't break its spirit.

He just added another dimension to Rice's.

Once over the rough spots ("I had to learn to listen to what he says and not how he says it," Rice says), a special relationship developed. Rice and Holtz even planned a post-season dart tournament. Holtz probably practiced.

Rice can take the abuse, then go back to the huddle and flash a knowing smile to his offense—everything's cool.

On good days, Rice will even initiate some of the teasing.

Holtz will sometimes jumble his names and Tony winds up "Ricky" as in Rickey Foggie, the quarterback under Holtz at Minnesota.

Rice will respond with a "Coach Bo" as in Schembechler.

"I'll show you 'Coach Bo,'" cracked Holtz. "Graham get in there!"

It's not wise to try to outpoint Holtz in wit. He'll get in the last word.

He also built himself a pretty fair quarterback.

"They Just Find a Way to Win"

—*Lou Holtz on the 1988 Irish*

Notre Dame did not head into its 1988 season opener against Michigan blind exactly, but it would be fair to say that the outlook was foggy. It was hard to tell then if all the bases were covered. The expectations were high, naturally, but it was difficult to know just where realism and optimism should part company. One of the bright sides: If the Irish didn't know what they had, how could Bo Schembechler? How to attack? Where to attack? It was a great guessing game then and the oddsmakers figured Notre Dame, ranked No. 13 then to Michigan's No. 9, as a 2-point favorite. You know why?

Lou Holtz knew: "It's because a lot of people don't believe they're Catholics unless they bet on Notre Dame."

The oddsmakers in this case turned out to be right on the money, but not before the crowd at Notre Dame Stadium and the national television audience had witnessed an incredibly tense and hard-fought game.

When later the Irish beat Miami and Southern Cal, they left the field knowing what the win meant, how significant it was at the time. The victory over Michigan kept getting bigger and bigger as the year wore on.

"If someone asked me who we could play in the country that would be the toughest opening opponent we could possibly have, I'd have to say Michigan," Holtz said a few days before the game.

"Someone was talking with me and said there were a lot of questions about whether we can move the ball or stop their running game. I thought that was good. Since there are still questions, at least no one has us conceding yet."

Controversy out of Ann Arbor in the weeks leading up to the opener centered around whom Schembechler would choose as his starting quarterback. The veteran Schembechler kind of played along, having fun with the question, and at one point named six possibilities. Six? That must have been something; six quarterbacks sharing practice time. In reality, it was going to be Michael Taylor or Demetrius Brown. Both had experience and a handle on the Michigan offense. Regardless of who it was, the game would be a collision of running games, not passing shows, so what did it matter? At least it gave sportswriters some good copy in the month-long buildup.

Notre Dame had no such quarterback dilemma. It was Tony Rice's job to keep. But there was something that kept everyone holding his breath.

Tony Brooks, the big 218-pound sophomore tailback from Tulsa, who had shown so much promise with 262 rushing yards as a freshman, had experienced some discomfort in his left foot during pre-season practice. X-rays were taken and it was diagnosed as a stress fracture. Distressing news. All of a sudden, visions of the injury to Ohio State's great tailback, Keith Byars, came to mind. His college career took a dive and he took a long time to recover. There were a lot of similarities. Brooks could not do any severe damage to his foot by playing on it, that was assured, so the Irish medical staff would experiment before putting him on the shelf. He either could play on it or he couldn't. Could he be effective and how high was his pain tolerance? When he would cut or kick it into another gear, he noticed it most. He was fitted with a special steel-reinforced shoe that looked like a workboot and kept playing. Notre Dame was considered to have the finest all-around backfield in the country at the start of the year but now some leaks were showing. Brooks wasn't as good as new but he was patched up, playing and contributing. Against Michigan he carried seven times for 48 yards as starter Mark Green's partner at tailback. A good sign, but no one could know then if it would hold. It was just something else to watch and worry about.

Schembechler figured to have his biggest advantage up front, where he likes it most, with a veteran offensive line paced by three seniors including All-America center candidate John Vitale. He would be going against Notre Dame's sophomore nose tackle Chris Zorich, who had never even been in a college game before. Defensively, the Wolverines had an All-American at nose in Mark Messner.

"We want them to rely on their young offensive linemen to knock us out of there," said Schembechler, reportedly drooling.

Emotions were running high by game time, neither team could wait to start hitting someone else, and they didn't. As Michigan finished their pre-game drills, they passed around (and through) the Irish, who were still running their pre-game drills. There was a minor confrontation between the two teams in the tunnel of the stadium even before the game began. Then things got interesting.

In their traditional, concussive style, only 23 passes were thrown, 12 by the Irish, 11 by Michigan. After a quarter and a half, the Irish were in position to rout, leading 13–0, without their offense even getting into the end zone.

Sophomore Ricky Watters, the occasionally brash tailback-turned flanker, transformed into Tim Brown for a few seconds and returned a first-quarter punt 81 yards for a touchdown. Schembechler only a week and a half earlier had said, "They've got a guy that could be more dangerous than Brown," in talking about Watters.

It was certainly Watters' moment, but not his night. The night and week after belonged to senior placekicker Reggie Ho, a Chinese-American from Hawaii who went out for football "so I wouldn't be looked at as a study Geek." He kicked in high school for a couple of years and played a little soccer but was on no one's recruit list. If the Fighting Irish were an unknown, Ho was the mascot. The most polite college kid you'll ever meet, he responds to all reporters as "sir," passes along credit to everyone he can think of, and takes the blame for all bad snaps or holds.

Actually, Ho was hoping for a stint with the Peace Corps instead of the NFL. He loved to kick, but left no room in his life for anything but academics for two years. He didn't go out for the team until the spring session of his sophomore year and at 5-5, 131 pounds, he was easy to lose in the shuffle. His passions were pre-med and placekicking. If he wasn't in the library working to maintain his 3.77 grade point average, Ho was off somewhere kicking up a storm, in the snow if there was no safe territory indoors.

The hours of work honed his own unique routine. Two steps back, two at a 45-degree angle, exhale a deep breath, nod to holder Pete Graham, drop both arms to the right side, then twitch the fingers as if typing on air. Ho leaned every ounce he had into his kick and never saw the results. The head was always down, as was the body with a long-striding (as long as it can get for a player 5-5) follow-through.

He was by no means a great kicker—anything beyond 40 yards was generally considered out of his range and he missed four PATs— but he was tough in the clutch and a breath of fresh air for big-time college football. He became another special member of Notre Dame history with his team-leading 64 points.

Holtz had chosen Ho through simple addition: Ho had been the most consistent and he had Billy Hackett to handle kickoffs and long field goals. Fame enveloped Ho in Notre Dame Stadium on September 10, 1988. He lined up four times and was true on each try, the last from 26 yards out with 1:13 to play, to give the Irish a 19–17 lead. As much as it meant at the time, it would have been nothing more than a buried footnote had the more recognized placekicker that day, Michigan's Mike Gillette, hit the game-winner from 48 yards out as time ran out. Ho was a reluctant hero ("I just want to be an ordinary, average person," he said), a shy individual uncomfortable with the limelight, but he was a fine example of college football's best side. Everyone rushed to do a story on the overnight success, including *Sports Illustrated.* "I would never want to be walking down the street and have people recognize me and think I'm somebody special," he said. "There are a lot of people who work very hard and don't get what I have gotten. Those are the people I want to help as a doctor."

When someone suggested that his heroics against Michigan might be worthy of his being placed on scholarship, Ho was shocked. "Oh, no sir," he said, seriously. "I'm doing this purely for Notre Dame. They've done so much for me here, no way would I ever take money from them."

Following Ho's final field goal, Tony Boles returned the kickoff from the 7 to the 37. Michael Taylor sandwiched two completions to Chris Calloway for 30 yards around an Irish sack and pushed the ball to the Irish 33. Schembechler didn't gamble. He sent Boles into the line and the tailback picked up one. The Wolverines stopped the clock three seconds short of the gun and wagered the game on Gillette's foot. The senior, who had grown up in St. Joseph, Michigan, less than an hour's drive from Notre Dame Stadium, had hit a 49-yarder earlier in the quarter and was considered one of the nation's top clutch performers. He appeared to have enough on the kick, but before it ever came to rest, an explosion went up in the south end zone. It had missed to the right and Notre Dame dodged its first bullet.

The Irish played well and got some breaks, like a pass interference call that helped set up Ho's last kick.

Schembechler said his team was outplayed. It was. Most encouraging for Holtz was that his team showed great potential defensively. Michigan didn't get a first down until the second quarter and was limited to 139 yards in 52 rushing attempts. Junior inside linebacker Michael Stonebreaker was all over the field and registered 16 tackles. What's more, there was a pass rush! Defensive end Frank Stams was credited with two sacks against a team that only threw 11 times. Notre Dame had yielded 17 points, but it actually was more dominant than it had been in the 26–7 victory in Ann Arbor a year earlier. Offensively there was no passing game at all with Rice hitting three of 12 with an interception, but the rebuilt line looked better than it had in any preseason scrimmage with the Irish picking up 226 yards in 43 rushes.

In weeks to come Michigan would prove just how good a football team it was with a narrow miss against Miami, a Big Ten championship, and a Rose Bowl victory over USC. The Irish found out a lot about themselves on September 10, but there was not exactly cause to start predicting a national championship in the making.

There weren't many scares in the next month—Michigan State, Purdue, and Stanford were handled with relative ease. The Irish did stumble around before finally shaking a monkey off their back at Pittsburgh. They won for the first time in the last four meetings, 30–20, thanks to the best stretch of luck a Notre Dame team has fallen into in years.

The first came on Pitt's first drive of the day. Within a couple of strides of the goal line, freshman star tailback Curvin Richards was separated from the football by cornerback Todd Lyght, and nose tackle Chris Zorich fell on it for the Irish at the 2.

Subtract 7, probably, or at least 3 from Pittsburgh's column.

Then late in the first half, with the Panthers trailing 17–14, scrambling Darnell Dickerson made a few cuts and weaved his way into the end zone on a 9-yard run. Unfortunately for him the ball wasn't in his hands at the time. It had slipped out at the 1 and scooted into the end zone where Dickerson was alone for several seconds trying desperately to pick it up. It squirted out once, then squirted out again, then came to rest under the body of Irish cornerback Stan Smagala.

Subtract 7 more.

In the final quarter with just under 10 minutes to play, the Irish were up, 23–20, but faced a fourth-down situation from their own territory and had to punt it away. A disastrous error on the play by Pittsburgh—12 players on the field—gave Notre Dame's offense another chance. Everyone knows what good teams do with second chances. "They will take advantage of it," Holtz said afterward.

Subtract 7 more.

With a second wind at the 47, the Irish rammed it home, with Mark Green going the final eight yards on a dazzling second-effort run. The first victory over Pitt in the previous four matches was a relief, but it also created some fears. There was no pass rush to speak of and the Irish secondary got beat deep twice, the second one covering 33 yards on fourth down. Maybe it was trouble. Maybe it was just a bad day.

The Irish were 5–0 and going home. The triumph set the stage for a week of football craziness South Bend probably hadn't witnessed since as far back as 1966, when eventual national champion Notre Dame met undefeated Michigan State.

Miami was coming.

Since the 58–7 thrashing the Irish accepted in Miami in 1985, the Hurricanes had become almost a test of Notre Dame's football manhood. The bad blood still flowed hot in Irish veins. One of linebacker Ned Bolcar's friends, a diehard Notre Dame fan from New Jersey, called to say he was so nervous, he hadn't slept all week. "One guy I know called and was crying on the phone," Bolcar related on the Wednesday before the game. "I thought, 'Geez, I don't get excited until Friday night.' I told him, 'Don't worry. Stop crying!'"

By the time Miami came up on the schedule, Notre Dame had moved up all the way to No. 4 in the Associated Press poll. Miami was 4–0 and solidly entrenched at No. 1, after pasting Florida State, 31–0, then escaping Michigan's grasp, 31–30. Under Jimmy Johnson's intensity and swagger the Hurricanes certainly had become college football's measuring stick, a defending national champion with the look of a dynasty. They had a pro-style passing assault and a defense good enough to completely throttle Florida State. Notre Dame had just as much motive. But did they have the horses?

Tickets were worth the mother lode and a record number of media requests had been filed with Notre Dame's sports information department.

For the student body, it was a week-long joyride taking shots at Miami. Jimmy Johnson's phone number had been printed in the student newspaper and the Miami head coach was getting crank calls. Before it was over, Holtz said he was getting them, too. Holtz wrote a letter to *The Observer*, the student newspaper, asking students to behave. The three captains did the same. How much it helped is difficult to judge. "Catholics vs. Convicts" signs were draped outside dorm windows and the same sentiment was printed on T-shirts by campus entrepreneurs. T-shirt messages were big that week. One read, "You can't spell scum without U.M." and another listed "Top Ten reasons to hate Miami." No. 1 was Jimmy Johnson. Darrell Gordon, senior defensive end, wore a

T-shirt to a Monday press conference that read, "Less talk, more play." Nobody listened.

The university tried to deflect at least a portion of the animosity the students aimed at Miami that week by designating it "Spirit Week" and developing such forums as "The Role of Christianity in Athletics." No one showed up.

Press conferences were scheduled daily and in bulk form because a number of players were involved in mid-term exams during the week leading up to the game.

Holtz tried to put the game in perspective—sort of. "It's a big football game but I think we need to keep in mind we're not talking about World War II. It's just a game—one you'll remember the rest of your life and have to live with the rest of your life—but it's still just a game."

The Hurricanes are fun to hate because generally speaking they're quite open about their attitude toward the media-created Notre Dame "aura." They could care less about Knute and Frank and Ara, unless they happen to be on the field that day.

"People say 'Notre Dame' like that's supposed to mean something," cornerback Donald Ellis said before the game. "I don't see Notre Dame as greater than Toledo or Wisconsin or anyone else. I don't see them any different than Central Florida."

Well, why not just spit on the "Rock's" grave?

What Miami lacks in respect, or, at the very least, diplomacy, it makes up for in confidence. The Hurricanes believe in themselves and could give a nickel about "Gipper's Ghost" and "the echos." The student body was on a roll taking shots at the renegade reputation. The Hurricanes shot back where it hurts the Irish most—right in the face of their hallowed tradition.

By game day, tension was seriously kicking in. There was a scuffle in the Notre Dame Stadium tunnel with some pushing and shoving before the game was even underway. Notre Dame players said it started because

Miami was playing its intimidation game. Holtz said it happened in the end zone when the Hurricanes ran through a Notre Dame formation, baiting and taunting the Irish. But both clubs obviously had a hand in it. The new and improved version of the Fighting Irish certainly didn't ignore it. Holtz had said a couple of times before they wouldn't be intimidated. He didn't say how far they'd go not to be intimidated.

"Yeah, (in the previous season's 24–0 loss) there was a lot of talking, a lot of pushing, a lot of shoving, and things along that line, which are completely illegal," Holtz had mentioned earlier that week. "There has been a strong emphasis this year that there will be no talking condoned on the field.

"The reason it was brought around, as I understand, was two games that specifically almost turned into ugly riots: One of them was the Miami-South Carolina game and the other was Miami-Oklahoma. I think that's the way some people play the game, but they're not going to be able to play that way. The emphasis was that there'd be penalties called for taunting and there have been this year."

With anyone hardly noticing, Holtz had expressed his view of Miami's reputation and who initiates what. Because he knew his team wouldn't back down (and he didn't want them to), he suggested after the game that some consideration should be given to interrupting the series for a "cooling down" period. Not much consideration was given to the idea.

Like an omen, earlier in the week Notre Dame's outstanding senior strong safety, George Streeter, had noted: "The thing we want to get established is that this is our field and our turf."

And, he might have added, "Our tunnel," too.

"When someone comes to South Bend to play us, we don't want to make it a pleasurable experience."

They made it pleasurable for anyone watching. Regardless of which side you were on, you had to appreciate

the coaching, the clutch performances, and the drama.
Two great teams and one of college football's great moments. Former Irish assistant coach, Tom Pagna, working the game as an analyst for Mutual Radio Network,
acknowledged it may have been the best game he had
ever witnessed. "We played well, they played great," said
Miami quarterback Steve Walsh. Holtz, like Joe Namath
in the 1969 Super Bowl, predicted a victory during a Friday night pep rally—this from a man who a couple weeks
later would say "(winless) Rice scares me to death." Talk
about going against the grain. Holtz must have been
caught up in the festivities, too.

"I can't believe I said it," he admitted later, "and no
one else could either."

It was like an Ali-Frazier war. The Irish drew first
blood late in the first quarter when Tony Rice scored on
a 7-yard run to cap a 75-yard drive. Miami countered to
tie it early in the second quarter when unflappable
Steve Walsh, who was on his way to a record performance
while going for his 18th victory in 18 college starts, connected with Andre Brown from eight yards out. Four
more touchdowns were scored in the second quarter,
the Irish scoring on Braxston Banks' 9-yard reception
from Rice and Pat Terrell's 60-yard interception return.
In the last five minutes Walsh answered, throwing a pair
of TDs, and the two teams started over at 21–all in the
second half. In the third quarter Rice threw his only interception, but on Miami's first play Frank Stams fell on
a fumble caused by defensive end Jeff Alm. The Irish
worked it to field goal range but the kick was blocked.
Again the Irish held and when Johnson ordered a fake
punt, the Irish stuffed it. The momentum turned, Rice
hit Ricky Watters on a 44-yard pass and Pat Eilers scored
from two yards out. The Hurricanes came right back
and drove to the Irish 25 before the 6-6 Alm picked off
a pass, one of seven Miami turnovers (Walsh fumbled
twice and threw three interceptions).

"I had to get around the guard," said Alm, "but I got

picked up by a double team from the center so I just took two steps back." And picked Walsh's pocket. The Irish eventually got a Reggie Ho field goal on the drive to open up a 10-point lead. In the fourth quarter Miami finally made it without a hitch to the Irish 17 where Carlos Huerta nailed a 23-yard field goal to pull Miami within a touchdown, 31–24. Then the fun started. After the Irish stalled, Miami drove to the 11 where it faced a fourth and 7 dilemma. The determined Johnson went for it and Walsh connected with Cleveland Gary at the goal line. But as Gary was hit by George Streeter, the ball squirted out—or did it?—and Stonebreaker recovered. Even from replays it was hard for anyone to tell with certainty, though once Johnson got a post-game look he said he had *no doubt* it was a non-fumble. There were still seven minutes to go and one of the three Irish turnovers was to follow. Tony Rice had the ball knocked out of his hands at the 21 and Miami recovered, setting up Miami's final score on Walsh's fourth-down pass to Andre Brown from 11 yards out.

"There was no doubt we would go for two, then or earlier," Johnson said. "We always play to win."

(A little more than two months later he said he *gave* Notre Dame a national title by going for two. The thank-you cards from Irish fans are in the mail. Holtz responded, "The only thing I've ever known Jimmy Johnson to give up is the check.")

Before the 2-point conversion attempt, Holtz huddled his entire defense on the sideline. "Coach Holtz called us over and just said we've got to believe," related linebacker Wes Pritchett, who led the Irish in the game with 10 tackles. "He said all we have to have is everybody doing what they're supposed to. We dropped eight guys on the play . . ."

On the conversion, Walsh dropped straight back. He was looking for his outside receivers Andre Brown or Dale Dawkins, who were supposed to be breaking in, but they got hung up on the outside. Walsh, getting pressure from tackle George Williams, finally threw toward the corner and halfback Leonard Conley. It floated in and Terrell, who had been a split end the previous year, stepped in front and knocked it down.

When Anthony Johnson recovered the onside kick with 45 seconds to play, Notre Dame had secured one of its greatest victories ever in Notre Dame Stadium.

"I am disappointed and feel sick about this," said Johnson, words that could only bring joy to Irish fans. "I thought that if we ever got in the lead, we would have the game won."

The Irish had pulled it off having to use eight offensive linemen, losing their two top guards, Tim Grunhard and Tim Ryan, for most of the game. They had pulled it off with Walsh throwing for 424 yards, but otherwise being badgered into mistakes, mostly by Stams. Frank was everywhere, tipping the pass that was intercepted by Terrell, causing two fumbles, and recovering another. They had done it with a two dimensional offense as Rice threw for a then-career-high 195 yards and one touchdown.

The Irish victory put them in the running for top ranking and a shot at the national championship. If Miami was going to defend its title, it would have to catch a break, and it later made a bid to put destiny back in its hands by lobbying for a rematch with Notre Dame in a bowl game. That idea never got past first base. There was so much bad blood that no bowl was likely to want the headache or the risk. Moreover, someone else—like West Virginia—would earn a right to get a crack at Notre Dame in the Fiesta Bowl. Should an undefeated contender be left out in the cold so that Notre Dame and Miami could carry on their private war? It might have been a bigger hit for television, but it would have done little for college football. Miami and Notre Dame, side by side all week in Tempe, Arizona— that's like fanning the flames.

Holtz wasn't worried about facing Miami again, ex-

cept that it would be trouble. As for the Miami sugges-
tion that Notre Dame won because of "breaks," he responded, "There were five questionable calls and four of
them went against us." He mentioned his own team's injuries and having to play without two offensive starters
for much of the game. He knew his club was much better at the end of the year than it had been in the sixth
game of the season. Then, before the Fiesta Bowl, he
told *Sports Illustrated*'s Rick Telander, "If we played
them [Miami] 10 times, we'd beat them eight." Lou Holtz
fights back, too.

With the victory immediately touching off talk of
the possibility of playing for a national championship,
Holtz cautioned that such talk might be a bit premature.

"I don't know how a team can win the national championship with only six victories. That's all we have now,"
he pointed out. Besides, UCLA was still No. 1 and would
be for a couple of more weeks.

Short of a total collapse, no one was going to test the
Irish until they came to the finals at USC. At a different
time, Penn State could have been a nasty roadblock, but
Notre Dame's 21–3 triumph closed out a 5–6 campaign
for the Nittany Lions. Even if Joe Paterno's Lions were
down, Irish fans relish their wins over Penn State.

The Irish would be heading west with a 10–0 mark
and No. 1 ranking. Southern Cal was No. 2 and undefeated behind Rodney Peete, the most celebrated quarterback in the country.

"I really like playing in games like this," said Mark
Green, "It sort of brings out everything inside you. You
go out and play against a team who can match up at
every position. It's sort of what it's all about."

It marked the 60th meeting between the two schools
and the first time they had ever met ranked 1–2 in the
country. The percentages were on USC's side. No team
in the illustrious series had won more than five in a row
and the Irish were shooting for No. 6. The Irish had few
people in their corner on this one—playing on the road

against a team that seemed to be carrying as much magic in their pockets as the Irish themselves.

The week leading up to the game was like a soap-opera script: "When we last saw the weakened Rodney Peete, he had bounced off a sick bed after a bizarre bout with the measles to deck UCLA. Now, before the big game he has suddenly come down with a case of laryngitis. Meanwhile, Trojan coach Larry Smith wrestles with the dilemma of playing with a voiceless quarterback. Will he call plays through a megaphone from the sideline? Will he hand out memos? Will his center bark out signals? Stay tuned for more . . ."

It was a weird week for the Trojans, who were relieved when Peete's voice started to return the day before Thanksgiving.

His illness sent the Irish to the infirmary to get their measles and flu shots. "I took my flu shot in front of some players and never flinched," said Holtz. "Passed out, but never flinched."

By week's end Holtz would have plenty of pain elsewhere. On Friday he had to make one of those gut-wrenching calls. His top rusher Tony Brooks and top receiver Ricky Watters went AWOL in California, reporting 40 minutes late for Friday's team meal. It was not a grave offense, but neither was it their first, and reportedly they had been duly warned. It was the last straw for Holtz. The gavel came down: One game suspension.

"He was like a steamed father," Brooks said of Holtz. "Sometimes when Coach Holtz chastises you, he'll come back later and console you. I was hoping that would happen."

It didn't, and Brooks admitted, "At the time I thought the punishment didn't fit the crime. Coach Holtz stood by his decision and I respect that. And I guess I stopped thinking so much about myself then and more about the team."

The next morning the two were put on a plane for

South Bend and they watched the game in an airport in Chicago.

"Now they're there to watch 'em prepare the meals," joked Holtz a few weeks after the suspension.

Holtz had to make a similar decision during the 1977 11-1 season at Arkansas. Before the Orange Bowl matchup against Oklahoma, he suspended three of his top players for their involvement in a dormitory incident. The Razorbacks went out and leveled the Sooners, 31-6.

The Irish went out and pounded the Trojans, 27-10.

Notre Dame didn't figure to be able to run it much. Brooks was gone, and the Trojans knew what to do with an option, limiting Oklahoma to 89 yards earlier in the season. Heck, Rice got 65 alone on the first series. Faking to fullback Anthony Johnson, Rice got to the perimeter, where he and tailback Mark Green played a little 2-on-1 with USC's Mark Carrier. It was no contest. Carrier went for Green—his assignment—and with no support in sight to stop Rice, the Irish quarterback went flying down the sidelines for six. Just like they draw it up on the board. That was it for offensive highlights for a couple of quarters as USC's highly-rated defense limited Notre Dame to 253 yards. The defense took it from there and took it out on Peete.

With blossoming confidence in the secondary, the Notre Dame staff decided to go top-heavy with man-to-man coverage. That freed up bodies for the big "B."

"We blitzed more than we have all year," observed Barry Alvarez, defensive coordinator. "We felt we matched up well in the secondary and when we're in man coverage, we can send five (rushers) all the time." Because Peete seldom looked toward his running backs as an outlet, as did Miami's Walsh, the Irish could even fire their middle linebackers on occasion. Peete was hurried and eventually battered. He was sacked three times, twice by Frank Stams. It was Stams' fumble recovery that set up a quick 19-yard scoring drive, capped by Mark Green's 2-yard run.

With the Trojans trying to cut into the deficit before the end of the half, they carved more trouble for themselves. Flanker John Jackson slipped making a cut on an out pattern, leaving Irish cornerback Stan Smagala as the primary receiver. The swift Smagala caught it on the run and outran the pursuit for a 64-yard TD. Peete never saw it. Just as he turned to chase Smagala, Stams laid him out with a shoulder. He was down on the turf for a minute or so until his wind came back. He passed for a total of 225 yards, but he was wobbly the rest of the day. Smagala's big play gave the Irish a 20–7 half-time lead.

Notre Dame's offense was still spinning its wheels in the third quarter when USC appeared to find some life. Aaron Emanuel's 21-yard run gave the Trojans first and goal at the 4. Emanuel got the call again and picked up one yard. Then he was slammed by linebacker Wes Pritchett for a yard loss. An offside penalty and incompletion followed as disheartened USC settled for a field goal.

Sparked by Anthony Johnson's running, the Irish took the kickoff and drove 70 yards as California product Mark Green plunged in from a yard out for the clinching score.

"Our football team is prettier than me, but that's about it," Holtz said, after the Irish managed eight first downs to USC's 21. "They just find a way to win."

Holtz had always said when they turned the corner defensively they'd have a chance. Against USC, Notre Dame's secondary played its finest game of the year and the best in years for an Irish team. The Irish had forced another four turnovers, giving them a total of 12 for their three big games against Michigan, Miami, and USC. They had battered Peete, just as they would Major Harris. They had allowed 356 yards, but prevented big plays and forced bad ones.

More importantly, they had picked each other up when the suspensions knocked them down.

It was a long road from Michigan to USC. "I'm completely beat right now," Holtz said afterward.

But his team was perfect.

A⁺ in Chemistry

Pre-season practices run together. One is rarely different from another, except in the mood of the coaching staff and the number of pounds of flesh it intends to extract that particular day. It only changes in degrees.

On August 29, 1988, a little less than two weeks before the opener at home against Michigan, head coach Lou Holtz had something out of the ordinary in mind. It was exam day. He had played and fiddled with his offense to find the right combination. Now was the time to play with their minds. With his team baking in the afternoon sun, Holtz turned up the thermostat. The plan was to tear them down and see what was ticking. It's not even easy for him to explain exactly what he was looking for, except he'd know it if he saw it. For a portion of the practice, "we put the whistles in the pocket," as he put it, making for a kind of free-for-all, Chinese fire drill with a football. Play didn't stop with a tackle. Backs got up and got hit again and tried to keep moving, the linemen kept blocking, and the coaches stayed in their ear. When it was over there was no sign of bad blood or breaking point. Holtz liked what he saw in their eyes and what he didn't hear from them.

"If we become a good team, mark down August 29th," he said, walking off the field with a little more bounce in his step.

"Never once," he explained later, "did this team ask why. They only said, what do we have to do?"

August 29 may have been the day they convinced Holtz of what they were made of, but the decision to put it on the line, at least by the seniors, was made several months before, in the dead of winter. That's when they set the stage.

Seniors, Holtz said, have to play the best football of their lives. They also have to accept a leadership role, no questions asked. And the pain that sometimes goes with it. Setting an example takes work, especially from the sidelines.

"When your players are freshmen," Holtz observed, "all they want to do is play. When they're sophomores, they want to start. Then when they're juniors, all they want to do is win. When they're seniors, they're wondering what legacies they are going to leave behind them."

More than a few seniors had reached the conclusion it was time to put up and shut up. Because they desperately wanted to win big, they were ready to set some standards. The bottom line was that they were coming off a solid season and had enjoyed a taste of success they had never experienced before, at least at the collegiate level. As freshmen and sophomores, they had been humbled with 5–6 records. Then came an 8–1 start and 0–3 finish for an improved, but hardly satisfying, 8–4 record.

"We were sick and tired of not reaching Notre Dame standards," said free safety Corny Southall. After the Cotton Bowl the coaching staff made it clear that some seniors would not be moving into starring or even starting roles. There was a good chance there would be little limelight and personal reward for three years of work. Their enthusiasm was a bust and they could feel it among themselves.

"A lot of guys were doubting themselves and we were

starting to split up and go separate ways," explained Southall, one of the most articulate and outspoken members
of the senior class and one who had ridden his own personal rollercoaster. "We knew we wanted to win but we
weren't sure which direction we were going." Or what
price they wanted to pay.

They had some big decisions to make, personally and
as a group. The three captains, Andy Heck, Mark Green,
and Ned Bolcar, along with Southall and a few others,
called for a senior meeting. One junior, linebacker Michael Stonebreaker, attended. They met at the off-campus
apartment of a friend, locked the door, and spilled their
guts. What was said was meant to be kept in private, but
suffice it to say they cleared the air and created their game
plan. First, they wanted to treat freshmen like people,
and teammates, quite unlike the way they recalled being
treated when they entered Notre Dame as freshmen.

"After all, we were supposed to be a team," said Green,
recalling the cold shoulder he received from upperclassmen.

"We'd accept our roles as leaders, but maybe not as
the guys on the field," explained strong safety George
Streeter, who was one of the seniors who played a major
role in both areas. "Some guys had to sacrifice their hopes
and dreams of being a Notre Dame star. They had to accept the role of being a teacher."

They truly meant the promises to mean more than
lip service. And, as suspected, a number of seniors were
put to the test. For the most part, they held true to their
pledge.

Defensive end Darrell Gordon was one. He had started
11 games as a fourth-year senior and expected to play as
prominent a role when he applied for and received a
fifth year of eligibility. Instead, he was replaced first by
sophomore Andre Jones, then later by freshman Arnold
Ale. The toughest pill to swallow was being benched,
completely, for the match with Miami. It was a game
in which he desperately wanted to be involved. "It was
devastating to me because I felt I owed Miami. I had

played against them before. I knew what they were all about." He had been to Miami in 1985 when the Irish were humiliated, 58–7, but in the 31–30 triumph he never even got on the field. To this day he's not sure why and he never demanded an answer. "Maybe they thought I wasn't playing up to my potential," he thought.

Ale, the freshman from California, got his first start that day and credits Gordon with calming him down and offering him encouragement every step of the way. Gordon could have gone off to hide. It would have been easy to understand.

"It was difficult, but the main concern is winning," he said prior to his start in the Fiesta Bowl. "I would always encourage the rest of the players. They're playing for all of us, just like I'll be playing for them. You don't get down on people or they can't respect you for who you are and what you represent."

Gordon held true to the promise and by the Fiesta Bowl he had earned his job back, getting his fourth start of the year. He made one of the critical plays in that game, stopping quarterback Major Harris for a 2-yard loss with West Virginia in position to mount a comeback.

"He never said a word," remarked Holtz of the benching. "He went out and busted his tail and earned his starting job back."

Gordon wasn't the only senior challenged. Most of them were in some way. Southall had been a starter as a junior until a knee injury sidelined him in the fifth game of the year. Then came Pat Terrell's move from split end to free safety in the spring, seemingly grooming him then for the post, and Southall's starting job was in jeopardy. Terrell finally took over the starting role in the fifth game of the year against Pittsburgh.

"I'm human—I was upset," Southall admitted. "But I never let it show in the locker room because I knew it could affect the other players around me. I was willing to help Pat as much as anyone." Terrell noted publicly that Southall's assistance was a plus and Terrell's big plays against Miami—the 60-yard interception return and knock down of the 2-point conversion pass—helped secure the victory. Holtz observed that Southall was among the first to greet Terrell after he knocked down Walsh's last pass. Southall continued to play, but his role diminished as the year wore on.

Ned Bolcar's diminished from day one.

As a junior Bolcar had finally made it to the top of the heap. The heavily recruited product from Phillipsburgh, New Jersey, had waited two years for a starting role and was thrust into prominence when Michael Stonebreaker was declared academically ineligible as a sophomore. Bolcar lived up to the potential placed on his shoulders coming out of high school, leading the Irish in tackles with 106 and earning second-team All-America honors. He also was named CBS Sports' Defensive Player of the Year and after the season was named a Notre Dame tri-captain. But that spring he would go from second-team All-American to second team. Stonebreaker, who had shown great promise as a freshman, returned to the Irish in the spring and fit in well physically with what the defensive staff wanted from its "eagle" linebacker, while Bolcar was on the sidelines nursing an ankle injury. At middle linebacker was Wes Pritchett, returning to the spot he had anchored opposite Bolcar the previous season. Only rarely did a defensive scheme call for all three and Bolcar wound up as the odd man out. He was considered a swing man, but Stonebreaker started the season with a 19-tackle performance against Michigan and Pritchett was playing better than he ever had before, winding up as the club's leader in tackles. At 6-6, 251 pounds, Pritchett had four inches and 30 pounds on Bolcar, and Stonebreaker, with better foot speed, rounded out a combination that was difficult for Bolcar to crack.

Things clicked too well defensively early in the year to force a change. Having his playing time drastically reduced certainly wasn't easy for Bolcar to take. A very friendly, talkative sort, Bolcar aired his feelings publicly at least once early in the season, then held his tongue the rest of the year, trying to maintain the role of loyal captain. Whatever difficulty Bolcar had in accepting the situation, it didn't hurt his performance level on Saturdays. He went from 12 starts as a junior to none as a senior but still finished as the club's fourth leading tackler with 59. He was second on the team in tackles for loss with five. At season's end Holtz praised his handling of the situation as Bolcar was presented with the Spirit of Notre Dame Award for the athlete who best exemplifies the Fighting Irish spirit.

Notre Dame, with its great linebacker tradition, won the '88 national championship with the finest trio of linebackers in the country. It showed in the Fiesta Bowl when Stonebreaker went to the sidelines early in the game with an injury to his Achilles tendon. Bolcar, who before the game had said he was leaning toward applying for a fifth year of eligibility, got more playing time than he had in any other game along the championship road. If it had been necessary, Stonebreaker could have played some more, but with Bolcar around, it wasn't.

"I loved playing that much," Bolcar said after the game. "We wouldn't have been here without Stoney and I hated to see him get hurt, but I was glad to be out there.

"Maybe I'll come back next year and play next to Stoney. That would be OK, wouldn't it?"

There were other seniors who were pushed into the background. Split end Steve Alaniz, a senior from Texas, waited four years to catch a pass and, in the sixth game of the season against Miami, gave up a starting job to freshman standout Raghib Ismail. Alaniz continually offered a helping hand to Ismail in practice as the former high school tailback got settled into the new position.

"These guys are a class band of individuals," Streeter said of the senior class.

It certainly saved Holtz a lot of headaches in trying to develop chemistry and keep his team together. The seniors had lived up to their promise. "You can't weigh it," Holtz said. "They're the ones who raised me."

Streeter, putting the four years in perspective, said, "There have been no bad times — just difficult ones."

At the annual football banquet following the completion of the regular season, Holtz paid tribute to Gerry Faust for the strong character he brought in with his final recruiting class.

Interviewed before the Fiesta Bowl, Gerry Faust remarked, "I don't think I had anything to do with what they're doing now. I recruited those kids because it was part of my job. I'm proud that I recruited quality kids. It makes me feel good to know that is a good bunch of kids. Kids I know will graduate.

"But Lou's the one that's taught them how to win."

The team's character surfaced after the eighth game of the year, a sloppy, lackluster 22–7 victory over Navy. It was about that time a year earlier when the Irish collapsed, losing the last three games of the season. The seniors had tried to keep their fingers on the pulse of the club and they felt it was time for another gut-check, entire team included.

"Things get kind of rough around here in November academically," said Streeter. "We didn't want it to get away. I, for one, stood up and dedicated myself to playing the best football of my life."

Streeter, a religious, introspective individual, hit like a hammer. Flanker Pat Eilers remembered an early meeting with the Chicago product. "George Streeter just knocked me up and down," Eilers said. "I can't even remember it so I don't know if it hurt. It took me more than a half day to get all my senses back."

Streeter was outstanding the rest of the way and there were similar promises made then to help keep things on pace. That was the kind of responsibility they took for their own mental direction.

Holtz, of course, also chipped in. Southern Cal coach Larry Smith believed that one of the factors that was particularly important in recharging the Trojans was to use the USC tradition and rich history and its past heroes to generate a sense of responsibility among the players. Ditto for Holtz.

"There's just so much tradition and mystique here," he has said.

In the pre-season, during a practice in the Stadium, he talked with them about the honor they should feel in playing in Notre Dame Stadium. He talked about the past, about making it their home, and taking pride in protecting it. He talked about Rockne and Leahy and the reputation they built. The players referred to it as "our house." By the close of the 1988 season, the Irish hadn't lost there in two years and the 12-game winning streak is the longest since the 1942–50 seasons, when they won 28 straight.

When freshman tight end Derek Brown contracted an illness late in the season, Holtz blurted out in a press conference, "It was the same disease that George Gipp died from," which it may or may not have been. After a practice later that week, he brought the club together and he mentioned Brown's illness, that George Gipp died from it, and said, "Let's win one for Derek." Of course, Brown was standing in the huddle at the time.

"I've seen the team from the worst to the best," fifth-year senior Darrell Gordon told Jack Etkin of the *Kansas City Star*. "We're more united, where before we were for ourselves. The glory was for ourselves."

Holtz invoked the past when he tried to inspire his club in the home game against Miami.

"Coach said before the game we were going out to play today not just for ourselves, not just for the team, but the players who played here the last 100 years," recalled flanker Pat Eilers. "You're representing something they've built. I felt more responsibility to play well. I knew what I was representing."

It's easier to sell to some teams than others. Holtz had no problem with a team that had struggled for so long and had been long out of touch with anything remotely related to a special part of history.

After the Miami game, defensive end Frank Stams said he looked up at the locker room wall and studied the names of former Notre Dame players. "I played the game for all those guys who had suffered in those defeats (to Miami). I played the game for the Notre Dame tradition."

Derek Brown said he had narrowed his college choices down to Notre Dame and Miami, when he tuned into a tape of *Wake Up the Echos*. That, he said "was when it finally hit me."

Holtz wanted the reverence back. He also wanted the fun to remain.

One of the big reasons it did was due to the antics of Frank Stams and Wes Pritchett—top defenders and Notre Dame's answer to comic relief. They grabbed center stage as much for their sense of humor and occasional pranks as they did for their outstanding performance. The fun multiplies with the victories, but part of the effect is in the timing.

"They knew when to get serious," said Alvarez. "If we really need a good practice on a given day, I'll go to Wes and Frank. When the kids see how serious they are, it rubs off. They listen to them. They were very aware of what they had to get done as a team and as individuals."

Neither the jokes nor their play fell flat.

Stams, who wears a pretty good poker face, first got his reputation for telling unsuspecting freshmen that Holtz wanted to see them. When Holtz caught on to the prank, he started telling the players to take it in. "They were all ends and I was the only one out there practicing," deadpanned Stams, kidding again.

There were other ways to lighten up the drudgery of practice. Pritchett, who always seems to be wearing the hint of a grin, literally "lit up." Planning his prank on the sidelines one afternoon, Pritchett hit up a reporter for a cigar. He then sneaked back on the field and started firing questions at defensive coordinator Barry Alvarez. Alvarez, with his back to Pritchett, turned around to find his middle linebacker ready for action, puffing away on a cigar.

Pritchett and Stams were more than just characters. In their own way, they had become leaders, although maybe not by example. (There wouldn't be enough cigars to go around.) Their spirit became a very functional piece of equipment—just like a helmet, providing it's a good fit.

"We feel like we're in a leadership role," Pritchett acknowledged. "We're like the grandpas of the team. I try to have a good time and keep everybody loose, but you've got to know when to turn it on and off. We'll try to set the serious tone, too. It's amazing how the younger guys have really responded. They'll up the tempo with everybody else."

There is a playful part of the game that gets lost easily in the enormity of the business. Major college football is serious stuff, hard work, and long hours. It's repetition. Pritchett and Stams had their way of tackling boredom. They broke up the monotony for themselves, sometimes for the rest of the club and, most importantly, helped ease some of the pressure from the backs of a very young football team.

They kept the fun in perspective, just as they kept the game in perspective. It is supposed to be fun, isn't it? They had paid their dues to get away with the zaniness and had been around long enough to know where to draw the line. Most days, they went by the book. And when duty called, they played for keeps.

"They know when to laugh and joke," Holtz said. "They know when to keep things loose. They are important for team morale."

Pritchett played as if he was possessed. He played well as a junior, playing alongside Bolcar, and as the third inside linebacker in his sophomore season. But Pritchett graduated to a higher level in his last season.

No performance was more indicative of the year than at Southern Cal. When the Trojans were threatening from the 3-yard line in the second half, Pritchett collided with the Trojans' tailback Aaron Emanuel and drove him back to the 4. There were 93,000 people in the Coliseum and everybody heard the hit. An offside penalty followed, then an incompletion, and USC settled for a field goal.

Pritchett made his presence felt everywhere as a senior. He had left Notre Dame in the spring of 1986 "for disciplinary reasons," but was serious when he returned in the fall. The former National Merit Scholarship semifinalist in high school explained, "I felt I had a point to prove that I could be part of it and graduate," he said. "I learned how much it meant to be here because I had that outside view." Soon after the Cotton Bowl, he decided to apply for a fifth year of eligibility and was granted the extra year to complete his degree requirements. The 6-6, 251-pounder, who called defensive signals, didn't waste it.

"I thought it would be more beneficial to me to come back and be at Notre Dame," he said. "I really felt this team had a chance to be good and I wanted to come out, have fun and enjoy it. I thought in the spring there was good chemistry on the defense and I think the (coaching) staff has great chemistry as well."

Pritchett prepared himself well. In the off-season he bulked up, trimmed the body fat and his 40-yard sprint time. With the size of a defensive lineman, he had the foot speed to play linebacker. He remembers coming to Notre Dame weighing 34–40 pounds less, yet being a step or two slower. A young Irish team needed his experience and he thrived on the extra year. His 117 tackles led the team, almost 50 more in the same number of games than he had posted in his junior season. By the nature of his middle-linebacking spot, Pritchett generally had to fight off an offensive lineman to get to the ballcar-

rier and Alvarez said he never before had a "mike-side"
linebacker lead the team in tackles. That was the kind
of dominant season Pritchett turned in. "I really think
people have overlooked the way he has played," Alvarez
said, nine games into the season.

Bolcar says he's crazy. "You don't know what he's going to do next," he said.

Like the time he grabbed the microphone at a 1988
Quarterback Club luncheon and recited 25 lines of Shake-
speare's Henry IV. "That just didn't seem like the Wes
Pritchett that I knew," said Holtz, dumbfounded.

The only thing certain about Pritchett during the national championship season was that he was on the
same wavelength as Stams. They had a lot of victims,
some not even associated with the team.

Late one evening the week of the Stanford game, Stams
was sitting around in the sports information department.
When the phone rang, he picked it up. The caller wanted
to know the time of the Stanford game. Stams said it had
been cancelled. When the ruse finally ended, the caller
wanted to know to whom he was talking.

"Michael Stonebreaker," Stams replied.

They played their share of jokes on each other and
their teammates, but they probably had the most fun
trying to spice up the press conferences and interview
sessions. When it was mentioned that his buddy Pritchett had broken his hand early in the Miami game, hero-
of-the-day Stams joked, "Yeah, Wes told me Sunday that
he could hear bones crunch every time he moved his
hand. I told him, 'Wes, that really had to fire you up.' I
wish he would have told me about it during the game.
That would have pumped me up, too. I could have turned
all that pain into energy. That would have been awesome." Stams did sustain an injury, getting poked in the
eye, "But nothing as good as Wes. I can't even show anybody any stitches."

At the end of the season, during the media blitz before the West Virginia game, Pritchett was asked to describe how the "Three Amigos"—Stonebreaker, Stams, and Pritchett—were different.

"Well, we're all friends, but we like different things," said Pritchett, grasping for a wisecrack. "I know Stoney likes jarts, velcro jarts, and Frank's good at badminton, and I'm into tetherball."

When another reporter asked Stams about the importance of having the extra year of eligibility as a fifth-year senior, he thought for a second and said, "Well, I've finally found out where the library is. And the ratio of girls to guys has gone up. That's important."

Was he a good fullback? "I was a great fullback," he responded with a straight face. "If I would have stayed at fullback, I'd have been a Heisman Trophy candidate."

When the television cameras went on, Pritchett and Stams went into their act. Standing off to the side, they'd give themselves a plug, as if it were coming from an assistant coach.

"Brian White (an Irish graduate assistant coach) told me that 10 or 15 years from now, people aren't going to look back at who got the most headlines or who made the big plays," Stams said. "They're going to remember the guy who practiced hardest, the one who had the most fun and cared about the other players."

Their humor obviously kept things from ever getting too dull, and that was part of their purpose, but Alvarez was always quick to point out it never got out of hand. "Our kids are at their best now when they see someone sliding and they have to get on a guy to get serious. They'll get after a guy to pick it up."

That was all part of the special chemistry they developed over the year. It was a lively bunch that made the game more fun than any recent Notre Dame team had. They carved for themselves a good learning atmosphere and practiced hard. Then they played harder. The change was essential.

From the perception of the coaching staff, the Irish

had some room to grow in becoming more physical. Always a big football team, the intimidating reputation had dissolved. Defensive coordinator Barry Alvarez labeled it a top priority.

"I got tired of people talking about Notre Dame not being physical," he said. "That's embarrassing to me as a coach and it should be embarrassing to them as players. I wanted to make sure when the season was over that image was changed. . . . That's what we demanded as coaches. But we still made it fun. We didn't abuse them. We never beat them up during the week. We wanted them to know when you play like this (hard) you have fun.

"But you can ask (assistant) Joe Moore — he'd heard some things (about Notre Dame not being physical) from some teams," Alvarez added. "Other coaches talked about it and I confronted the team about it in the spring. And I reminded them of it when those teams came up."

It took hold during spring practice. Team speed was up and so was the collision meter. The youth didn't make anyone shy.

"What you try to do is build a pride among the guys on defense," Alvarez stated. "The holdovers have to have that pride in themselves that whoever steps in continues to play the same way. I want that brand of football — kids that can run on a field and knock the hell out of someone. It's sure nice as a coach when you work on those things in practice and you see it on Saturday."

His Irish obviously took it to heart and sometimes even got carried away. But there's a wisp of a line between what's perceived as hard-nosed aggressiveness and what is looked on as a cheap shot — Notre Dame was credited with the former and accused of the latter before the season was over.

What has always been interesting is how many people believe that Notre Dame plays with a halo instead of a helmet. Not only does Notre Dame have to be the best, it has to be the nicest. If Notre Dame commits a personal foul, it was a questionable call. If Notre Dame is whistled for unsportsmanlike conduct, the other guy must have done something first. What was the burning question after the Fiesta Bowl? What was West Virginia doing to get the Irish so riled up that they committed four personal fouls in the final minute and forced Lou Holtz out on the field to calm them down? "Hey, those Mountaineers must have really been playing rough out there, huh? They must have really been mouthy."

What were they doing, taunting the Irish about the score?

A letter to the editor in a *Sports Illustrated* issue even blasted the Irish "by the manner in which they won. Why must a talented and clearly superior team resort to bush-league tactics like personal fouls and the taunting of opposing players?"

Ironically, the season ended in similar fashion the season before, when Tim Brown dashed across the field to corral an Aggie who had swiped his towel. Maybe that's the day Notre Dame started fighting back.

But let's polish off a few myths. Notre Dame's name does not make it exempt from occasionally crossing the line. Nice doesn't cut it on a football field and Notre Dame now knows better. Nice is what you place in the locker as you undress. Was Notre Dame nice to Miami in the end zone before their game? It doesn't matter who started mixing it up, both had a hand in it.

"We just refused to be intimidated this year," Pritchett agreed. "I think it was just a situation where we had sacrificed so much and we didn't want to lose what we worked so hard to gain like that."

Defensive tackle George Williams concurred. "We saw what happened at Miami and against Texas A & M last year. Michigan tried to intimidate us, Miami tried . . . most teams did. We learned you can't win if you're intimidated. It means they've already got the mental edge if you are."

A chip on the shoulder and physical tactics aren't bad

tools to have. Notre Dame became a big winner after it became more physical, more willing to fight back and not be intimidated. It's as simple as that. It doesn't have to get out of hand, but sometimes it does. Holtz didn't excuse his team for its occasional extra-curricular play in the Fiesta Bowl—he said, "We were completely wrong"—but he felt it came out of frustration. The Irish felt they were being held and getting little satisfaction from the officials. That's when they crossed the line; more wrong than right, but that's the reason. Holtz doesn't want his club getting a reputation as thugs, but emotion is valuable. A touch or more of intimidation can work—ask Miami—though that's not a label Notre Dame prefers to own.

About developing a pass rush, Holtz even kids, "You have to have four guys take the most direct route to the passer and arrive there in a bad mood."

Against West Virginia, Holtz said, "I felt we got away from things we really believe in in the latter part of the game . . .

"But our players do play hard and do play aggressive. We are not trying to intimidate. We just want to play hard and play clean."

Sometimes it's just plain hard to have the cake and eat it, too.

Going the Distance

On the day the final chapter was written on Notre Dame's national championship season, the significance of it all was tragically put in perspective.

Bob Satterfield, a backup cornerback who had worked his way up from a walk-on player to earn a scholarship as a senior, collapsed and died only hours after returning from the trip to the White House on Wednesday, January 18. A fine, wiry athlete, Satterfield had toiled as a prep team tailback before getting the opportunity to work with the second unit defensively. He was not a star and seldom got into games, yet he played a big part.

"Bob always accepted his role and went about it with enthusiasm," defensive backs coach Chuck Heater said. "He was a walk-on for most of his career here, even though he could have started at a lot of Division I schools."

Satterfield, from Encino, California, was with teammates Mark Green and Darrell Gordon at a local nightclub when he collapsed and died. Alcohol or drugs was ruled out as a factor and a congenital heart defect was listed as the cause of death.

"He was a very quiet individual. He was dedicated to

his work," said Gordon. "He inspired a lot of people. He was always happy, even during the bad times."

A memorial Mass was held a couple of days later and campus flags flew at half-staff.

Team chaplin, Rev. James Riehle, CSC, said, "He served his time and now he's with God. God wanted him because he was a virtuous man."

Satterfield's hall rector, Brother Edward Luther, CSC, said, "He was always a very happy person. . . . He was looking forward to getting his national championship ring."

It was difficult for anyone who knew Bob and anyone associated with the club to accept. His loss never would be fully understood. Notre Dame's football team had lost a member of the family, a family which had become very close. They all had shared in the sacrifices. Bob would not be able to share in all the glory—in the near future and down the road at reunions and gatherings that regularly honor such accomplishment.

Satterfield represented a part of the program that's always overlooked—the players paying the same heavy price behind the scenes. They had their own special kind of chemistry. They looked after each other.

When Chris Shey, a walk-on who had transferred into the Irish program from Loras College, was unable to attend the Fiesta Bowl because of eligibility guidelines and didn't have the money to pay for the trip himself, a group of players pitched in and paid his way to Tempe. That was the style of the '88 team. It's the attitude senior defensive end Darrell Gordon spoke of before his start in the Fiesta Bowl: "They're (teammates) playing for all of us, just like I'll be playing for them."

It was the attitude that head coach Lou Holtz nurtured from the first day he arrived.

"There was no emotion toward other players as there is now," remarked defensive end Frank Stams about football life before the new regime. "The team concept suffered."

"He (Holtz) made us a closer team, much closer than

we were before he got here," says Stams' buddy, Wes Pritchett.

"We needed discipline," explained Stams. "Maybe we didn't know it then but we know it now."

Holtz could develop discipline rather quickly, too— although, he wouldn't describe it as discipline. He would call it good working habits. Of course, he could lead by example in that area. What he couldn't teach or devise or manufacture was speed, the kind that keeps coming from all angles, the kind that Miami puts on a field. There was only one way to get it and that was through recruiting, but that would require time.

Patience is not Holtz's greatest virtue.

The philosophy that should endear Coach Holtz to any senior who has ever played for him is that he does not build for the future. He never uses the term "rebuilding" and goes with anyone who gives his club the best chance to win, regardless of the record. When the Irish went to the Cotton Bowl to play Texas A & M, Holtz had a difficult decision to make about which quarterback to use. Terry Andrysiak, coming back from a broken collarbone, hadn't played in almost three months while Tony Rice was the Irish future and the guy who had actually gotten the then 8–3 Irish to the bowl. A victory wasn't going to push the Irish into national championship contention. Why not play the young guy? Holtz went with his gut feeling that Andrysiak gave his club the best chance against the Aggies, though another start under his belt certainly couldn't have hurt Rice. On the flip side, he wasn't afraid to give a younger player an opportunity. In the Cotton Bowl he started sophomore John Foley at tackle for the first time after he had made a late-season switch from linebacker.

From the day he arrived, Holtz let it be known the high value he placed on speed. Among his first moves in '86 was to shift outside linebacker Robert Banks to defensive tackle for his senior season. Banks was eventually drafted by the Houston Oilers.

Heisman Trophy winner Tim Brown sent the Irish off in the right direction in 1987 with this phenomenal touchdown catch at Michigan. In front is Allen Bishop and behind is Erik Campbell. (Photo credit: Vince Wehby, Jr.)

Lou Holtz relaxes in his mode of transportation after an early-season practice that must have gone pretty well. (Photo credit: Vince Wehby, Jr.)

Irish sophomore nose tackle Chris Zorich gets an arm on Michigan quarterback Michael Taylor. Zorich debuted with 10 tackles. (Photo credit: Joe Raymond. Courtesy of the *South Bend Tribune*.)

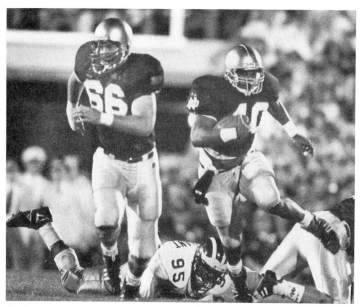

Sophomore tailback Tony Brooks is led downfield by All-American tackle Andy Heck against Michigan. (Photo credit: Joe Raymond. Courtesy of the *South Bend Tribune.*)

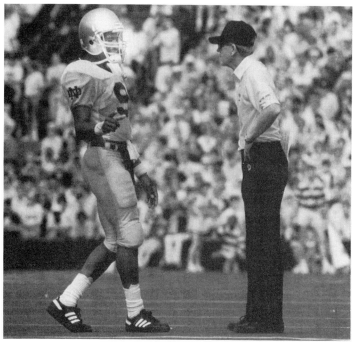

Lou Holtz has a few questions for quarterback Tony Rice at Michigan State. (Photo credit: Barbara Allison. Courtesy of the *South Bend Tribune.*)

Freshman tight end Derek Brown gets a play from head coach Lou Holtz against Purdue. (Photo credit: Barbara Allison. Courtesy of the *South Bend Tribune*.)

Junior fullback Anthony Johnson soars over Pittsburgh defender Cornell Holloway. (Photo credit: Joe Raymond. Courtesy of the *South Bend Tribune*.)

Notre Dame's unity was showing against Miami. (Photo credit: Vince Wehby, Jr.)

Tony Rice gets set for a handoff against Miami. (Photo credit: Vince Wehby, Jr.)

Against Miami, Tony Rice threw for a then-career best 195 yards on eight completions in 16 attempts. (Photo credit: Vince Wehby, Jr.)

Notre Dame's defensive line squares off against Miami's front. (Photo credit: Vince Wehby, Jr.)

All-American defensive end Frank Stams made it a miserable year for opposing quarterbacks and made his presence felt against Miami's Steve Walsh. (Photo credit: Barbara Allison. Courtesy of the *South Bend Tribune*.)

Free safety Pat Terrell celebrates with fans and teammates after knocking down the 2-point conversion pass that secured Notre Dame's 1-point victory over Miami. (Photo credit: Joe Raymond. Courtesy of the *South Bend Tribune*.)

The country's No.1-ranked team came up short against the Irish. (Photo credit: Vince Wehby, Jr.)

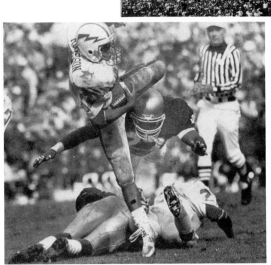

Strong safety George Streeter moves in to make the tackle on Air Force's Anthony Roberson. (Photo credit: Barbara Allison. Courtesy of the *South Bend Tribune*.)

Ricky Watters caught four passes for 108 yards and two touchdowns against Air Force. (Photo credit: Barbara Allison. Courtesy of the *South Bend Tribune*.)

He would have received a lot
of votes. (Photo credit:
Vince Wehby, Jr.)

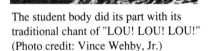

The student body did its part with its
traditional chant of "LOU! LOU! LOU!"
(Photo credit: Vince Wehby, Jr.)

The Irish take the field in the fourth game of the season at home against
Stanford. (Photo credit: Bill Leheny.)

Senior tailback and captain Mark Green had a 22-yard touchdown run against Penn State and has only safety Eddie Johnson to beat here. (Photo credit: Bill Leheny.)

Senior placekicker Reggie Ho, team leader in total points scored with 64, completes his trademark ritual prior to a PAT against Penn State. Holder Pete Graham awaits the snap. (Photo credit: Mari Okuda.)

Junior defensive tackle Jeff Alm celebrates after the Irish cap a perfect season at home with a 21-3 victory over Penn State. (Photo credit: Joe Raymond. Courtesy of the *South Bend Tribune*.)

Irish cornerback Stan Smagala picks off a Rodney Peete pass and sails down the sideline for a 64-yard TD to give ND a 20-7 halftime lead over USC. (Photo credit: Mari Okuda.)

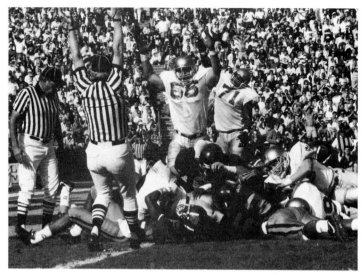

On the first possession of the fourth quarter, the Irish drive 70 yards and Mark Green scores from the 1 to secure an impressive 27-10 win against the Trojans. Andy Heck (66) and Dean Brown (71) affirm the referee's call and ND's claim to #1. (Photo credit: Mari Okuda.)

Inside linebacker Wes Pritchett puts the heat on West Virginia quarterback Major Harris. (Photo credit: Barbara Allison. Courtesy of the *South Bend Tribune*.)

Freshman speedster Raghib "Rocket" Ismail runs away from the West Virginia defense. (Photo credit: Barbara Allison. Courtesy of the *South Bend Tribune*.)

Nose tackle Chris Zorich gets double-teamed by West Virginia's front line. (Photo credit: Vince Wehby, Jr.)

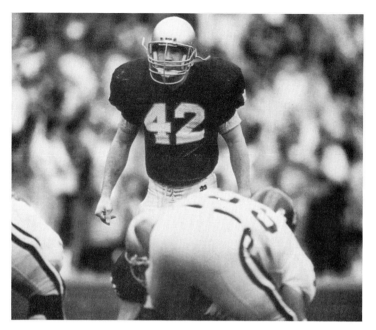

All-American linebacker Michael Stonebreaker sizes up the situation. (Photo credit: Vince Wehby, Jr.)

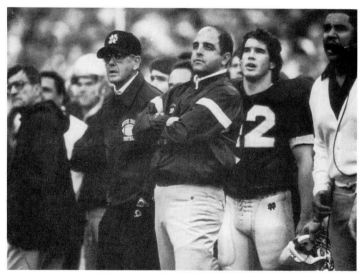

Lou Holtz and defensive coordinator Barry Alvarez watch the Irish take it to West Virginia. (Photo credit: Vince Wehby, Jr.)

Frank Jacobs applied the finishing touch to West Virginia with the touchdown catch. (Photo credit: Barbara Allison. Courtesy of the *South Bend Tribune*.)

Back on top. (Photo credit: Vince Wehby, Jr.)

If Holtz didn't have all the time in the world to re-cruit the speed he needed to win now, he would just shuffle the pieces around a little and milk as much as he could from what he had. For years, Gerry Faust had great size and strength in his offensive line—there were some impressive specimens along the line—but the game was changing and generally passing the Irish by. It was a game of speed with a fragile balance of size and quick-ness. Holtz eyed a player's feet before his biceps. That's how Tim Ryan went from a non-playing 240-pound line-backer to a starting offensive guard. That's why Holtz turned big tight ends into tackles. In two seasons, Tom Rehder went from a seldom-seen tight end to a third-round NFL draft selection as a tackle, and in one year Andy Heck went from a tight end with 16 receptions in three years to a first-team All-American at tackle.

Rarely one to show much emotion, Heck was the gifted and reticent leader. He appeared to take almost an unusually cerebral approach to the game. He did not wear his emotions on his sleeve or anywhere else. From the look on his face in a post-game locker room, one was hard-pressed to guess whether it was a win or a loss. He took a no-nonsense approach all year, as if to remind his fellow linemen, "Don't get excited, the work's not done and people are still wondering about us."

In years ahead, when Holtz sits down with a new pla-toon to talk about making sacrifices, he'll mention Heck and the unselfish approach. Late in the season, after the awards came in, Heck talked about what the move meant to him—he said it meant the Irish would be better off at tight end with Frank Jacobs and Derek Brown.

After his junior season, he had a feeling he would be pushed over a spot. "As a freshman I roomed with Tom Rehder when he was starting at tight end," Heck related. "I admired the way he played and tried to emulate him. I remember telling him when he was moved to tackle, 'Gee, Tom, I sure hope that doesn't happen to me.'"

He could see the writing on the wall when Holtz

brought in the country's top tight end prospect in Brown. When the move came, Heck went to work—and then he went to the table. In January of '88 his 6-7 frame was covered by 239 pounds. He started eating four, sometimes five, meals a day until he got sick of eating. He was never hungry and the change in wardrobe was getting expensive.

"I gained 20 pounds and had to go out and buy new clothes," he said, "then I gained 20 more and had to buy another set of clothes." Forty pounds and he still didn't look fat—because he had little of it. He pushed his bench press up to 400 pounds and he kept his quick feet. He had done a lot of blocking as a tight end the three previous seasons, but now he was locked in and blossoming under the tutelage of first-year assistant coach Joe Moore, a veteran of the trenches. Heck's weight finally leveled off at around 270 and he was ready to carry it.

What he wasn't ready to accept were all the questions and doubts raised about the offensive line. As a lone senior, he felt like a mother hen, quite protective and defensive. He also made the rest understand there was only one way to make people believe.

"I'm getting sick and tired of hearing people say, 'I just don't know how the offensive line is going to be,'" he said. "Coach Moore has been talking to us a lot about being winners," he said at the start of the season. "If you've noticed, winners in life usually have the best-looking girlfriends, the money, and the best jobs. And I'll tell you one thing about our offensive linemen: We have some pretty darn good looking girlfriends."

Heck had some company at tackle from another former tight end. Mike Brennan, once an outstanding lacrosse player, gave up the chance to play at a college well-known for its lacrosse to join the Irish as a walk-on tight end. Likeable and determined, Brennan kind of came out of nowhere and, when he bulked up from 225 pounds to nearly 250, the coaching staff knew he was serious. He had some quickness and finesse still in him from his lacrosse days and it served him well as the staff used him as a kind of troubleshooter up front. He was awarded a scholarship prior to the start of the '88 season and was worth every penny. He played in every game and started in two. He went from tight end to tackle, then to guard . . . well, anywhere the Irish happened to need him at the time. He was no giant, but he had what the Irish staff valued: good feet.

Mike Heldt, a 255-pound sophomore, was just 18 years old when he won the job at center. It was hardly a wall of behemoths up front and, overall, probably one of the smallest lines Notre Dame had played with in some time. But they came to play and could move.

The Irish defense featured its share of position changes. Tackle Jeff Alm had been an outside linebacker in his first year at Notre Dame, nose tackle Chris Zorich had started out as a linebacker, free safety Pat Terrell started as a split end, and swift cornerback D'Juan Francisco as a tailback. Obviously, the most successful change was moving Frank Stams from fullback to defensive end. Stams had started every game as a fullback in his sophomore year, but wasn't asked to carry the ball often in Faust's tailback-oriented offense. At 230 pounds he had more than ample size for the position and he had good straight-ahead speed. But the moves were missing, the ones he wouldn't need as Notre Dame's rush end.

Holtz brought in the most speed of any Notre Dame recruiting class ever and spread that around. Former tailback Raghib "Rocket" Ismail—his speed was legendary in the East where a promoter tried to get him to run against a racehorse as a publicity stunt—gave the Irish a "Smurf-like" split end and Rod Culver made a successful switch from tailback to fullback.

All of the moves generated speed, most notably on defense. West Virginia tried often but just couldn't get deep on the Irish. Either the receivers couldn't beat the defensive backs or quarterback Major Harris couldn't beat the rush. That was the big switch for Notre Dame, the key to getting over the hump and reacquainted with its rich heritage.

One of Ara Parseghian's great coaching traits was in knowing where his personnel best fit. Three of his top defensive players on the 1966 national championship team—Tom Schoen, Pete Duranko, and John Pergine— had shifted from the offense. Coaching experience must help. Holtz showed the same knack.

Some other parallels were drawn between Ara and Lou in the course of the season, and some startling similarities between the 1973 national championship team and the '88 team were brought to light. For one, both teams were coming off convincing defeats in bowl games the previous year—the 1973 team to Nebraska, 40–6, in the Orange Bowl and the '88 team to Texas A & M, 35–10, in the Cotton Bowl. Not too many fans who remember Tom Clements would compare him in style to Tony Rice, but through six games some of the comparative statistics were fascinating. Clements and Rice had each thrown 71 passes at that point and Clements' average was 99.5 yards a game to Rice's 99.3. The running attack was a carbon copy—Parseghian spreading the load with Wayne Bullock, Art Best, and Eric Penick, and Holtz with Rice, Mark Green, and Tony Brooks. Freshmen like Ross Browner, Willie Fry, Luther Bradley, and Al Hunter made great contributions for Parseghian, while freshman like Raghib Ismail, Derek Brown, and Arnold Ale made them for Holtz.

The two coaches kept in close touch. In fact, Holtz invited Parseghian to speak to the team on occasion. Holtz calls on Parseghian regularly for his thoughts. Parseghian called to wish him luck the Friday before the opener against Michigan. Superstition kept him calling every Friday after that.

Going into the season the Irish were considered, at best, a year away from being able to contend. They didn't have the earmarks of a national champion. Senior numbers were down (only two started on offense) and Tony

Rice was thought to need at least a full year under his belt before he could really make an impact. The season before he hadn't convinced everyone that he was even the answer. They started the season ranked 13th in the Associated Press poll.

"We're always going to be in the pre-season Top 20 in the magazines because there are so many Notre Dame fans around," Holtz said then. "The minute they see you're in the Top 20 they want to buy that magazine."

At the time Holtz applied his rating system to the rankings. "If they think we're any good, they put us in the top three. If they think we're going to be decent, we're going to be in the top six. If they think we have a chance of being pretty good, we're in the top 10. If they don't think we're going to be very good, we're going to be in the top 15. And if they think we're going to be horrendous, we're somewhere in between 15 and 20."

Three years had taught Holtz all about the line on Notre Dame. In his first season as Irish head coach, his unranked club dropped a 24–23 heartbreaker at home to Michigan. The next week they were ranked No. 20, a first for the polls.

Notre Dame's schedule (you know, the one that everyone had decided was too difficult week-in and week-out for the Irish to win it all) didn't change much in degree of difficulty, except the Irish lost Alabama and Boston College from the previous season's schedule and picked up Stanford and Rice. Circumstances also gave the Irish the bonus of seven home games (only five are scheduled for 1989), the most in Notre Dame history. The Irish originally were scheduled to visit Southern Methodist, but because of that school's elimination of football for two years by the NCAA's "death penalty," the Irish added a home game with Rice. That eliminated another game from being played on artificial turf, something Holtz didn't mind a bit. If his team plays on artificial turf he feels a team must practice on it—"It changes the speed and a back can make cuts he'd never make on natural grass," Holtz says—and in the last couple of years the Irish injury reports always multiplied on the harder surface. Only two of the five away games (including the Fiesta Bowl) were played on artificial turf, at Michigan State and Pittsburgh. The Irish didn't play particularly well in either spot, but they did escape without any long-term injuries.

Every big winner will admit it takes a piece of luck to pull it off—the Irish got it by staying healthy most of the season. Fullbacks Anthony Johnson and Braxston Banks were ailing off and on throughout the season, but only in the Michigan State game, when Tony Brooks stepped in at fullback, were they both out of commission simultaneously. Holtz wondered if they drew straws at the start of the season to see whose turn it was to be healthy on a given week. Brooks had the stress fracture in his foot, but never missed a game. The offensive guards were hampered by occasional injuries, Tim Grunhard missing starts against Miami, Navy, and Penn State, but saw action in all but the Navy game. The Irish were also missing Banks and tight end Frank Jacobs that day. Guard Tim Ryan also missed a start in the Miami game but played that day. Grunhard and Ryan both checked out with injuries in the fourth quarter against Pittsburgh, but sophomores Joe Allen and Winston Sandri fell right in line and helped the Irish to a critical 14-play scoring drive.

Depth made up for what injuries the Irish did suffer. Once into the season (defensive tackle John Foley was sidelined before the season started) only freshman offensive tackle Justin Hall was lost for any great length of time. The near 300-pounder broke an ankle a couple of games into the season and sat out the rest of the year. He was missed. He had shown enough potential early in the season that it was thought he could press for considerable playing time. But all in all, the Irish stayed healthy, and their most durable performer was Rice, who had 134 carries, second on the club.

As special as the chemistry Holtz credits with putting his team over the hump was the coaching combination, infused by three new members. The staff has changed a little each season and only four remain from the original group Holtz hired as he came in—line coach Tony Yelovich, wide receivers coach Pete Cordelli, defensive end coach George Stewart, and recruiting coordinator Vinny Cerrato. Joining the staff coming into the championship season were seasoned Joe Moore, who took over the tight ends and tackles, Chuck Heater in the secondary, and John Palermo, the defensive line. Palermo, Cerrato, Stewart, backfield coach Jim Strong, and Cordelli had been with Holtz while he was at Minnesota.

All the position coaches defensively were new and coordinator Alvarez mentioned, "I think the chemistry of the staff and how the new guys fit in was very important."

Holtz does not make anything easy on his assistants. They're expected to hustle as much as the players. During combat drills such as three-on-three, the coaching staff will jump in, pull players off the pile, give 'em an earful or a pat on the back. Immediate feedback. It generates excitement for the players. It spreads.

Holtz went out of his way during Fiesta Bowl week to pass on the majority of credit to his assistants and the relationship they developed with the players. He kidded one day, "I think Barry Alvarez will make a great head coach—but I think he's a year away."

He probably would like to have everybody back for 1989. The Irish will need all the help they can get with a Kickoff Classic matchup against Virginia added to a rugged schedule with six away games and no weekend breaks. They'll be expected to win them all, of course.

They were expected to sign another wonderful crop of incoming freshmen as Cerrato entrenched himself as one of the country's best. "If he ever gets married, we're in trouble," Holtz said, referring to the time Cerrato spends on the road.

Tom Lemming, who publishes *Prep Football Report*

and is one of about a dozen persons who follows football recruiting around the country, says, "Notre Dame has a really smooth recruiting machine. Before Holtz and his staff, it was Faust and a prayer. Notre Dame was organized under Brian Boulac (recruiting coordinator under Dan Devine and in Faust's first year). When he left, Faust tried to do it all himself.

"Now, I'd have to say there's no better recruiting coordinator than Vinny Cerrato. Plus Notre Dame has another four or five coaches on its staff who are outstanding recruiters too."

And as far as a closer, it's hard to top Holtz. As Lemming says, "You can't beat his magic tricks."

Holtz measures his recruiting classes over two seasons. Since there is no way to fill all needs in a given recruiting class, it is important to balance one year with the other. As an example, in 1988 Holtz filled a need for running backs and skill position players, minus a quarterback. In '89 he signed two of the best quarterbacks in the country in Rick Mirer and Jake Kelchner and did well in recruiting linebackers and linemen. That made it a good recruiting stage.

That, combined with the experience in hand, will make Notre Dame a team to beat, a lofty pre-season status it hasn't enjoyed (or suffered) in some time.

Holtz has already started preparing his lines.

"I think it will be very, very difficult for this team to rebound.

"I will be shocked if we have a good year next year."

Only 16 starters were scheduled to return.

"I know you're probably thinking 'There he goes again' and I probably wouldn't believe it if I were you either."

Not even Holtz is that good a salesman.

Part Two

THE PERFECT SEASON
A Recap

Game 1
MICHIGAN
September 10, 1988

Hands tucked deep in his pants pockets, windbreaker collar up, and the ever-present baseball-styled Notre Dame hat pulled low over his head, Lou Holtz looked relaxed, walking and chatting with Irish basketball coach Digger Phelps, while surveying his club on the Monday before the Michigan game.

Later that afternoon he acknowledged, "I just can't tell right now. I'm just glad we're playing a night game Saturday so we'll have more time to mature." A little gallows humor never hurt.

Holtz's pre-season clues were encouraging—"I think we'll play well, surprisingly well for a lot of young players," he said—but would they hold up when Michigan called?

Michigan vs. Notre Dame, Holtz vs. Schembechler make for flavorful first-game clashes. In 1986 Lou Holtz made his debut as Notre Dame's head football coach at home against Michigan. The Wolverines had one of the strongest teams in the country and Holtz had his first team ready, too. In one of their more memorable battles, Michigan won by a point, 24–23, when John Carney's 45-yard field goal missed with 18 seconds to play. In

1980 it was Harry Oliver's 51-yard field goal that won it for the Irish. In 1988 it was Reggie Ho's kick and Mike Gillette's miss in the final 1:13 that decided it.

Every year Holtz acknowledges the challenge of opening with Michigan because of Schembechler's preparation. Schembechler might say the same of Holtz. Until Holtz came along, Michigan had lost only one season opener in Schembechler's 18 seasons. With the late-night thriller in Notre Dame Stadium on September 10, the Irish made it two in a row.

"Are we good enough?" Holtz questioned prior to the game. "Are we strong enough? Are we mature enough? I think we'll play good for us, but is that good enough? I don't know."

The Irish were ranked 13th coming in and Michigan No. 9. The quarterback decision was still hovering over Ann Arbor early in the week—it was down to Michael Taylor or Demetrius Brown. A year earlier in Notre Dame's 26–7 victory in Ann Arbor, Brown ran the show and Holtz said, "If somebody beats him out they must be awfully, awfully good."

Taylor performed well in the '88 matchup with eight completions, but threw only 11 times as Michigan didn't get a first down until the 13:03 mark of the second quarter. By that time, the Irish had 13 points on the board, but not because their offense was a machine, smooth or otherwise. It was because of sophomore Ricky Watters, the 6-3, 200-pounder who was playing his first game in Tim Brown's shoes at flanker and as the deep man on punts. Earlier in the week, Schembechler cautioned that Watters could be Brown's equal as a big-play threat and, in no time, his point was proven. Five minutes into the game, Watters gathered in Mike Gillette's 53-yard punt, took a couple steps up the middle, broke to the outside, then made one more cutback at the 35-yard line to complete an 81-yard touchdown run. Reggie Ho's PAT made it 7–0. Two series later, Michigan punted again to Watters. The strong-legged Gillette nailed a

51-yarder and Watters had time to find a seam and returned it 16 yards to the Irish 42. With Tony Brooks breaking a counter for 19 and Rice keeping on an option for 16, the Irish pushed it to the 15 before stalling. With 35 seconds to go in the first quarter, Ho kicked the first of his four field goals, from 31 yards away. On Bill Hackett's kickoff, Leroy Hoard was hit by D'Juan Francisco and the ball popped out. Freshman Arnold Ale recovered, giving the Irish the ball at the Michigan 22. The Irish lost ground on a penalty, gained it back, and went no further as Ho hit a 38-yarder for a 13–0 Irish lead.

Another special teams' gem set up the Wolverines' first score when Tony Boles took Hackett's kickoff at the 3 and returned it 59 yards to the 38. Francisco made the tackle from behind. From the Irish 38, Michigan chipped away, twice converting on third down and long situations. On fourth and 1 from the 5-yard line, Schembechler gambled and Taylor sneaked for two and a couple plays later Hoard dived in.

Rice's interception, a pass that bounced off Watters' chest, stopped the next Irish drive inside Michigan territory, but the ND defense held and the Irish went into the half with a 13–7 lead.

At the start of the second half, Michigan punted away and Gillette's 56-yarder was fumbled by Watters into the end zone. He picked it up and got it to the 8, and from there the Irish went nowhere. Jim Sexton got off a 41-yard punt and Michigan took over at midfield. The Irish held, but Gillette's next punt hit Watters and Michigan recovered at the Irish 14. In six plays the Wolverines were in (helped by a penalty on third and 7 from the 11) and holding a 14–13 lead with 4:44 to go in the third quarter.

Notre Dame responded and Rice got the drive off to a good start when he hit Steve Alaniz for 23 yards, one of his three completions on the day. The rest was done on the ground, Green getting 16 in one chunk. On second and 5 from the Michigan 5, the Irish went nowhere and with less than a minute gone in the fourth quarter, Ho hit from 26 yards for a 16–14 Irish lead.

The lead was short-lived, as Michigan took over at the 20 and drove to the Notre Dame 32, the big play coming on Taylor's pass to Chris Calloway for 17. Big defensive plays by Ned Bolcar, Bryan Flannery, and Chris Zorich brought Gillette out to try a 49-yarder. The drive took 8:38 and, with 5:39 to play, Michigan was back out in front, 17–16.

The Irish took over at the 20 and got an interference call on first down. Then Rice turned the corner for 21 and followed with a flip over the middle to Tony Brooks, who turned it down the left sideline for 18 — first down at the Michigan 25. Rice had another key 4-yard run on third and 4 from the 19 for a first down, but the drive stalled at the 4. Ho lined up for the 26-yarder and became the fifth placekicker in Irish history to hit four in a game. The Irish celebrated, but the Wolverines weren't done.

Hackett's kick was fielded at the 7, dropped by Tony Boles, then returned out to the 37. With 1:06 to play, Taylor went to work, hitting Calloway for 11. On second down from the 49 with 43 seconds to play, Taylor's pass sailed through two pairs of Irish hands and Calloway nearly made the catch at the 25. But on the next play, Taylor hooked up with Greg McMurtry for 19 yards. From the 32, Taylor threw again, incomplete, then Boles was stopped for no gain and Michigan called a timeout with three seconds to play.

Gillette was called out again and his kick fell short and to the right as Notre Dame Stadium exploded.

"We played poorly," said Schembechler, "and in my judgment Notre Dame deserved to win. They outplayed us."

Holtz, encouraged by his defense, which allowed no drive longer than 48 yards, said following Monday's practice, "I'm not real happy. I can't tell you what this (a close victory) means to us. I know we've got a lot of problem areas to resolve. I expected us to play better than we did in some areas."

Rice had completed only three of 12 for 40 yards and Holtz noted, "Some of the passing problems were not necessarily his. We had receivers running at the wrong depth, in the wrong spots. It was pure chaos. We can't win with that."

Notre Dame 19, Michigan 17

Game 2
MICHIGAN STATE
September 17, 1988

Nothing about the Irish victory over Michigan did much to relieve Lou Holtz of all the concerns he had going into the season—at least not publicly.

Another game without a passing attack and a very close call. Another game with more turnovers (2–1) than the opposition and another narrow miss.

"This is one I'm worried about," Holtz said the day before his club took off for East Lansing and a Saturday morning start to a match with Michigan State. "They're very quick, they're very physical, and with our young offensive line . . ."

The Irish offensive line had made enough creases against Michigan to net the Irish 226 yards on the ground, more impressive when considering Michigan's veteran front could squeeze only 139 yards out of its running game. Still, Holtz saw a chance to improve and that week he decided to move Tim Ryan, who had been the backup center, to guard. He would start against Michigan State.

Michigan State was coming off a loss to Rutgers and Holtz remarked, "There's two things you don't want to do: Play a winning team coming off a loss or play a losing team coming off a win."

The Spartans were coming off a 9-2-1 season, a Big Ten title, and a Rose Bowl win. Defensively, they had seven starters returning to a defense that limited opponents to only 61.5 yards rushing a game. There also was the added concern of playing on the artificial turf. "They're going to see backs make cuts they don't think they can make," Holtz said. At Spartan Stadium the Irish were only 9-9-1 going into the contest.

"We just have a hard time beating them up there," observed Holtz, who had lost in three previous trips to East Lansing. "We just haven't played well up there for a long time.

"We never have been able to run the ball against Michigan State," he added, "but I don't feel bad, nobody else does either."

On September 17, No. 8-ranked Notre Dame played well enough.

All along, the Irish had to adjust. On the first series of the game, Holtz lost his top two fullbacks—Braxston Banks to a knee injury and Anthony Johnson to an ankle injury.

"Our team never flinched, that's a credit to them," Holtz said afterward. Minus his fullbacks, the Irish still ran. They had no choice with a passing game that bottomed out. (Tony Rice and Kent Graham were a combined 2-of-11 with two interceptions.)

The Spartans opened up a 3–0 lead on John Langeloh's 39-yard field goal midway through the first quarter. After Langeloh was wide to the left on a 29-yard attempt early in the second quarter, the Irish finally got moving. Tailback Mark Green, who finished with a game-high 125 yards on 21 carries, took a swing pass and picked up 38 yards to key the drive that finally stalled at the MSU 14. Reggie Ho was good on a 31-yard attempt to tie the score at 10:07 of the second quarter.

As troubled as the Irish offense seemed early, it was no picnic for the Spartans. After Ho's kick tied the score, they managed only one first down the rest of the half.

With MSU forced to punt from its own 19, Notre Dame's Raghib "Rocket" Ismail took off from his spot on the corner and got all of Josh Butland's punt, giving the Irish the ball at the MSU 7. In three plays they went two yards and Ho salvaged three points with a 22-yard field goal. Mike Stonebreaker intercepted a Bobby McAllister pass in the end zone and returned it 42 yards as time ran out in the first half with the Irish nursing a 6–3 lead.

Offensively, the Irish got their act together in the second half—sort of—but had only seven points to show for it. They only had to punt once in the second half, that on the last series of the game, but a comedy of errors made things messy and look a lot worse than they were. There were two flubbed field goals, a Rice run covering 34 yards that was nullified by a penalty, and a fumble on fourth and 1 inside the 20. Lucky for the Irish the defense never budged.

Michigan State coach George Perles loves to count on his running game, but had only 89 yards to total up. The longest MSU drive covered 63 yards—that in the final 1:20—and after that there were harmless drives of 38, 34, and 31 yards. Playing from behind, McAllister threw 31 times and completed 18 for 207 yards, but Mike Stonebreaker intercepted him twice.

Early in the third quarter, the Irish started to click. Tailback Tony Brooks, who took over for the injured fullbacks, broke a first-down play for 37 yards and the Irish needed only five more plays to get in as the option game opened up.

"We hadn't been able to make our power game go, so we had to go to the option more in the second half than we wanted to," Holtz said. Then he added, "We think we're going to break some things on some people."

Green picked up 20 yards in the drive and Rice, who rushed for 53 in nine carries, went the final eight yards for the score. In all the Irish totaled 245 yards on the ground and impressed Perles. "It has been quite some time since someone has gained that many yards on us," he said. "Notre Dame is the best option team we have faced. They got a lead where they could play ball control. It was great execution."

Rice threw only twice in the second half, as the Irish ground out 195 second-half yards.

"We made a few adjustments at half, but all we were trying to do was hang on," Holtz said.

No one had rushed for more than 200 yards against the Spartans since the 1984 Cherry Bowl and Green's 100-yard performance made him only the second back in two years to do that on MSU, the other being former Michigan great Jamie Morris. The offensive line may have been new, but it was passing some early tests with flying colors.

Junior linebacker Mike Stonebreaker dominated for the second straight week. He was credited with 17 tackles and broke MSU's back with his 39-yard return of a McAllister interception for a touchdown with 5:18 to play. Stonebreaker, who finished third in balloting for the Butkus Award, was named the Midwest Defensive Player of the Week for the performance.

In neither of the first two games did the Irish look pretty, but they had survived against two teams expected to contend for the Big Ten title. Both would go to bowl games and Michigan would wind up beating USC in the Rose Bowl.

Still, the Irish were showing a few leaks.

Notre Dame 20, Michigan State 3

Game 3
PURDUE
September 24, 1988

After two close calls the Irish were due for a week off. Purdue obliged.

But before the September 24th date in Notre Dame Stadium, there was a fullback to train and an idea to run by Tony Rice. Braxston Banks was on crutches and out indefinitely. Anthony Johnson would rest if the Irish could afford it. With 218-pound Tony Brooks coming off a fine day at fullback against Michigan State, that's whom Holtz selected to shore up the area. He would have an exceptional day with 110 yards in 11 carries, but he wanted no part of the position as a permanent move. "I've learned you've got to get your pads lower a lot quicker," he said. "I still like tailback a whole lot better."

Holtz, at the start of the week, was again forced to measure his club's passing game. It was a new situation for him. Never before had he had a team look so inept for two straight weeks. Purdue figured to make it three in a row even if it was a sizeable underdog going into the game. The Boilermakers' pass defense in its first two games against Washington and Ohio University had been their strongest suit. "Thirty-four passes have been thrown against Purdue, eight have been completed and six have been intercepted," Holtz said. "That's a 23 percent completion rate. We should be comfortable, that's right at our percentage." That was Rice's completion rate. The accumulative Irish passing game measured a bit lower. "We're going to try to be diversified," Holtz promised. "Some day we're going to be.

"We don't have anybody who's natural out there and understands everything about the (passing-game) reads. All we can do is keep trying."

Holtz didn't mention it at the time, but with an idea offered by a fan, he suggested to Tony Rice that he start throwing darts. At that stage of the game there was nothing to lose. It certainly couldn't hurt his motion or release. But better for confidence than the darts, though, were a few completions.

He didn't get his first against Purdue until his third pass when he hit a sliding Pat Eilers for 13 yards. He didn't miss again that day, connecting on six straight. Maybe he didn't set the world on fire, but it was the best sign Rice had shown in his career up to that date. Purdue, of course, was overmatched, hampered by injuries coming into the game, and worse off going out.

The Irish put 42 points on the board in the first half and before it was over Holtz used more than 80 players.

Rice, who put the first points on the board when he broke an option for a 38-yard touchdown run, completed a 72-yard drive with his first touchdown pass of the season. It was an 8-yard flip in which freshman tight end Derek Brown needed to stretch his 6-7 frame to haul it in. With Reggie Ho converting, the Irish were up 14–0 in the first quarter. They scored four times in the second quarter, two of which came on one-play possessions, lasting no longer than 12 seconds.

The first came off a play-action fake when Rice hit frosh split end Raghib Ismail in midstride at the Purdue 13 and he easily won the race to the end zone. Then Ricky Watters added his six points. Gathering in Shawn

McCarthy's 45-yard punt at the 34, Watters backtracked to get behind the wall, then kicked in down the sidelines for his second punt return for a touchdown in three games. Ismail came between Watters and McCarthy for the final break in the return. "He (Ismail) stopped him and then I yelled at him not to do anything because I know we've had some called back before (in previous years)," Watters said later. "He heard me and said 'I'm cool.' It really came together."

That was about the last of it for the offensive starters as Holtz called off the assault.

"I thought Tony Rice threw the ball more today like he does in practice," Holtz said. "Don't get me wrong, he isn't ready to play on Sunday yet."

"The passing keeps improving every week and everyone is behind me, especially the fans, and I have confidence I can throw the ball," Rice remarked.

Watters added, "I don't think anyone will be talking about Tony Rice's arm anymore. I know he can throw the football and I keep telling him to have confidence. He's a great quarterback and has a great arm."

All that, and Rice was only four of six.

Steve Belles stepped in for Rice late in the first half and hit Brooks with a 34-yard pass for a touchdown and freshman fullback Rodney Culver broke off a 36-yard run in the fourth quarter to complete the Irish scoring.

"Notre Dame had more speed than we did," said Purdue coach Fred Akers. "We are trying to get to that point. They are much quicker than a year ago. Today they were awfully good, but I doubt they are going to have another first half like they had against us."

Holtz didn't allow himself to get too excited. "We have to keep this game in perspective," he said. "Although we played well, Purdue was banged up coming into the game." The Irish weren't at full strength, either, with the top two fullbacks sidelined, but it didn't matter and the depth was showing.

Offensive guard Tim Grunhard, who got to rest the

second half, mentioned what was on every player's mind, if no one else's, at the time. "We have to realize that every game is for the national championship and we can't allow for a letdown. We have to win the games we're supposed to win like this and carry it into the games we have to win."

The 468 yards on offense overshadowed another great performance by the Irish defense, which allowed only 100 rushing yards and 267 in all with five interceptions. Senior strong safety George Streeter was credited with two, the others all came from second-unit players at the time—strong safety Greg Davis, free safety Pat Terrell, and linebacker Ned Bolcar.

"The reason I feel good is because we had an opportunity to play against a passing attack and our secondary responded to the challenge," Streeter said. "We feel we have a great defense and we will challenge anyone to line up against us."

Notre Dame 52, Purdue 7

Game 4
STANFORD
October 1, 1988

Going into the fourth game of the season, Tony Rice was a new man.

Lou Holtz was his old self.

When it came to selling Stanford, Holtz should have been hired by the university public relations department. He would have earned them a game or two on a major network. First of all the Cardinal was 1–2 coming in, losing a season opener to Southern Cal by four points when quarterback Brian Johnson was injured in the fourth quarter and another to Oregon, 7–3, when they just couldn't score. That was enough for Holtz to take and run.

"Talent-wise, they're an excellent football team," he said. "For all the more I know, Southern Cal is the best team in the country and for all the more I know Oregon (still undefeated at the time) may be No. 2. Hey, for all we know Stanford may be No. 3."

Did all that add up? Well, maybe not, and Stanford wasn't getting any votes in the poll as the No. 3 team in the country, but Holtz figured (at least on paper) with a break here or a breakthrough there, the Cardinal could have been 3–0 and on top of the world coming into South Bend. A master craftsman, Holtz could build up

William and Mary (which he did) as long as he was playing them and not coaching them on Saturday.

"And we haven't played them (in recent years) so we
don't know where we stand against them," Holtz added.

The fourth game of the season was a kind of hump
game for the Irish, a mini-jinx over the previous three
seasons since they hadn't won in the fourth game of the
season.

"At this point, you've got to guard against the same
things you do in your personal life," Holtz cautioned,
"fatigue and inflation."

It is obvious by the previous statements that a big
head is out of the question. And there was no question
about the mood of the club. More than 80 players saw
action against Purdue, which meant a breather for the
starters and a breath of life for those who had previously
been doing nothing but watching from the sidelines.
Getting playing time for some other players was just
what the Irish needed after a month and a half of football.

"But we just have to get better," Holtz noted the Monday before the Stanford game. "We've come a long way
as an offensive football team and as a defensive football
team. Now we've got to go to the next plateau in all
areas. I don't know if we can get to the top, but I think
we can get to the next plateau."

Standing in their way would be the next opponent,
no matter who it was.

When Holtz said a little confidence would help Tony
Rice, he hit it right on the button. All it took was four
completions in six passes against Purdue to loosen up
the junior from South Carolina, and on the evening of
October 1, in Notre Dame Stadium, Rice put the two
phases of a quarterback's game together like few players
can. Notre Dame was No. 5 going into the contest and
Stanford was overwhelmed.

Rice was like a basketball player with a hot hand. He
couldn't miss no matter what he did. He completed his
first six passes of the night, giving him 10 straight to

tie a ND record. His 11th pass was completed deep, but out of bounds to Raghib Ismail.

"Their quarterback did an excellent job running the option and his throwing just gives them another dimension," said Stanford coach Jack Elway, who knows a lot about passing quarterbacks. "Right at this point, I'd have to say they're the best we've faced." (Someone should have remembered that when the Irish went out to USC.)

Of Notre Dame's four touchdown drives in the first half, none lasted longer than three minutes and the Irish had to punt only once. The quickness was too much for the Cardinal to contain.

Rice got his day rolling with a 30-yard touchdown run on the first Irish possession. With a 26-yard completion to Steve Alaniz, Rice maneuvered the Irish to the 5 on the next possession but Reggie Ho missed a 21-yard field goal. Then the Irish were stopped on a great Stanford goal-line stand at the 1, but on the first play from there quarterback Brian Johnson was hit by Chris Zorich, fumbled, and Ned Bolcar recovered. Mark Green went over the top for the TD and, since Ho had missed the first PAT, the Irish went for two. Rice ran it in.

Rice's completion string was kept alive on the next series by a penalty after he had overthrown Tony Brooks on a screen. The Irish eventually completed a 46-yard drive, with Tony Brooks scoring, and a healthy Anthony Johnson scored the final TD before the half.

By halftime, Rice had thrown for 83 yards and rushed for 49 with a TD and 2-point conversion. He was just getting warmed up. The real serious damage came at the start of the second half when he guided the Irish 73 yards in 10 plays.

On first down from the 27 he connected with Ricky Watters for 16 yards. Then two plays later on first down from the 42, he optioned to the short side of the field, faked a pitch to trailing back Tony Brooks, and turned it up for an 18-yard gain. He gained seven more in the drive on the ground and got the final three in the air.

He faked to Johnson, then flipped a pass toward Derek Brown, who had yet to turn around. The ball was there when he did, and he made the reception.

Because Stanford got a nice performance off the bench from Jason Palumbis, stepping in for Brian Johnson, Rice had to stick around for one more series. He completed two passes in the drive and scored his second touchdown of the day from six yards out.

"I thought Tony for the first time executed in a ball game the way he has in practice," Holtz said afterward. "The most pleasing thing was that we played the whole game without a turnover."

The ball was in Rice's hands most of the time. He completed 11 of 14 passes for 129 yards and one touchdown and ran for 107 yards and two touchdowns plus a 2-point conversion. For the third straight week a different back rushed for over 100 yards. It was Watters' best day as a receiver with four catches for 51 yards.

The Irish defense set the tone early against Johnson as he was harrassed into a 7-for-18 performance for only 57 yards and an interception. "The Notre Dame defense did a great job on the pass rush," he said. "I felt a lot of pressure."

Stanford's rushing attack mounted only 59 yards for a total of 274 to Notre Dame's 467.

Nevertheless, Holtz said afterward, "I have a lot of concerns. I don't know how good we are or how good we are on defense. We're on the road to Pitt next week and they have an explosive offense. We are back to square one.

"We are not a great defensive football team. People have tried to make us out to be one, but everything you do here is magnified. I still don't know how good we are on defense."

Notre Dame 42, Stanford 14

Game 5
PITTSBURGH
October 8, 1988

The excitement was beginning to build. The Irish were 4–0, ranked No. 5, and had Miami within its sights. But before that, they had a Pitt stop to make. They almost got sidetracked.

With No. 1 Miami a couple Saturdays away, it was hard for Irish fans to get excited, let alone worried, about playing 2–2 Pittsburgh. Early in the week, Holtz wanted to make his point.

"What I'd like the news media and all the fans to understand is that the only thing I want to talk about is Pittsburgh," he stated. "We're climbing the ladder, taking it a step at a time and everyone else is taking an elevator.

"I'm even hearing it from my own sister (Vicki)," he added with a smile. "She was telling me, 'I just have this good feeling.' But all she has to do is get a seat and buy a hot dog."

It was her brother Lou who had to keep his club's head on straight and focused on Pittsburgh, which had made the previous couple of seasons miserable for Holtz. In his first season with the Irish, they played in Notre Dame Stadium and suffered a 10–9 setback. A year later, they went to Pittsburgh with a 3–0 record and an offense that was rapidly improving. They left with their first loss and a young and new starting quarterback in Tony Rice, after senior Terry Andrysiak suffered a broken collar bone.

History, at least, was on Holtz's side in trying to keep his club in line. Still, there was a lot of Miami talk to deflect on campus. "I know I'm not the greatest speaker in the world and I know what the players are hearing all the time and you worry about who they are listening to."

Pitt, which appeared to serve notice of its strength with an early-season victory over Ohio State, had lost to West Virginia and Boston College, in which, in the latter, the Panthers blew a 12-point lead in the final eight minutes. Like the Irish, Pitt was coming off an 8–4 season with great expectations. "They're so strong against the run," Holtz said, "you have trouble moving the ball on the ground."

The day started in sunshine, ended in rain, and the Irish sweated out a 30–20 triumph. Same old hard-headed, stubborn Pitt—new surge of Irish luck.

The Panthers got a good idea of the kind of day they were in for when they drove deep into Notre Dame territory and freshman star Curvin Richards fumbled at the 2. The ball rolled under Chris Zorich and the Irish took over. But on third down from the 21, Rice was intercepted by Alonzo Hampton and Pitt took over at its own 46. It only took four plays to score, as Darnell Dickerson hooked up with Reggie Williams on a 42-yard touchdown pass. The Irish then helped add to what had become a trademark. Going into the Fiesta Bowl against West Virginia, the Irish had scored immediately following an opponent's score on 15 of 26 occasions.

Taking over at the 40 on the ensuing kickoff, they scored in four plays. Tony Brooks had the big play with a 52-yard burst up the middle and Rice carried it in from two yards out. Ho added the kick to tie it at 7–7.

The Irish added a 14-play, 86-yard touchdown drive before the end of the first quarter, Anthony Johnson carrying four straight times and scoring on fourth down from the 1 with 42 seconds to go.

Pitt drew even in the second quarter as Dickerson hooked up with Henry Tuten for a 33-yard TD pass on fourth and 4 from the 33. Again the Irish responded, driving 30 yards to set up Ho's 37-yard field goal and a 17–14 lead.

It stayed that way into the half when Dickerson, after carrying the ball into the end zone from nine yards out, fumbled at the 1, tried to scoop it, then tried again and couldn't find the handle as the ball squirted into the end zone. Irish cornerback Stan Smagala finally landed on it with 58 seconds to go in the half.

"In a game like this momentum goes back and forth," said Holtz. "And if we would have been down four at the half (Dickerson's fumble), it wouldn't have been the end of the world."

Pitt had been held to 98 yards in 20 carries in the first half, but Dickerson had thrown for 180 yards and two TDs. He would get only 29 in the second half.

"Give Pitt some credit," defensive coordinator Barry Alvarez said. "They did a real good job of changing things up on us. Give them credit for keeping us off balance. They really have an outstanding offensive line."

The Irish were driving on their first possession of the second half when they turned it over at the 33 on Ricky Watters' fumble. Pitt marched to the 27 and got a 44-yard field goal from Scott Kaplan to tie it up. Holtz was pacing the sidelines. Rice couldn't wait to get on the field.

"Boy, Coach, this is a heckuva game," he said, smiling.

Then, for the third time that day, the offense responded to Pittsburgh points.

Braxston Banks, coming back from an injury, provided a big spark when he caught a Rice pass for 30 yards, then finished off a 14-play drive with back-to-back dives. When Ho's kick failed the Irish led only 23–17 going into the final quarter. The next Pitt drive was fueled by a personal foul and a pass interference flag and Kaplan's 34-yard field goal attempt was good to pull the Panthers within 23–20.

With guards Tim Grunhard and Tim Ryan on the sidelines with injuries and sophomores Joe Allen and Winston Sandri stepping in, ND ran off 14 plays and almost six minutes off the fourth-quarter clock. The Irish faced a fourth and 13 situation from their own 32 in the drive, but Pitt was whistled for too many players on the field and the Irish got a second shot. From the 47, they chipped away and Mark Green finally banged it in on a second-effort run from eight yards away.

"The fourth quarter penalty is a mistake that just shouldn't happen," said Pitt coach Mike Gottfried. "It kept a drive alive. Someone just confused a call and we didn't have enough time to call a timeout."

"If you give somebody a chance, any good team will take advantage of it," Holtz said of the penalty.

With 4:32 still to play and the Irish up 10, Pitt tried to stage a rally and drove from its own 35 to the Notre Dame 29, where Dickerson was intercepted by Arnold Ale. The Irish had it locked up and Miami was waiting in the wings.

"We're going to enjoy this one first," said Green. "I'm just not thinking about it (Miami) yet."

Tackle Dean Brown remarked, "I want to enjoy this one first. We'll take next week as it comes and put our faith in the coaching staff."

The coaching staff hoped there was still a little Irish luck left.

Notre Dame 30, Pittsburgh 20

Game 6
MIAMI
October 15, 1988

Super Bowl week, or something nearly equivalent to it, overtook South Bend. Miami was 4–0, No. 1, and looking very much invincible after throttling Florida State in the season opener, then quite unbeatable three weeks later after mounting an incredible comeback (17 points in six minutes) for a 31–30 victory at Michigan.

"I knew we had talent and we had a chance to be good," Johnson said of his club, which had lost a number of great players from the national championship team and returned nine starters in all. "But there was a concern how consistent they'd be. . . . There's no question that next year we'll be a more veteran football team.

"The Michigan win no doubt helped our team grow up," said Johnson. "We had four turnovers and they didn't have any that day."

To be sure there weren't many votes in Notre Dame's corner despite the 5–0 record and No. 4 rating. Against most any other team the Irish could count on a home-field advantage. In five years Johnson teams had lost only once in regular-season games out of the Orange Bowl.

"In 1984 when we went to South Bend, we felt there

144

was as much electricity in the atmosphere as any game
I've been around," Johnson remarked before the game.
"The people are close, there are a lot of seats on the field
and some right next to our bench. With the enthusiasm
and importance of this game I feel it will be as emotional as any game all year long.

"But we were down 30–14 at Ann Arbor with 105,000
people screaming at the top of their lungs. It doesn't affect us except to put more adrenalin in our veins."

The dyed-green Irish followers and student body needed
no adrenalin. Their blood was flowing just fine, although
a little warm. Since the 1985 whipping in Miami, Notre
Dame had had only one other chance to get even, but
in '87 the Irish still weren't in Miami's league and lost
24–0. This was another chance and the first time Miami
had to visit Notre Dame since 1984, when the Hurricanes
coasted, 31–13. In fact, the Irish hadn't won since 1982
and Miami's streak was at four games.

Anyway, the student body had been licking its chops a
long time to apply its special brand of hospitality—"How
do I hate Miami? Let me count the ways." There was no
way of keeping it all clean but Notre Dame officials
hoped for control. Lou Holtz and his captains wrote letters to *The Observer*, the student newspaper, asking
for enthusiasm in the true spirit of sportsmanship. It
couldn't hurt. It didn't help. The student body was too
into it, expressing themselves with funny, but mostly
tasteless, T-shirts and the slam-a-Hurricane banners.

The players themselves changed the subject. "People
talk about hating Miami," remarked tri-captain Ned Bolcar. "I think that's mostly because of the press. There's
no hatred between me and Miami.

"It's not Miami's fault they beat us 56–0 (actually
58–7—What's in a score?) and 24–0 the last couple years.
That's their job. If people are upset at Miami, fine, but
maybe they should be upset at Notre Dame. I guess if
it helps them get excited and get ready for Saturday,
that's great."

Inside linebacker and fifth-year senior Wes Pritchett said of their recent encounters, "There hasn't necessarily been a lot of taunting at us. Their players just have done a lot of celebrating. It angers me in that they were moving the ball and had reason to celebrate."

Enough said.

The weather was ideal and pre-game drills ended with that tuneup in the tunnel. No one was hurt, but the tone was established.

Earlier in the week, Holtz was busily preparing an offense without his first string offensive guards, Tim Ryan and Tim Grunhard, who were injured against Pitt. In their places to start were Mike Brennan, who had begun the season as a backup tight end, and Joe Allen. Both were getting their first starts. So were two freshmen, split end Raghib Ismail and defensive end Arnold Ale. Ryan and Grunhard eventually got in as eight offensive linemen played. "I told him (Holtz) I have to play," said Grunhard, following the game. "This is the game I've worked for all my life. I'm glad he gave me a chance."

With the Irish mixing it up well offensively and free safety Pat Terrell returning a Steve Walsh interception (tipped by Frank Stams) 60 yards for a touchdown, the Irish opened up a 21–7 lead with 5:42 remaining in the first half. Notre Dame Stadium was rocking and in a matter of minutes Walsh put them back in their seats. He drove Miami to the Notre Dame 23 and, instead of attempting a field goal on fourth and four, Johnson decided to go for the first down. The Irish blitzed and Walsh slipped the ball to Leonard Conley, who beat Todd Lyght to the end zone. With 2:16 to go in the half, the Irish were stopped and Jim Sexton's punt from the 29 traveled only 25 yards.

After one first down, Miami faced third and 10 from the 37 when Walsh hit Andre Brown over the middle for 22. From the 15, Walsh hooked up with Cleveland Gary and the Irish lead was history. Fourteen points in five minutes and Walsh had made it look easy. In the previous four games no opponent had laid a hand on him and that's about all the Irish could do. He threw a couple of interceptions and fumbled once in the first half or the Irish would have been playing from behind.

"They could throw for all they wanted but we had to make them pay for throwing," Holtz said. "There were some mistakes, but many of them were made by great plays. It was a game of two great teams that just competed as hard as anything I've seen."

In the first series of the second half, Rice was intercepted. In the first play following the turnover, Miami gave it back on Conley's fumble. Stams recovered. The Irish moved into field goal range on the next possession only to have Bill Hackett's 43-yard field goal attempt blocked.

Neither team was going to win any awards for execution and Miami shot itself in the foot one too many times midway through the third quarter. When Jimmy Johnson gambled on fourth and 3 from the 47 and faked a punt, reserve quarterback Steve Belles was there to make the stop.

"It was a mistake," Johnson noted later. "It was supposed to go right, but we went left instead and they stuffed it. I thought that at the time we could make it and then take the lead. And if we got the lead, I thought we could control the game."

On first down from the 46, Rice connected on a 44–yard pass play to Ricky Watters, who went out of bounds at the 2. Flanker Pat Eilers took a pitch on the next play, cut back, and found a seam to score.

The next Miami drive started at the 32 and Walsh pushed the Hurricanes to the Irish 23 before 6-6 defensive tackle Jeff Alm made the interception at the line of scrimmage. Hitting Florida freshman sensation Derek Brown for 26 yards on second down, Rice guided the Irish to the Miami 11, where Reggie Ho came through with a 27-yard field goal and a 31–21 lead heading into the final quarter. Ten points wasn't much cushion and

Miami cut into it two minutes into the final quarter on Carlos Huerta's 23-yard field goal.

The Irish were in good shape and moving on third and 1 from the 41 on the following possession when Watters dropped Rice's pitch and Tony Brooks had to recover 15 yards behind the line of scrimmage. After the punt, Miami took over on its own 46 with 10:28 to play.

In five plays the Hurricanes were at the Irish 7. On second down, Todd Lyght broke up a pass and on third down a pass intended for Brown was in and out of Michael Stonebreaker's hands. On fourth down with seven minutes still to play, Johnson elected to try again. Walsh hit Gary inside the 5, but he was hit by George Streeter inside the 1 and fumbled. Stonebreaker recovered. Johnson argued that Gary should have been ruled down, but the fumble stood.

Then things really got interesting.

First Miami wasted another opportunity when Walsh was hit by Stams and fumbled, Zorich recovering, at the Irish 28. Then, on third down from the 21, Rice fumbled and Greg Mark recovered for Miami at the Notre Dame 14 with 2:10 to play.

After three plays and three yards, the Hurricanes faced another fourth down and goal situation from the 7. With excellent protection Walsh waited, then threw to the front right corner of the end zone, where Brown made the lunging TD reception with 51 seconds to go. Johnson said there was never any doubt about attempting the 2-point conversion. Walsh dropped back and floated it to the corner of the end zone as he started to get pressure from tackle George Williams. This time Terrell had Conley in man-to-man coverage and stepped in front to knock the pass away. The onside kick that had worked at Michigan was recovered by Anthony Johnson to preserve the upset.

"It was a win by the spirit of a group of guys who just refused to fold, and believed," Holtz said.

The brilliant Steve Walsh threw for 424 yards, a record

by an Irish opponent, but was intercepted three times and suffered his first loss as a starter.

Notre Dame had climbed the mountain. Its program was back and standing eye-to-eye with the best.

Notre Dame 31, Miami 30

Game 7
AIR FORCE
October 22, 1988

What Irish fans remember first about the pre-Holtz era is the thrashing their football team took in Miami. What they remember second is four straight losses (1982–85) to Air Force, a solid program but generally quite overmatched, at least always on paper, against Notre Dame. Notre Dame had won 11 straight before suffering that first loss in '82.

In Holtz's first two encounters with the Falcons the Irish won by a combined 66–17 count.

Not that the Irish could afford to take Fisher DeBerry's club lightly, but it was one of those games on the schedule they were "supposed" to win.

There were, of course, some new circumstances with which to deal. The Irish were 6–0, ranked No. 2, with their head in the clouds following the victory over Miami. Air Force attacks by ground.

"That's unusual for a football team to be involved in a big game like that (Miami) for the first time and win," Holtz remarked the following Monday when the dust had settled. "It's equally hard to come back.

"But if we aren't ready to play we don't deserve to wear the gold helmets. That's the way I feel."

The Irish defense had to switch gears. Against Miami they faced the finest passing attack in the country. Against Air Force, it was the country's best ground game, unless you consider a pitch a pass. The wishbone made the Falcons fly. They were averaging 521.7 yards a game, a national-best 432 of that on the ground, and 46.4 points. Mighty mite quarterback Dee Dowis (5-10, 155 pounds) was averaging almost eight yards a carry and had rushed for 132 yards the year before against Notre Dame.

"The verdict is still out, but I think this offense has a chance to be the best one we've had," admitted DeBerry, who was in his fifth season as chief of the Falcons.

His defense just had little chance. Hurt by injuries and graduation losses, the Falcons were in trouble without the football. They were allowing almost 500 yards a game, 307 through the air, and 32 points.

"We know it will take a superhuman effort," DeBerry said. "Notre Dame has a lot of tradition along with being just a great challenge. It's something like David and Goliath."

To Holtz and the Irish defense, the wishbone is not a foreign object. He dabbles in it, throws it in from time to time, which means the defense sees a little of it in practice, particularly in the spring session.

"I don't think there's any doubt we (coaching staff) have a much better understanding of the wishbone than the average coach," Holtz admitted. "Maybe we know enough about stopping the wishbone to really be scared."

Holtz likes it because it's an offense of execution and precision and you don't walk up to a chalkboard and say this is the way you stop it. It takes a disciplined defense to handle it.

By halftime, Air Force had 168 yards and 13 points, the TD following a 26-yard drive after Anthony Roberson's 60-yard kickoff return in the second quarter.

Linebacker Wes Pritchett felt the first-half defensive execution was sloppy. "We overcompensated a little too much," he said. "We weren't taking care of our own responsibilities."

Cornerback Todd Lyght agreed. "I think at times we had people trying to do too much and playing other positions," he said. "I think we were more disappointed than concerned. . . . The seniors just let us know there's way too much on the line."

Pritchett was one of the seniors who had a few words for the rest of the club after the coaches left the locker room at the half. "We just said this is our house and let's crank it up," Pritchett said in the post-game interview. "We worked too hard and had come too far to go out there and get sloppy."

The talk worked. The Falcons managed a mere 48 yards in the second half as the Irish scored three times without a return.

On the ninth play of the first second-half series, quarterback Tony Rice flipped a flare pass to Tony Brooks, who carried it 42 yards for the touchdown. Reggie Ho's kick gave the Irish a 27–13 lead and control.

After nose tackle Chris Zorich stopped Andy Smith short of a first down on a fourth-down play from the Notre Dame 34, the Irish needed only four plays to add to their total.

Backup quarterback Steve Belles entered the game as a tailback and, on second and 7 from the 50, took a pitch from Rice and flung a pass downfield to Ricky Watters. He hauled it in at the 7 then dragged an Air Force defender with him into the end zone.

It was only the fourth pass of the season for Belles, but two had gone for touchdowns covering 84 yards. Holtz also liked the way he ran from the tailback slot. "He's not back there just for the fun of it," he said. "He's got good eyes. He can see the field."

"If I can produce (running the ball) at tailback, it gives us two passing threats," Belles noted. "I think Coach Holtz just wants to use his players' talents the best he can."

Watters struck again in the fourth quarter on second and 22 from the Air Force 28 when Rice found him in the back corner of the end zone to complete the day's scoring.

After seeing his offense completely shut down in the second half, DeBerry left impressed.

"We had to go back out there in the second half and make something happen," he said. "Notre Dame did what they had to do. They did what the No. 2 team in the country can do; they took charge of the game.

"I really believe that the most improved part of the Notre Dame program is their defense. Their defense is playing as good as any Notre Dame defense I've seen. Their defense might be the unsung part of their football team."

The 170 rushing yards was a season low for the Falcons and Mike Stonebreaker led the Irish in tackles with 12.

With his 36 rushing yards against Air Force, Rice became Notre Dame's all-time rushing leader for quarterbacks. The mark was previously held by Joe Theismann with 384 in 123 carries. Rice had 404 in 91.

Notre Dame 41, Air Force 13

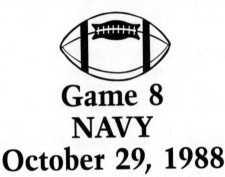

Game 8
NAVY
October 29, 1988

With seven down and Navy up, Lou Holtz wasn't worried about a letdown, heading to Baltimore's Memorial Stadium.

"I don't expect it to happen against Navy or anyone else," he said, "because I think this team understands what it's up against every week. We're not the most talented team around, but I think our players know what it takes to win."

Notre Dame has done that against Navy for a long time. Not since Navy's Roger Staubach team of '63 had the Irish been on the losing side and the streak was at 24 heading to Baltimore. It didn't appear in any kind of jeopardy even with three starters sidelined by injuries. Guard Tim Grunhard made the trip but did not play while fullback Braxston Banks and tight end Frank Jacobs both remained home.

That didn't figure to matter. Navy was 3–4 and coming off a 52–6 loss to Pittsburgh. Head coach Elliot Uzelac was in his second year and retooling the Midshipmen for the wishbone. Considering the Irish had just shut down the country's best in Air Force, it would appear they would be well prepared for what Navy might do.

"They're much bigger than Air Force," Holtz countered. "And it's a case of an Academy team that's well disciplined. They'll play hard and they'll be physical.

"We're delighted to be where we are, but we've got a ways to go. We're not where we need to get defensively."

From the time the Irish left South Bend, they were out of sync. Because of airline problems they arrived in the Baltimore area Friday night six hours later than planned.

A Northwest charter developed problems en route to South Bend from Minneapolis and turned back. A second plane was prepared but a brake problem was discovered. The third plane arrived in South Bend six hours later and the Irish didn't get to the hotel until after 9:30 P.M. Game time was the earliest of the season: 11:10 A.M. South Bend time.

On the first series of the game, Navy quarterback Gary McIntosh fumbled, Jeff Alm recovered, and the Irish were on their way to a 27-yard touchdown drive. Tony Rice passed to Anthony Johnson for 23 yards to set up a 10-yard touchdown pass to Derek Brown four minutes into the game. That was the end of anything coming easy.

"Notre Dame is as good as the media makes it," charged Navy fullback Deric Sims, "which means you build them up to be Superman and put an 'S' on their shirt. That's what everybody is going to see them as. But we did the best we could and we proved they are not as strong as the media builds them up to be."

That came after a 22–7 victory.

The game was played in cool, but sunny conditions. The Irish made it look like they played in a downpour. At least five very catchable passes were dropped, but those mistakes were just a piece of the problem.

There were 90 yards in penalties, including one in which the Irish had too many men on the field. It had been a long time since anyone had seen that one out of Notre Dame.

The kicking game contributed to the day's headaches with one missed extra point, a 10-yard punt, and some very short kickoffs. Despite all the troubles the Irish generated a 16–0 halftime lead.

"The kids played hard and competed," Holtz said. "We just weren't all on the same page. That togetherness you have to have wasn't there."

Freshman fullback Rod Culver snapped through a couple of tackles on his way to a 22-yard touchdown run and on the following drive the Irish got to the Navy 12, where Reggie Ho kicked a 29-yard field goal as time ran out.

The practice the Irish defense got against the "bone" the previous week against Air Force was showing. Notre Dame didn't allow a first down until the second quarter and, on the third series of the game, Uzelac replaced McIntosh with Alton Grizzard. The Middies managed only 46 yards on the ground, none in the air, and only two first downs by halftime.

Even if Notre Dame wasn't sharp, it appeared in full control.

The Irish got their final touchdown on the first drive of the second half, going 67 yards on eight rushing plays. Sophomore fullback Ryan Mihalko powered his way in from a yard away for the score and Tony Brooks was stopped short on the 2-point conversion run.

That was the last anyone heard from the Notre Dame offense. Jim Sexton punted six times in the game, more often than in any of the previous six games.

"It's hard to put your finger on it," said fullback Anthony Johnson. "It didn't seem like everybody was in the game. I kind of felt we'd get things going and we never did. We were confident, maybe overconfident in some sense."

Navy finally got on the board with 3:30 remaining in the third period. With the Irish stopped on downs from their own 23, Sexton's shanked punt traveled only 10 yards, giving Navy the ball at the 33. On first down from the 22, Grizzard swept to the right and went all the way.

On its next series Navy drove into Notre Dame territory when Pat Terrell recovered an Alton Grizzard fumble. But the Irish handed it right back when Paul Day fell on Mark Green's fumble. From its own 35, again Navy marched into Notre Dame territory.

Facing a fourth and 2 at the 32, Uzelac sent Sims up the middle for what appeared to be a first down. After a lengthy consultation over the measurement, the ball went back over to the Irish.

"A lot of things happened out there today and I don't want to overshadow the performance by the officiating, but the officiating stunk," said an angry Uzelac. "I ask any member of the press when they ever saw that many members of the officiating crew get over the ball and get that many opinions. Notre Dame does not need help from the officiating."

It would have taken a couple of big breaks for Navy to battle back. It had absolutely no passing game. Even its last possession with the clock winding down, Grizzard threw only once in seven plays.

"They lived up to their reputation," Frank Stams acknowledged. "One thing you've got to give them credit for, they kept coming with their stuff. . . . I thought they'd come out and pass a little more."

The Middies threw only five passes all day, completing one for nine yards.

"Most teams would be satisfied (with a 22–7) victory," remarked free safety Corny Southall. "We can't be."

"Offensively, they just whipped us up front," Holtz observed. "We're not a very good football team right now. . . . Our team was not mentally alert. That's no one's responsibility but mine.

"Fortunately, our defense played well and really competed."

After a frustrating day, there was a reward waiting for the Irish. UCLA suffered its first setback and Notre Dame was destined to climb to the No. 1 ranking in the country for the first time since 1981.

Notre Dame 22, Navy 7

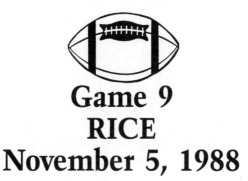

Game 9
RICE
November 5, 1988

"Here we are No. 1 and I'm scared to death about a team that hasn't won," Lou Holtz said of Rice after an early-week practice.

If it was any consolation, the players took it upon themselves to be concerned. It was only a year before that everything faded away with three straight losses at the end of the season. They recognized the hump. As reflective senior strong safety George Streeter related, they rededicated themselves and their concentration.

As you might expect, Holtz was not a happy camper coming back from Baltimore and made his players feel like they were back in pre-season practice. The days were long and the contact unusually constant for a team going into its ninth game of the season. Holtz made one slight change early in the week. He built a fire under tackle Dean Brown by inserting Mike Brennan in his spot. Brown would eventually start.

"The kids have responded this week," Holtz said, following Thursday's practice. "Some of our practices were a little hard to control the tempo. But we didn't have to get after them. The intensity and concentration have been real good."

Said tackle Jeff Alm: "It was not a hard week, it was an intense week; a good physical week that we hadn't had in a while."

It also was the first week the Irish got to deal with the No. 1 ranking. "If they're looking for guidance, they're looking at the wrong guy," Holtz joked. "It's new for me, too.

"Our team's no different," he observed. "You've got to be able to handle success. Some people can't handle success. We're asking ourselves the same questions we did when we were 1–4 in our first year: What are we going to do now?

"If our players are under the conception that we are No. 1, then we're dead. . . . What it means is that we have the chance to control our own destiny. What we're doing is fighting for a championship. Let's just put it in perspective."

That meant Rice went up on a pedestal. Rice was on the schedule and playing in Notre Dame Stadium because Southern Methodist's "death penalty" scratched that series. Even if the Owls hadn't won a game in seven tries, they had been competitive in their last five after head coach Jerry Berndt (now at Temple) returned Quentis Roper to quarterback and quarterback Donald Hollas to safety. In Little Rock the week before meeting the Irish, Rice had come within a touchdown of undefeated Arkansas.

Lou Holtz spent seven seasons at Arkansas and he still had his contacts. "The players at Arkansas thought Rice was one of the better teams they played. I don't care what their record is, they're playing well. They were not out of a single (Southwest) conference game."

Against Texas Tech, the Owls had over 600 yards in total offense and Roper featured a double threat. Despite the record Rice had an opportunity to make some kind of mark.

"You have to be excited about playing Notre Dame," remarked Rice's outstanding center, Courtney Hall. "It's probably the closest we will get to playing for a championship. This will be the ultimate, supreme test."

It wasn't for the Irish. They had a long week and a productive Saturday with a 54–11 victory.

On its first possession of the day, Rice drove 70 yards in 10 plays and got a 23-yard field goal from Clint Parsons for a 3–0 lead.

It lasted all of about 13 seconds. On a damp field, Raghib Ismail left a lasting impression. On the ensuing kickoff Ismail caught the ball at the 13, broke to the right side and through a couple of arm tackles before picking up a key block from Steve Belles on his way to an 87-yard return for a touchdown.

"Rocket" wasn't quite finished. Eighteen seconds into the final quarter he did it again. Gathering in a groundball kick at the 17, Ismail found a seam in the middle and was gone. Not since 1922, when Paul Castner did it, had a Notre Dame player returned two kickoffs for touchdowns in a game. He was later awarded the NCAA statistical title for kickoff returns though he had two fewer returns than necessary to qualify. His average of 36.1 going into the Fiesta Bowl was so good that even with two more returns for no yardage, he would have won the title.

"We wanted to come out and hit with them," said Hollas. "After Ismail's runback, it was like a snowball effect."

After the first series, Rice struggled to get anything going against the Irish defense. Roper had 197 yards passing, but the best Rice could do was three field goals. The scoring ended on a weird note when Bill Stone scooped up a blocked PAT and went all the way for the two points. The rule had just gone into the books and the return marked the first time such a play occurred at the Division I level.

With the Irish sacking Roper four times and getting another eight tackles for losses, the Owls' net rushing total was only 32 yards and 229 overall.

Chris Zorich rose to the challenge. Going against All-American Courtney Hall, he had six tackles, two for losses, with one sack. And Jeff Alm and D'Juan Francisco got their second interceptions of the season.

"They took it right at us," Hall said. "They're a very good team. They have a good defense because they play well together and they have a bunch of good solid players."

Notre Dame didn't have to get fancy. They wound up with 439 yards in offense, 294 on the ground, as 14 different backs got a piece of the pie. The Irish only punted twice all day.

"If you told me that would be the score, I would have never believed that," Holtz remarked. "I think we were a little too strong for them overall and we were ready to play, I'll say that."

It was the roughest day of the season for flanker Ricky Watters, who obviously was struggling to get comfortable with his role. He fumbled a handoff and also a punt when "Coach Holtz said to calm down and keep my composure," Watters recalled. "It was some time after the second fumble when he told me I'm going to be a tailback. That's my natural position and Coach Holtz knows that."

Watters would play both positions in the final week, primarily at flanker, but Holtz said Watters would be back at tailback in the spring.

No. 1 wasn't very lucky for Florida State, Miami, or UCLA. Notre Dame survived its first test. "Let's hope the luck of the Irish holds up," Holtz responded.

Notre Dame 54, Rice 11

Game 10
PENN STATE
November 19, 1988

No one wanted to stop now. Just when the Irish game got revved up again it was time to slip into idle and take a week off. A year earlier they would have killed for a week off, heading into the 10th game of the season against Penn State.

Now, with the depth much improved, the health better, and a 54–11 victory only a couple of days old, Holtz and even his players wanted to keep the rhythm going.

"I'd like to keep going," acknowledged tackle Dean Brown. "Our confidence is slowly getting stronger and stronger."

"If I had a preference, I'd like to continue to go," Lou Holtz said. "But we've got an off-week and we've got to continue to make the best of it and try to get better."

Holtz felt that Reggie Ho got better and, after replacing him with Bill Hackett on PATs against Rice (he had two blocked), Holtz said the senior Ho would be back in his spot for the final home game of the season.

Penn State, which had developed into an intense rival in recent years—the previous two Irish defeats were by six points—would close out the home schedule for the

Irish and in two years the two clubs had done an about-face. The last time the Nittany Lions were in Notre Dame Stadium, they were on their way to a Fiesta Bowl bid and a national championship, while the Irish were in their first season under Holtz and on their way to a second straight losing season for the first time in almost a century. The Irish threw in quite a scare before the Lions survived, 24–19—the last loss the Irish were to suffer in Notre Dame Stadium.

Now the Irish were 9–0, ranked No. 1, and about to accept a bid to the Fiesta Bowl, while Penn State was 5–5 and on the verge of its first losing season in a half-century.

"They've been close against some good teams, a mistake here, a mistake there," Holtz cautioned. "I know they're capable of playing very well. And everyone's telling me they're dancing in the streets and all fired up because they don't want to be the first losing team in 50 years."

Penn State had had a hold on Notre Dame. Only once since the series resumed in '81 had the Irish won and the Lions had won three straight, giving them a 6-5-1 edge in the series.

The Irish had to stop Penn State's rushing game, which they hadn't done a year ago in a 1-point loss, and had to be concerned that the Lions were allowing only 132 yards a game on the ground, more than 100 yards under what the Irish were averaging. And of their five losses coming in, three were by a touchdown or less.

"Penn State matches up very well with us in terms of personnel," Holtz noted.

There was no letdown and the 21–3 score didn't do justice to what the Irish did to the visitors.

"We finally beat a team that eluded us for three years," said George Streeter. "It would have been a shame for us to lose to a 5–5 team and mess up the season we've got going. We didn't take them lightly at all."

The Notre Dame totals were impressive on both sides. Offensively: Thirty-eight minutes of possession time, 502 yards, 301 on the ground with Tony Rice throwing for 191 yards, then the second best total of his career. Defensively: Penn State completed only five of 24 passes—the Irish experimented with considerable man-to-man coverage—managed only 105 yards on the ground and turned the ball over three times.

"As a unit we were really focused in," said tackle George "Big Boo" Williams. "We used a lot of movement. We knew their quarterbacks (Lance Lonergan and Tony Sacca) were young and we thought the movement might mess them up."

The Irish had two interceptions, one by tackle Jeff Alm and another by nose tackle Steve Roddy, giving the Irish ends and tackles six for the season.

Nevertheless, Penn State hadn't lost its stubborn streak.

"I credit Joe Paterno," Holtz said. "You have no idea how he can keep a team in a football game when it's getting outgained in everything."

Some of that was of Notre Dame's own doing. It had an uncharacteristic three turnovers, including Rice's first interception since the Miami game, a TD called back by a penalty, 94 yards in penalties, and a missed 35-yard field goal.

From the outset, it looked like a romp. The Irish took over at the 13 on their first possession and rammed it 87 yards in 12 plays, the big gainer coming on Rice's pass to Watters, good for 31 yards. From the 2, Rice faked a handoff, rolled left, pump faked to tight end Rod West, then carried it in.

"You have to give Notre Dame a lot of credit," Paterno said. "They play hard, they play clean, and they play with a lot of enthusiasm. I wish them the best. . . . They're just a good football team."

The Irish put seven more points on the board before the end of the half (they had a TD from Tony Brooks taken off by a penalty), when they marched 60 yards in only five plays and senior tailback Mark Green won a 22-yard footrace down the right sidelines.

Notre Dame let another opportunity slip away with a half-minute to go in the half. When Jeff Alm forced a fumble and Wes Pritchett recovered, the Irish took over at the Penn State 24. But an interference call on ND and another interception gave it back to Penn State at the 32 with 22 seconds to play. The half appeared to be over, when tailback Leroy Thompson was stopped at mid-field as time expired, but the Irish were nabbed for a facemask penalty, giving Penn State the ball at the 35 with no time showing. Paterno sent in his kickoff man, Eric Etze, who had yet to attempt a field goal all season. He connected from 52 yards out on the final play of the half.

The Irish, who had allowed 69 yards on the ground in the first half, were even better in the second and the Lions completed only two of 12 passes.

"They're awesome," Mark Green said of his defensive teammates. "I'm glad I'm on their side. When I'm watching from the sidelines, I can empathize with the opponents because they really hit."

In a third quarter possession starting at the 33, Notre Dame went for it all. On an audible call on first down, Rice stepped back and lofted it down the right sideline. Raghib Ismail ran under it near the 20 and shed Eddie Johnson's arm tackle for the longest touchdown pass of Rice's career. Rice, as a precautionary measure, was taken for X-rays of his ribs after the game. Fortunately the results were negative, and a positive sign for the upcoming matchup against the Trojans.

"Ever since I've been here I've dreamed about this," offensive tackle and captain Andy Heck said of the upcoming meeting with No. 2-ranked Southern California. "We're No. 1 and 10–0 going into the last game against our greatest rival—I couldn't ask for more. Maybe it will be the game of the century."

Notre Dame 21, Penn State 3

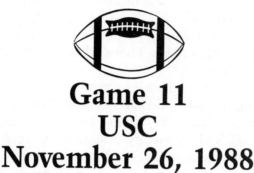

Game 11
USC
November 26, 1988

For five straight years, Notre Dame had had Southern California's number to match the longest streak in a storied history that was coming up on its 60th anniversary. For the first time ever two of college football's giants were heading into the matchup with one ranked No. 1 and the other No. 2.

"It's THE game," Holtz said, following Monday's practice of that week. "When the series started you could buy a Ford for $500 and Tunney was fighting Dempsey. . . .

"It's about two fine institutions with great traditions. . . . There have been a lot of All-Americans who have played in this series."

It was Super Bowl week II. Like the week of the Miami game, Holtz closed his practices. Unlike the week of the Miami game, he phoned Jimmy Johnson to tap his brain on his club's incredible run of success on the road. Holtz also decided to alter the usual itinerary from the two previous season-ending trips. Going to Miami in '87 and to USC in '86, the Irish arrived the Wednesday before Thanksgiving. He felt that was too much time in the sunshine and, as a result, his club's concentration drifted. This time the Irish would not arrive in their motel at Newport Beach until Thursday evening and would have only one full day away from home before game day.

Following that Monday's practice, Holtz remarked, "They were sharp today. That's what it's all about. It's Southern Cal week."

It had its share of oddities. On Monday, Rodney Peete had laryngitis and could barely speak above a whisper. He had played heroically against UCLA, completing 16 of 28 in USC's 31–22 victory, despite being weakened by the measles. He only practiced one day that week. For the week of the Irish game, he was practicing, but freshman quarterback Todd Marinovich was standing behind him calling out the snap count.

"I know it's an unusual way of practicing, but at least Rodney is out there this week, unlike last week when he missed all but one day of workouts," USC coach Larry Smith said. By Thursday Peete was talking again and the Irish had received their measle shots.

Holtz's developing reputation of downplaying his own club's talents and building up the opposition preceded him into LA. After taping a Friday afternoon interview with Holtz, one television station in its evening show "beeped" every time Holtz played up USC. In the minute or so interview the "beeps" were well into double figures and sounded like a telegraph message.

"If it's a high-scoring game, we're going to lose," Holtz announced. "When you go on the road, you better take your defense, discipline, quickness, and kicking game."

If not overmatched, the Irish did figure to have their hands full. The strength of the Irish offense was its running game, averaging 267 yards a game. USC was allowing only 68.1 and had held Oklahoma's powerful option game to only 89 yards.

"I think in terms of their offense, I don't think there's any question this is our biggest test," Smith said. "They combine the power game with the option game. When we played Oklahoma, we really didn't have to concern ourselves that much with getting hurt by the pass like we do against Notre Dame."

The Trojans really got hurt only once. On USC's first punt Chris Sperle buried the Irish on their 2-yard line. On first down Tony Rice faked well to Mark Green and stepped back to the back of the end zone and lofted a pass to Raghib Ismail near midfield. He made the catch before stumbling and the Irish were out of trouble.

The Irish had proven earlier they could run, when Rice broke off a 65-yard TD run on an option. But could they sustain it without their top rusher (Tony Brooks) and leading receiver (Ricky Watters) on hand? That Friday, when the pair was 40 minutes late for an evening meal, Holtz docked them one game and sent them home on a plane to South Bend. It wasn't their first infraction and Holtz reportedly had issued an ultimatum Thanksgiving night after they were late for a team meeting. Where were they? They couldn't find their car in a California mall parking lot, so the Irish would be shorthanded against the No. 2 team in the country.

"I think I would have felt the weight of that loss on my shoulders," Brooks said later. Most other members of the club didn't want to comment on it. They looked at it as an injury. "People go down, other people step in," said cornerback Stan Smagala.

Heisman Trophy winner Tim Brown, playing with the Los Angeles Raiders, was in the post-game locker room and remarked, "That's Lou Holtz. If you're not going to do it his way, you're not going to be around. He was preaching that for two years."

Big plays carried the Irish all afternoon in front of almost 94,000 in the LA Coliseum. Offensively, it was every bit the struggle it was expected to be, Rice's run notwithstanding. After Rice and Ho made it 7–0 with almost five minutes to go in the first quarter, the defense came up with the first of several big plays. On the Trojans' possession following the score, defensive end Frank Stams fell on the ball at the USC 19 and in five plays the Irish were in on Mark Green's 3-yard run. Ho's kick made it 14–0 and the Irish were off and running. Well, maybe not.

For the next two quarters the Irish offense was nearly motionless with only one first down and 17 yards. After the Trojans put together a 66-yard drive to pull within a touchdown, Stan Smagala picked off one of Peete's 44 passes and used his 4.4 speed to go the 64 yards down the sidelines with 41 seconds to go in the half. The PAT failed for a 20–7 lead, but more important was the battering Peete had taken.

Peete had made a tackle on George Streeter following his interception and 23-yard return earlier in the quarter. With the Irish blitzing regularly, Peete was under pressure most of the first half. He was slammed by Stams on a block after Smagala's interception, knocking the wind out of him. Then with 16 seconds to go from the USC 47, Stams nailed him for an 8-yard loss and put him down on his shoulder. He got up slowly and watched the final play of the half from the sidelines as the Irish led 20–7 at the break. There was some question whether Peete would even return in the second half.

The Irish depth helped. Defensive coordinator Barry Alvarez used five defensive ends and six different players from tackle to tackle. "We wanted to keep them fresh — we felt we had to keep the pressure on Peete," he said. "We felt you've got to keep him off-balance. You can't let him in the groove and I think we did that."

Smith admitted, "We didn't handle the blitz today. We had handled it all year, but today it was like we were playing in a fog."

USC's best opportunity to rally came in its second possession of the third quarter. After being buried deep in their own territory, the Irish punted away and USC took over at its own 44. Peete got the drive going with a couple of his 23 completions and Emanuel picked up 32 yards in the drive and his 21-yard run gave the Trojans a first down at the 4. But Bolcar stopped Emanuel after a gain of one, then Pritchett stepped up and nailed him for a 1-yard loss and Peete's pass on third down was incomplete. USC had to settle for a field goal and it turned the tide.

The Irish, who had yet to get a first down in the quarter—Holtz acknowledged they may have been a little conservative—finally got it going from the 30. On first down Rice gained 13. Then on third and 3 from midfield, Anthony Johnson gained 10 and, on third and 6 from the 36, picked up 23 yards on Rice's screen pass. From the 13 the Irish drove it in, Green going the final yard with three minutes gone in the fourth quarter.

The Trojans got to the Irish 10 in its final possession but only 57 seconds remained.

The Irish were outgained 356–253 and had the ball only 25:53 to USC's 34:07, but a defense that kept getting better carried the Irish just as Holtz said it would have to.

"I've never had a year as gratifying as this," he said. "They've been underrated all year and just find a way to win."

"Now we're 60 minutes from a national championship," Green said. "We're going to let it all hang out."

Notre Dame 27, USC 10

Game 12
FIESTA BOWL
WEST VIRGINIA
January 2, 1989

Lou Holtz calls it another season, mostly because it's hard to know if a team can pick up where it left off. A month is a long wait between games and the Irish were ready to keep playing.

"In all honesty, deep down," Holtz acknowledged, "we didn't think we'd be sitting there, although you always hope for it."

They were on a roll, and their defense had reached national championship caliber. Rodney Peete and USC would agree.

Like good pitching in baseball, good defense usually wins out, but West Virginia's offense had been unstoppable all year, led by sophomore quarterback Major Harris' free-wheeling talents and an offensive line that was large, seasoned, and strong.

"West Virginia has completely dominated in the offensive line against everybody they've played," said Holtz. "They run power and their offensive line is so big and strong you have to do a variety of things to offset that—which we can do and have done.

"But then you put in the mobility of Major Harris and the option, that's where you get in trouble."

"We feel like we can run the ball against anybody," WVU tackle Rick Phillips said. "The thing that makes us comfortable is we can play option football, or we can play power football. If one thing doesn't work, we can go to something else."

The Mountaineers moved it on everyone, to the tune of 282 yards a game on the ground and almost 500 total. Thirty-six Mountaineers bench-pressed 400 pounds or better compared to five for Notre Dame and WVU had produced more than 3,000 yards on the ground for the season. They had averaged 42 points a game, 10 more than the Irish.

That still didn't mean coast-to-coast respect for the No. 3-ranked Mountaineers. There were questions about the strength of their schedule and Don Nehlen's team had Jimmy Johnson in the background, lobbying for votes for his Miami team should West Virginia beat Notre Dame.

"We're fairly well-respected by the people who know us, honestly," proclaimed Nehlen, during a mid-week press conference.

Holtz, who was born in West Virginia, had great respect.

The Irish were generally in good health going in, though they were down to two tight ends with reserve Rod West sidelined by a leg infection and offensive guard Tim Ryan was nursing a pulled groin.

Holtz was feeling good about his club's practices in Arizona and even mentioned that Tony Rice was throwing the ball well. There was considerable contact work in the first couple days of the week—some of the more physical practices they'd had all year, according to some players—before they started easing up.

Tailback and tri-captain Mark Green said, "I feel better about our offense than any point in the season. Things are really crisp. Just the concentration—it's been really good. There haven't been that many mistakes."

"When you get to this stage I think you're prepared for everything," Holtz said. "There are just a lot of unanswered questions. Is their offensive line as dominating as they've been against everybody else? How much have we improved since the end of the season? . . . How will we play after a six-week layoff? That's a big question."

Nehlen, a former quarterback, likes testing the big-play approach. He does not live by the philosophy that when you throw three things can happen, two of which are bad, especially when you throw deep. He includes interference calls and simply keeping a defense honest as a big hand to an offense. It certainly had worked so far.

The juggernaut was jumbled in Sun Devil Stadium. The Mountaineers rushed for only 108 yards and added another 174 through the air for only 282.

Mountaineer fans, no doubt, will claim the third play of the game as the big difference. On third and 3 from the WVU 33, Harris kept the ball to his left and was tripped up by Michael Stonebreaker. Tackle Jeff Alm finished the job and bruised Harris' left shoulder. He wasn't the same and neither was the Mountaineer offense as Nehlen was forced to cut back on his option game.

But would it have mattered? Trying to go deep several times, WVU had a hard time getting behind Notre Dame's swift defensive backs and Harris had little time to set up. And offensively, as Green had said earlier, the Irish were on, rolling up 455 yards and mixing things up to perfection. Tony Rice was more dangerous than Harris, throwing for 213 yards, running for 75, and leaving with Most Valuable Player honors.

In the first series of the game, he scrambled for 31 on a third-down play to set up Bill Hackett's 45-yard field goal.

On the next Irish scoring drive, he hooked up with Derek Brown for 23 of the 61 yards, capped by Anthony Johnson's plunge from a yard out on fourth down. Going into the second quarter, the Irish had nine points and the Mountaineers nary a first down.

"In a situation like this, he wants to be the man," Ricky Watters said of Rice.

The Irish youth stepped to the front offensively in the second quarter, when freshman Rod Culver scored on a 5-yard run to complete an 84-yard drive and classmate Raghib Ismail hauled in a 29-yard scoring pass from Rice as the Irish went 63 yards in eight plays. The Mountaineers squeezed out a couple of field goals, including one with no time showing on the first-half clock, and trailed 23–6 at the half.

"Before the game," Green said, "they were talking about how their offense was unstoppable. It was kind of the other way around."

The Irish were up 26–13 late in the third quarter when West Virginia's only opportunity knocked. The Mountaineers had just scored their TD on Harris' pass to Grantis Bell from 17 yards out when ND took over at the 20. On second down, Rice was intercepted by Willie Edwards and returned to the 26. A year earlier, Rice would have been chastised, maybe even pulled. Holtz told him to forget it and later accepted blame for making a mistake on the play call.

The defense didn't let it hurt, stopping WVU cold, and the sack of Harris by defensive MVP Stams and freshman Arnold Ale even knocked the Mountaineers from field goal range.

"That was the turning point," Nehlen said. "If we could have put some points on the board, we would have been in business."

They would have needed a lot more points because the Irish went 80 yards in seven plays and Rice's flip to Frank Jacobs tacked on six points. Rice's 2-point run ended the Irish scoring. WVU added a TD with 1:14 to play on a drive that featured four unsportsmanlike conduct penalties, including one on Holtz who went into the huddle to find out what was going on. "We got frustrated," Holtz said. "Our players were complaining about being held. But our players were completely wrong."

Now that the Irish had knocked off their fourth top 10 team, Holtz could say it: "Yes, I know I have been hesitant to put the stamp of greatness on this team, but no one proved that we weren't. They all had a shot at us, but this team knows what it takes.

"We did it as a team. We are a real family. And as long as I live, I'll always remember this team."

Notre Dame 34, West Virginia 21

THE 1988
SEASON STATISTICS

Team Statistics by Game

GAME 1
At Notre Dame Stadium

	ND	MICH.
1ST DOWNS	15	13
Rushing	12	7
Passing	2	5
Penalty	1	1
RUSHES	43	52
Yardage	234	151
Yardage lost	8	12
RUSHING YDS.	226	139
PASSING YDS.	40	74
Passes	12	11
Completed	3	8
Intercepted	1	0
TTL. PLAYS	55	63
TTL. YDS.	266	213
Average gain	4.8	3.4
PUNTS-avg.	3–43	6–46.1
FUMBLES-lost	2–1	1–1
PENALTIES-yds.	3–24	3–30
POSSESSION	24:11	35:49
3RD DOWNS	4–11	6–15

Scoring by Quarter

| **NOTRE DAME** | 10 3 0 6 – 19 |
| **MICHIGAN** | 0 7 7 3 – 17 |

GAME 2
At Spartan Stadium

	ND	MSU
1ST DOWNS	16	17
Rushing	13	7
Passing	2	10
Penalty	1	0
RUSHES	54	35
Yardage	290	124
Yardage lost	45	35
RUSHING YDS.	245	89
PASSING YDS.	50	207
Passes	11	31
Completed	2	18
Intercepted	2	2
TTL. PLAYS	65	66
TTL. YDS.	295	296
Average gain	4.5	4.5
PUNTS-avg.	4–43.5	8–42.9
FUMBLES-lost	2–1	0–0
PENALTIES-yds.	6–55	10–74
POSSESSION	30:40	29:24
3RD DOWNS	4–13	5–15

Scoring by Quarter

| **NOTRE DAME** | 0 6 7 7 – 20 |
| **MICH. STATE** | 3 0 0 0 – 3 |

GAME 3
At Notre Dame Stadium

	ND	PUR
1ST DOWNS	20	15
Rushing	13	6
Passing	6	9
Penalty	1	0
RUSHES	57	29
Yardage	328	100
Yardage lost	7	0
RUSHING YDS.	321	100
PASSING YDS.	147	167
Passes	14	42
Completed	8	19
Intercepted	1	5
TTL. PLAYS	71	71
TTL. YDS.	468	267
Average gain	6.6	3.8
PUNTS-avg.	4–37.7	9–41.3
FUMBLES-lost	1–1	0–0
PENALTIES-yds.	4–30	8–49
POSSESSION	30:30	29:30
3RD DOWNS	9–17	2–14

Scoring by Quarter

NOTRE DAME	14	28	3	7	—	52
PURDUE	0	0	0	7	—	7

GAME 5
At Pitt Stadium

	ND	PITT
1ST DOWNS	27	23
Rushing	17	8
Passing	7	10
Penalty	3	5
RUSHES	72	34
Yardage	343	180
Yardage lost	33	9
RUSHING YDS.	310	171
PASSING YDS.	96	209
Passes	14	25
Completed	8	12
Intercepted	2	1
TTL. PLAYS	86	59
TTL. YDS.	406	380
Average gain	4.7	6.4
PUNTS-avg.	1–37	3–48
FUMBLES-lost	1–1	4–2
PENALTIES-yds.	8–83	6–50
POSSESSION	39:49	20:11
3RD DOWNS	8–14	2–9

Scoring by Quarter

NOTRE DAME	14	3	6	7	—	30
PITTSBURGH	7	7	3	3	—	20

GAME 4
At Notre Dame Stadium

	ND	STAN
1ST DOWNS	27	16
Rushing	16	5
Passing	10	9
Penalty	1	2
RUSHES	61	23
Yardage	341	77
Yardage lost	9	18
RUSHING YDS.	332	59
PASSING YDS.	135	215
Passes	15	41
Completed	12	23
Intercepted	0	1
TTL. PLAYS	76	64
TTL. YDS.	467	274
Average gain	6.1	4.3
PUNTS-avg.	1–41	4–25
FUMBLES-lost	0–0	2–1
PENALTIES-yds.	4–45	6–80
POSSESSION	33:59	26:01
3RD DOWNS	9–13	6–15

Scoring by Quarter

NOTRE DAME	6	22	7	7	—	42
STANFORD	0	7	7	0	—	14

GAME 6
At Notre Dame Stadium

	ND	MIAMI
1ST DOWNS	16	26
Rushing	8	2
Passing	7	23
Penalty	1	1
RUSHES	49	28
Yardage	162	73
Yardage lost	49	16
RUSHING YDS.	113	57
PASSING YDS.	218	424
Passes	18	50
Completed	10	31
Intercepted	1	3
TTL. PLAYS	67	78
TTL. YDS.	331	481
Average gain	4.9	6.2
PUNTS-avg.	4–37.7	1–25
FUMBLES-lost	3–2	4–4
PENALTIES-yds.	6–34	5–39
POSSESSION	28:59	31:01
3RD DOWNS	7–14	8–16

Scoring by Quarter

NOTRE DAME	7	14	10	0	—	31
MIAMI	0	21	0	9	—	30

GAME 7
At Notre Dame Stadium

	ND	AF
1ST DOWNS	23	13
Rushing	18	10
Passing	5	3
Penalty	4	0
RUSHES	52	45
Yardage	283	195
Yardage lost	16	25
RUSHING YDS.	267	170
PASSING YDS.	177	46
Passes	15	11
Completed	9	5
Intercepted	0	0
TTL. PLAYS	67	56
TTL. YDS.	444	216
Average gain	6.6	3.9
PUNTS-avg.	3–40	5–37.6
FUMBLES-lost	1–1	1–1
PENALTIES-yds.	6–50	7–35
POSSESSION	33:47	26:13
3RD DOWNS	5–10	3–12

Scoring by Quarter

NOTRE DAME	7	13	14	7 —	41
AIR FORCE	3	10	0	0 —	13

GAME 8
At Memorial Stadium

	ND	NAVY
1ST DOWNS	21	10
Rushing	13	9
Passing	6	0
Penalty	2	1
RUSHES	49	52
Yardage	284	203
Yardage lost	17	20
RUSHING YDS.	267	183
PASSING YDS.	129	9
Passes	25	5
Completed	13	1
Intercepted	0	0
TTL. PLAYS	74	57
TTL. YDS.	396	192
Average gain	5.4	3.4
PUNTS-avg.	6–33	7–35
FUMBLES-lost	3–2	3–1
PENALTIES-yds.	7–90	4–45
POSSESSION	32:35	26:25
3RD DOWNS	7–14	3–15

Scoring by Quarter

NOTRE DAME	7	9	6	0 —	22
NAVY	0	0	7	0 —	7

GAME 9
At Notre Dame Stadium

	ND	RICE
1ST DOWNS	24	16
Rushing	16	4
Passing	7	10
Penalty	1	2
RUSHES	52	34
Yardage	299	91
Yardage lost	5	59
RUSHING YDS.	294	32
PASSING YDS.	145	197
Passes	18	36
Completed	9	21
Intercepted	0	2
TTL. PLAYS	70	70
TTL. YDS.	439	229
Average gain	6.3	3.3
PUNTS-avg.	2–32	6–34
FUMBLES-lost	2–2	2–2
PENALTIES-yds.	6–59	6–58
POSSESSION	26:28	33:22
3RD DOWNS	6–11	6–17

Scoring by Quarter

NOTRE DAME	14	17	7	16 —	54
RICE	3	3	0	5 —	11

GAME 10
At Notre Dame Stadium

	ND	PSU
1ST DOWNS	24	11
Rushing	17	6
Passing	6	3
Penalty	1	2
RUSHES	63	31
Yardage	313	128
Yardage lost	12	23
RUSHING YDS.	301	105
PASSING YDS.	201	74
Passes	19	24
Completed	11	5
Intercepted	2	2
TTL. PLAYS	82	55
TTL. YDS.	502	179
Average gain	6.1	3.25
PUNTS-avg.	4–39	8–41
FUMBLES-lost	1–1	2–1
PENALTIES-yds.	8–94	5–33
POSSESSION	38:57	21:03
3RD DOWNS	6–14	3–14

Scoring by Quarter

NOTRE DAME	7	7	7	0 —	21
PENN STATE	0	3	0	0 —	3

GAME 11
At Los Angeles Coliseum

	ND	USC
1ST DOWNS	8	21
Rushing	6	8
Passing	2	11
Penalty	0	2
RUSHES	41	40
Yardage	194	168
Yardage lost	32	37
RUSHING YDS.	162	131
PASSING YDS.	91	255
Passes	9	44
Completed	5	23
Intercepted	0	2
TTL. PLAYS	50	84
TTL. YDS.	253	356
Average gain	5.1	4.2
PUNTS-avg.	8–41	6–37
FUMBLES-lost	2–1	4–2
PENALTIES-yds.	8–52	6–50
POSSESSION	25:53	34:07
3RD DOWNS	5–13	8–19

Scoring by Quarter

NOTRE DAME	14	6	0	7	—	27
USC	0	7	3	0	—	10

GAME 12
At Sun Devil Stadium, Fiesta Bowl

	ND	WVU
1ST DOWNS	19	19
Rushing	13	4
Passing	6	10
Penalty	0	5
RUSHES	59	37
Yardage	245	141
Yardage lost	3	33
RUSHING YDS.	242	108
PASSING YDS.	213	174
Passes	11	30
Completed	7	14
Intercepted	1	1
TTL. PLAYS	70	67
TTL. YDS.	455	282
Average gain	6.5	4.2
PUNTS-avg.	4–37	7–45
FUMBLES-lost	2–0	0–0
PENALTIES-yds.	11–102	3–38
POSSESSION	36:43	23:17
3RD DOWNS	8–15	4–14

Scoring by Quarter

NOTRE DAME	9	14	3	8	—	34
WVU	0	6	7	8	—	21

Final Statistics

TEAM STATISTICS

	ND	OPP
Total offensive yards	4723	3365
Total plays	833	790
Yards per play	5.67	4.26
Yards per game	393.6	280.4
Rushing yards	3080	1344
Attempts	652	440
Yards per rush	4.72	3.05
Yards per game	256.7	112.0
Passing yards	1643	2021
Attempts	181	350
Completions	97	180
Had intercepted	10	19
Comp. percentage	53.6	51.4
Touchdown passes	12	9
Yards per attempt	9.08	5.77
Yards per completion	16.9	11.2
Yards per game	136.9	168.4
Punting yards	1691	2757
Number of punts	44	73
Average punt	38.4	37.8
Had blocked	0	1
Punt return yards	373	170
Number of returns	30	22
Average return	12.4	7.7

TEAM STATISTICS (*continued*)

	ND	OPP
Kickoff return yards	738	1258
Number of returns	31	71
Average return	23.8	17.7
Interception return yards	344	69
Number of interceptions	19	10
Average return	18.1	6.9
Number of penalties	76	70
Penalty yards	723	576
Fumbles (lost)	20–13	23–16
Total first downs	240	200
By rushing	162	76
By passing	66	103
By penalty	12	21
Third-down conversions	79–161	55–173
Percentage	49.1	31.8
Possession time	384:43	335:17
Minutes per game	32:04	27:56
Team scoring	393	156
Average	32.8	13.0
Touchdowns	51	16
By rushing	32	7
By passing	12	9
By returns	7	0
By recovery	0	0
Field goals (made-att.)	14–18	14–16
Safeties	0	1
PAT-kick	39–46	14–14
PAT-run	3–5	0–0
PAT-pass	0–0	1–2

RUSHING

	TC	Yds	Avg	TD	Lg
T. Rice	134	775	5.8	9	65
M. Green	148	707	4.8	7	40
T. Brooks	128	702	5.5	2	52
A. Johnson	74	302	4.1	6	22
R. Culver	34	215	6.3	4	36
B. Banks	36	141	3.9	1	28
S. Belles	20	80	4.0	0	18
R. Watters	33	76	2.3	0	14
R. Setzer	11	24	2.2	0	12
P. Eilers	6	22	3.7	1	7

RUSHING (*continued*)

	TC	Yds	Avg	TD	Lg
K. Graham	8	18	2.2	0	5
R. Mihalko	6	14	2.3	1	4
P. Graham	5	9	1.8	0	9
B. Satterfield	2	9	4.5	0	6
J. Jarosz	3	4	1.3	1	6
M. Gatti	1	4	4.0	0	4
C. Southall	1	3	3.0	0	3
R. Ebert	1	−4	−4.0	0	−4
Team	1	−21	−21.0	0	−21
ND	654	3080	4.7	32	65
OPP	440	1344	3.1	7	31

PASSING

	Att	Com	Pct	Int	Yds	TD
T. Rice	149	77	51.7	8	1389	10
K. Graham	26	17	65.3	2	154	0
S. Belles	4	2	50.0	0	84	2
P. Graham	2	1	50.0	0	16	0
ND	181	97	53.6	10	1643	12
OPP	350	180	51.4	19	2021	9

SCORING

	TD	PAT	R-ps	S	Fg	Tp
R. Ho	0	34	0	0	10–13	64
T. Rice	9	0	1-r	0	0	56
M. Green	7	0	0	0	0	42
A. Johnson	6	0	1-r	0	0	38
R. Ismail	5	0	0	0	0	30
R. Watters	4	0	0	0	0	24
T. Brooks	4	0	0	0	0	24
R. Culver	4	0	0	0	0	24
D. Brown	3	0	0	0	0	18
B. Hackett	0	5	0	0	4–5	17
B. Banks	2	0	0	0	0	12
P. Eilers	1	0	0	0	0	6
J. Jarosz	1	0	0	0	0	6
R. Mihalko	1	0	0	0	0	6
P. Terrell	1	0	0	0	0	6
M. Stonebreaker	1	0	0	0	0	6
S. Smagala	1	0	0	0	0	6
F. Jacobs	1	0	0	0	0	6
ND	51	39	3–r	0	14–18	393
OPP	16	14	1-p	1	14–16	156

SCORING BY QUARTERS

ND	109	142	70	72 – 393
OPP	16	71	34	35 – 156

RECEIVING

	PC	Yds	Avg	TD	Lg
R. Watters	16	343	21.4	2	57
M. Green	15	190	12.7	0	38
D. Brown	14	220	15.7	3	47
R. Ismail	13	360	27.7	3	67
A. Johnson	8	147	18.4	0	28
T. Brooks	7	121	17.3	2	42
P. Eilers	6	70	11.7	0	15
B. Banks	5	56	11.2	1	30
S. Alaniz	4	74	18.5	0	26
R. Mihalko	2	8	4.0	0	6
F. Jacobs	2	17	8.5	1	14
A. Robb	1	11	11.0	0	11
R. Culver	1	10	10.0	0	10
J. Jarosz	1	10	10.0	0	10
R. Smith	1	4	4.0	0	4
K. Graham	1	2	2.0	0	2
ND	97	1643	16.9	12	67
OPP	180	2021	11.2	9	42

PUNTING

	No.	Yds	Avg	Lg
J. Sexton	38	1469	38.7	53
P. Hartweger	4	159	39.8	49
S. Conner	2	63	31.5	34
ND	44	1691	38.4	53
OPP	70	2757	39.4	68

PUNT RETURNS

	No.	Yds	Avg	TD	Lg
R. Watters	22	291	13.2	2	81
R. Ismail	5	72	14.4	0	38
P. Eilers	3	20	6.7	0	15
ND	30	373	12.4	2	81
OPP	22	170	7.7	0	40

KICKOFF RETURNS

	No.	Yds	Avg	TD	Lg
R. Ismail	14	469	33.5	2	87
B. Banks	4	65	16.2	0	22

KICKOFF RETURNS (*continued*)

	No.	Yds	Avg	TD	Lg
D. Francisco	3	58	19.3	0	28
D. Grimm	3	34	11.3	0	15
R. Watters	2	42	21.0	0	24
A. Johnson	2	27	13.5	0	16
M. Green	1	25	25.0	0	25
R. Smith	1	14	14.0	0	14
S. Belles	1	4	4.0	0	4
ND	31	738	23.8	2	87
OPP	70	1234	17.6	0	59

INTERCEPTIONS

	No.	Yds	Avg	TD	Lg
G. Streeter	3	39	13.0	0	23
J. Alm	3	8	2.7	0	5
P. Terrell	3	84	28.0	1	60
M. Stonebreaker	2	71	35.5	1	39
D. Francisco	2	17	8.5	0	9
S. Smagala	1	64	64.0	1	64
G. Davis	1	31	31.0	0	31
A. Ale	1	17	17.0	0	17
D. Gordon	1	7	7.0	0	7
N. Bolcar	1	6	6.0	0	6
S. Roddy	1	0	0.0	0	0
ND	19	344	18.1	3	64
OPP	10	69	6.9	0	22

DEFENSE
Tackles

	No.	Fc	Fr
W. Pritchett	117	0	2
M. Stonebreaker	105	1	1
C. Zorich	74	0	3
N. Bolcar	59	0	0
F. Stams	54	3	2
G. Streeter	54	1	0
J. Alm	51	2	1
G. Williams	45	1	1
S. Smagala	44	1	1
T. Lyght	42	0	0
P. Terrell	40	0	2
D. Francisco	35	1	0
D. Gordon	30	1	0

DEFENSE (*continued*)
Tackles

	No.	tc	tr
A. Ale	24	0	1
A. Jones	19	1	0
D. Grimm	16	0	0
C. Southall	15	0	0
B. Flannery	13	0	0
S. Kowalkowski	10	0	0
T. Ridgley	9	0	0
B. Dahl	8	0	0
G. Davis	6	0	0
M. Jurkovic	6	0	0
M. Smalls	5	0	0
D. Jandric	3	0	0
S. Roddy	3	0	1
S. Belles	3	0	0

PASSES BROKEN UP
Lyght 10, Stams 8, Streeter 8, Stonebreaker 5, Smagala 6, Southall 4, Zorich 3, Alm 3, Pritchett 2, Williams 2, Terrell 2, Jurkovic 1, Francisco 1, Gordon 1, Jones 1, Ale 1, Flannery 1, Bolcar 1.

QUARTERBACK SACKS
Stams 9–76, Williams 5½–42, Zorich 3½–17, Pritchett 2–19, Stonebreaker 2–3, Kowalkowski 1–10, Dahl 1–6, Bolcar 1–2.

TACKLES FOR LOSSES
Alm 8–25, Pritchett 4–4, Lyght 3–8, Stonebreaker 3–4, Zorich 4–8, Bolcar 5–12, Stams 2–5, Streeter 2–7, Williams 3–17, Smagala 2–4, Lyght 3–8, Jones 2–3, Flannery 1–3, Gordon 1–2, Francisco 1–1.

Final 1988 Rankings

AP RANKINGS

1.	Notre Dame	12–0
2.	Miami (Fla.)	11–1
3.	Florida State	11–1
4.	Michigan	9–2–1
5.	West Virginia	11–1
6.	UCLA	10–2
7.	Southern Cal	10–2
8.	Auburn	10–2
9.	Clemson	10–2
10.	Nebraska	11–2
11.	Oklahoma St.	10–2
12.	Arkansas	10–2
13.	Syracuse	10–2
14.	Oklahoma	9–3
15.	Georgia	9–3
16.	Washington St.	9–3
17.	Alabama	9–3
18.	Houston	9–3
19.	LSU	8–4
20.	Indiana	8–3–1

UPI RANKINGS

1.	Notre Dame	12–0
2.	Miami (Fla.)	11–1
3.	Florida State	11–1
4.	Michigan	9–2–1
5.	West Virginia	11–1
6.	UCLA	10–2
7.	Auburn	10–2
8.	Clemson	10–2
9.	Southern Cal	10–2
10.	Nebraska	11–2
11.	Oklahoma St.	10–2
12.	Syracuse	10–2
13.	Arkansas	10–2
14.	Oklahoma	9–3
15.	Georgia	9–3
16.	Washington St.	9–3
17.	(tie) N.C. State	8–3–1
17.	(tie) Alabama	9–3
19.	Indiana	8–3–1
20.	Wyoming	11–2

USA TODAY/CNN RANKINGS

1.	Notre Dame	12–0
2.	Miami (Fla.)	11–1
3.	Florida State	11–1
4.	UCLA	10–2
5.	Michigan	9–2–1
6.	West Virginia	11–1
7.	Southern Cal	10–2
8.	Nebraska	11–2
9.	Auburn	10–2
10.	Clemson	10–2
11.	Oklahoma St.	10–2
12.	Syracuse	10–2
13.	Oklahoma	9–3
14.	Arkansas	10–2
15.	Washington St.	9–3
16.	Georgia	9–3
17.	Alabama	9–3
18.	N.C. State	8–3–1
19.	Houston	9–3
20.	Indiana	8–3–1

Notre Dame Football
Honors and Awards/1988

MICHAEL STONEBREAKER—junior ILB
—Butkus Award finalist;
—AP, Football Writers Assoc. of America, Newspaper Enterprise Assoc., Walter Camp Foundation, *Football News* All-America (all first team);
—UPI and *The Sporting News* All-America (second team);
—AP Midwest Defensive Player of the Week vs. Michigan State (17 tackles, two interceptions);
—*The Sporting News* Defensive Player of the Week vs. Michigan (16 tackles).

ANDY HECK—senior OT
—AP, UPI, *The Sporting News,* Newspaper Enterprise Assoc. and *Football News* All-America (all first team);
—Nick Pietrosante Award (by vote of teammates, to player who best exemplifies the courage, teamwork, loyalty, dedication and pride of the late All-America Irish fullback);
—Japan Bowl participant.

FRANK STAMS—senior DE
—AP, UPI and *Football News* All-America (first team);
—*The Sporting News* and Newspaper Enterprise Assoc. All-America (second team);
—Notre Dame Lineman of the Year, Moose Krause Chapter of National Football Foundation Hall of Fame;
—CBS/Chevrolet Notre Dame MVP vs. Miami (two forced fumbles, one recovery);
—AP Midwest Defensive Player of the Week vs. Miami;
—Hula Bowl participant.

TONY RICE—junior QB
—Notre Dame Monogram Club MVP (by vote of teammates);
—AP, *The Sporting News* and *Football News* All-America (honorable mention);

—CBS/Chevrolet Notre Dame MVP vs. Penn State;

—ABC/Chevrolet Notre Dame MVP vs. USC.

CHRIS ZORICH—sophomore NT

—Newspaper Enterprise Assoc. All-America (first team);

—*Football News* All-America (third team);

—AP and *The Sporting News* All-America (honorable mention).

GEORGE STREETER—senior SS

—*The Sporting News* and *Football News* All-America (honorable mention);

—Hula Bowl participant.

TIM RYAN—sophomore OG

—AP All-America (honorable mention).

STAN SMAGALA—junior CB

—AP All-America (honorable mention).

WES PRITCHETT—senior ILB

—*The Sporting News* All-America (honorable mention);

—AP and UPI All-America (honorable mention);

—Hula Bowl and East-West Shrine game participant.

TODD LYGHT—sophomore CB

—AP All-America (honorable mention).

PAT TERRELL—junior FS

—AP All-America (honorable mention).

MARK GREEN—senior TB

—AP, UPI and *The Sporting News* All-America (honorable mention);

—ABC/Chevrolet Notre Dame MVP vs. Michigan State (125 yards rushing on 21 carries);

—Japan Bowl participant.

NED BOLCAR—senior ILB

—*Football News* All-America (honorable mention);

—General Foods Spirit of Notre Dame Award.

RICKY WATTERS—sophomore FL

—*Football News* All-America (honorable mention).

REGGIE HO—senior K

—*Sports Illustrated* Special Teams Player of the Week vs. Michigan (four field goals, including game-winner at 1:13);

—CBS/Chevrolet Notre Dame MVP vs. Michigan;

—Hesburgh/Joyce Hall of Fame Scholarship Award (postgraduate grant for walk-on who has contributed significantly to the football program; maintains 3.77 in pre-med);

—Toyota Leadership Award on CBS national telecast vs. Miami;

—CoSIDA Academic All-America (second team).

RAGHIB ISMAIL—freshman SE

—*The Sporting News* All-America (honorable mention);

—AP Midwest Offensive Player of the Week vs. Rice (kickoff returns for 83 and 87 yards for TDs);

—*Sports Illustrated* Special Teams Player of the Week vs. Rice.

DEREK BROWN—freshman TE

—*The Sporting News* All-America (honorable mention).

TIM GRUNHARD—junior OG

—*The Sporting News* All-America (honorable mention).

GEORGE WILLIAMS—sophomore DT

—*The Sporting News* All-America (honorable mention).

TOM GORMAN—senior OG

—Toyota Leadership Award on CBS national telecast vs. Michigan;

—Notre Dame Club of St. Joseph Valley Student-Athlete Award (3.13 grade-point average in government).

BRAD ALGE—senior SE

—Hesburgh/Joyce Hall of Fame Scholarship Award. (Maintains 3.31 in management).

PAT EILERS—senior FL

—Toyota Leadership Award on CBS national telecast vs. Penn State.

LOU HOLTZ—head coach

—UPI Coach of the Year;

—*Football News* Coach of the Year;

—CBS Sports Coach of the Year;

—American Football Coaches Assoc. Kodak Region 3 Coach of the Year;

—Football Writers Assoc. of America Coach of the Year;

—Touchdown Club of Columbus (OH) Woody Hayes Award (for contributions to college football) and Robert A. Zuppke Award (for coaching the best college football team in the nation in 1988).

Part Three

DEFENDING CHAMPIONS
The 1989 Season

What Tho the Odds . . .

Whan Lou Holtz gathered his football team in a half circle around him on the warm late December afternoon in Miami, all he wanted was a few minutes alone for a private heart-to-heart chat. What he got was coast-to-coast headlines and a headache requiring a case of Excedrin.

Notre Dame's head football coach probably should have known. Things had been too quiet for too long—meaning all of a couple of weeks. For just about all of 1989, the season following Notre Dame's first national championship in 11 years, the Fighting Irish limped along with one kind of handicap or another. Just as one sore would heal, something would happen to open up a new one. None were tragic either to school or football team, but all were as irritating as a pebble in a jogger's shoe. Notre Dame lived with it, found one way or another to get to 11-1 in the regular season, and settled in Miami to prepare for the Orange Bowl matchup against No. 1-ranked and undefeated Colorado on New Year's night.

As Holtz gathered his team around him after some pre-practice drills and calisthenics, his purpose was to pump up his team, make it feel good about itself, and generally prepare it to peak emotionally for the her-alded Buffaloes. Seldom has a pep talk worked so well—especially for the opposing team.

What no one in the Notre Dame camp realized at the time was that a Denver television station, on hand to get some clips of the pre-practice drills, had the tape run-ning and the microphone open at the time and picked up everything Holtz had to say. Allen Funt would have been proud, except this candid camera caper wasn't very funny to the Irish—or to Colorado for that matter—when the episode found its way back to Miami, com-pliments of the Denver television station.

Before Holtz mapped out for his team how it would beat the Buffaloes, he voiced to the squad his opinion of what was being read into the quotes of Irish quarter-back Tony Rice by some of the Colorado players. They claimed Rice was showing no respect by saying "if we just go out there and put our minds to it, we'll get a 'W.'" Rice said his remarks were taken out of context and Holtz felt the Colorado players were taking liberties with their interpretation, going out of their way to make much more of it than was apparent, and wondered who was baiting whom.

It wouldn't have been a new trick for the Buffaloes. Earlier in the season, prior to Colorado's match with Illi-nois, Illini quarterback Jeff George was reported to have made disparaging comments about the Buffaloes dur-ing an interview on a television station and word spread quickly through the Colorado camp. Trouble was, George was never even interviewed by that TV station and com-ments attributed to him were, in fact, bogus. Illini coach John Mackovic addressed the situation and understood it to be a fabrication of one of the Colorado assistant coaches. Wherever it came from, the Buffaloes were ticked off by game time and thumped the Illini convincingly.

Holtz didn't want what he felt was a similar situation to be ignored.

"Let me tell you what," he said, "they've been living

a lie. They've been living a lie all year. Remember I told ya . . . The coaches had problems with Illinois . . . They're over there telling 'em you guys say this, you're saying that . . . that's fine. They can't be any more sky high than what they're going to be. But we just have to make sure we take care of our football team. They're expecting an outstanding football team and they're going to see one. They're going to see the best Notre Dame . . . and we're going to whip 'em.

"Number one, they're used to scoring a lot of points," Holtz went on. "They ain't playing a Kansas State. We've got to be patient on defense. Just play our football game . . ."

Holtz was shocked to learn someone had taped the speech and more shocked to learn that by the next day a bulk of the transcript had been provided to all media members in Miami. When Holtz walked into the press conference the following day, he admitted he had "more problems" than he did when the day started. Somehow it was a twisted but fitting end to a season that included an agonizingly long list of such episodes.

More was made of it by the media than by Colorado. Coach Bill McCartney chose not to respond "because Lou said those things within the confines of his squad" and, when baited, outside linebacker Alfred Williams responded, "It doesn't anger me at all. It sounds like something a coach would say to his team."

Truth be told, by the time the "Lou Holtz incident," as Holtz described it, hit the fan in Miami, the Irish were relatively numb to such circumstances anyway. Holtz himself didn't wait long to bounce back, issuing an apology to Colorado and looking more excited than ever for game time to roll around.

"I'm proud to say I'm a first," he joked. "It's the first time it's happened in the history of football. From now on, this will be known as the 'Lou Holtz incident.' Furthermore, I want you to know this—it will probably hurt my speech requests tremendously." When asked what he told Colorado coach Bill McCartney about the incident, Holtz joked, "I assumed it was taped."

Actually Holtz may have just been putting into practice some lessons that the long season had taught him. After the regular season, Holtz had a moment to catch his breath and put into perspective all the hassles the Irish encountered for one reason or another during the course of the season. He came to the conclusion that Notre Dame is forced to play by a different set of rules.

It was there in black and white. He saw Miami's grand entrance into the Orange Bowl, accompanied by pointed fingers and challenges/threats (whatever), hurled toward the Irish, go completely unnoticed in newspaper accounts, while the Irish were sauteed nationally for their part in the pre-game bout with USC in Notre Dame Stadium. It took some seasoning for Holtz to accept the difference.

Maybe his acceptance was convenient rationale. But hey, if it worked . . .

"Notre Dame is judged by a different standard by members of the media and by the public than is any other school—and I think that's great.

"At the time I said, 'this isn't fair.' But, in the future, I think I'm better equipped to understand the Notre Dame situation. I said at the time we were not treated fairly, but we were. My only regret is that I let it bother me at times."

Up to that time, the players had taken enough offense to what had been said and written to take some sort of stand. They seemingly banded together and took an "us against the world" approach.

"We just realized that we're playing for the guys in here," Ned Bolcar said, looking around the locker room after one game, "and our families and friends."

At the end of the season, in fact, the players had chosen to deny interview requests from *Sports Illustrated* because of the image the publication had painted of the Irish that included 1) accusations of taunting opponents; 2) complete blame for the scuffle against USC; 3) a label as the bad guys against Miami.

Much is expected in the name of sportsmanship. Particularly from an institution relishing its squeaky clean image. Especially when it's at the very top.

Notre Dame did not take its fall from grace lightly, nor did it stumble easily. If there was something truly special about the '89 team it was its stubborn streak. It could ignore personnel losses and personal setbacks and keep trudging along the long track. It spoke mightily of the machine Lou Holtz put into place and impressively of the character of the senior class.

It wasn't until a November evening in Miami that the story hit a snag. When the Irish reached back for something extra, they found an empty bag. The Hurricanes' execution was superb and Notre Dame watched too much of it happen in the 27-10 setback. Not even an impressive 21-6 victory over Colorado in the Orange Bowl could undo the Hurricanes damage to ND's claim to a second straight national championship. The loss to Miami in the high decibels of the Orange Bowl ended a school-record 23-game winning streak against the country's strongest schedule. As Holtz reminded in his one-shot campaign speech for No. 1 after the victory over Colorado, the Irish beat champions of the Big-10, Pac-10, ACC, and Big Eight while also crushing two of the East's best in Pittsburgh and Penn State. That's doing it the hard way.

"For what they had to go through, when most of it wasn't their doing, they'll always be a special team. Always," Holtz said with reverence.

"I told the squad (before the season) that if they were playing to win the approval of the media or the adoration of the fans, this would be the most miserable year of their lives and, by the time it was over, they would grow to dislike the game of football, because no matter what they did, it wouldn't be good enough. I told them if they played the game because they like to play, they like to compete, and they like their teammates, then it would be a very fun year for them and they would enjoy it. Then they would be able to look back on it and see that they did things they might not have thought possible because of that closeness."

Problems started popping up for the Irish before the celebration for the 1988 national championship had even died down. In February, All-American linebacker Michael Stonebreaker was involved in an accident in which he suffered injuries to his knee and hip and was charged with driving with a blood-alcohol level above the legal limit. Late in the summer, when he was expected to be cleared physically to play, he was charged with a violation of the probation on campus and he was suspended for the football season.

With Stonebreaker, the Irish were expected to have one of the finest linebacking corps in the country—Ned Bolcar starting opposite Stonebreaker and Donn Grimm supplying an experienced hand off the bench. Without Stonebreaker, Bolcar and Grimm played nearly full time for more than half the season. Until defensive coordinator Barry Alvarez felt comfortable spelling them, they went the distance and, by the middle of the season, they were in need of a rest. They finally got it when the Irish hit a stretch against Navy and SMU, but Alvarez knew the Irish were fortunate that the pair stayed healthy for the year.

No sooner had Stonebreaker's case left the front pages, when another star fell from grace. A number of problems landed tailback Tony Brooks in trouble and eventually caused his withdrawal from school.

In late February, Brooks was involved in a hit-and-run accident and charged with leaving the scene of a property damage accident and driving with a suspended license. He later was suspended from spring football practice for disciplinary reasons and eventually withdrew from Notre Dame.

Brooks returned to summer school and apparently

was in good standing academically, but was not admitted in the fall term for undisclosed reasons. After looking into the possibility of transferring, Brooks decided to pursue his goal of graduating from Notre Dame. He registered at Holy Cross Junior College, a school across the highway from Notre Dame, and hoped to be readmitted in the fall of 1990.

Losing the 220-pound Brooks was a big blow to Holtz's offensive plans. Brooks had rushed for nearly 6.0 yards per carry as a sophomore and would have finished as the club's top rusher were it not for a one-game suspension at Southern Cal. The absence of Brooks, coupled with the graduation of Mark Green, forced the Irish to start from scratch at tailback.

Sophomore Ricky Watters had made it pretty clear in the championship season that he never felt at home at flanker and wanted to return to tailback. After the loss of Brooks it was a moot point, since there was no other option.

Before the season got underway, more personnel problems cut into the Irish depth offensively.

The first came following spring practice, when quarterback Kent Graham, Rice's backup in the championship season, saw there was little opportunity for playing time behind Rice and decided to leave. Graham still dreamed of playing professional football and knew he would have, at best, only one college season as a starter under his belt. With two years of eligibility remaining, he transferred to Ohio State, hoping to win a starting job when he became eligible in 1990.

Braxston Banks, a tailback-fullback with some starting experience, never went through spring practice because of a knee injury and he elected to rest it the entire season and hoped to return at full strength in '90. He eventually decided not to pursue his final year of eligibility. The backfield concerns were further compounded by the loss of Kenny Spears to academic suspension. Spears wasn't about to replace Watters or senior fullback Anthony Johnson, but he had impressed the Irish staff with his work in spring drills.

Despite the losses, there really wasn't any reason to push any panic buttons because Watters and Johnson were backed up by sophomore Rod Culver, who had an exceptional freshman season when he rushed for over 200 yards and a 6.5 average. What the Irish probably couldn't afford in trying to maintain the rushing output was a serious injury to any of the three. They never had to find out. With durable quarterback Tony Rice handling the option and four of the five starters back on the offensive line, the Irish ran for 287.7 yards a game during the regular season. Flanker Raghib Ismail did his part to inflate that when Holtz occasionally used his fastest player—of placekicker size (5-10, 175 may be stretching it)—at tailback.

Sustained drives like their 8:55 march in the Orange Bowl were the trademarks of the '89 Irish. While trying to put the Buffaloes away, the Irish buried them, running into the teeth of the defense and marching 82 yards in 17 plays for the TD that put it on ice.

Despite having the four offensive linemen returning and Mike Brennan stepping in adequately for graduated All-American Andy Heck, no one was certain the Irish would dominate on the ground as they did—and certainly not in August when the thinning ranks in the backfield put Holtz on edge.

But the offensive line was the diamond in the trench. It was as fast as any Notre Dame line of the past and after 20-plus starts together, it was simply a group that made few assignment errors.

After Notre Dame rushed for 425 yards against Penn State—a record allowed by the Nittany Lions—free safety Sherrod Rainse couldn't believe how often he had a lineman in his face. "Too many times," he said, "probably five to seven times.

"And I should never encounter a guard or tackle downfield. But I think they have a lot of skim blocking—I'm not an offensive lineman so I don't know the terminology—where they get their initial man but then come off him and, with their speed, they were getting down on me. That happened too many times. If those guys get down on me, there is something wrong."

Even if opponents knew what was coming, they couldn't do anything about it. Holtz varied little from his approach—admittedly conservative—in regard to how often he wanted the ball in the air. Against Virginia in the opener, the Irish threw 19 times for 177 yards. Against Michigan a couple of weeks later, they threw only twice and the rhythm for Rice and the receivers never happened.

"He competes very, very well and he's made the throws when he's had to." Holtz said, "He protects the football and we play it rather conservatively in our approach."

Notre Dame was just as good as it had to be through the air because of the strength of the running game. As much as the passing game was a non-factor for the Irish in three and a half quarters against Southern Cal (Rice was 4 of 15 with one interception), it was actually what made the difference. With the Irish trailing, 24-21, in the final quarter and facing a second and 8 situation from the 44, Rice lofted a perfect strike to Ismail and hit him in stride at the 25. He carried it to the 15 and Rice carried the rest of the way on the next play to lock up the victory. With the running game the Irish seldom needed to throw. Rice averaged only 11.4 passes a game as a senior and the product wasn't very sound, with Notre Dame accounting for only two touchdowns through the air against 10 interceptions.

If pre-season questions about the running game were serious, they were easy when compared to the question marks facing the defense.

Stonebreaker was the first in a long line of serious losses. Early in pre-season camp, sophomore defensive end Arnold Ale walked away from a starting position on a defending national champion to return home to California and UCLA. Ale, who got his first start in Notre

Dame's 31-30 upset of Miami and may be best remembered for his co-sack of Major Harris in the Fiesta Bowl that helped lock up the national crown, had never been truly comfortable at Notre Dame and decided it was in his best interest to leave.

That was another jolt to the Irish staff and it came on the heels of the loss of defensive tackle George Williams to academic suspension. Williams had been a rock as a sophomore, finishing second on the club in sacks, and his 290 pounds was a considerable loss. There also was no help from John Foley, who was trying to make a comeback from an injury suffered in the Cotton Bowl in '87. He had sat out '88 because of nerve damage in his bicep. After a few practices he realized he couldn't protect himself and his career was over.

A year earlier, when the Irish won it all with such a young team, they were considered ahead of schedule. Now with all the unexpected personnel losses, they were back to square one.

Before the Kickoff Classic matchup against Virginia, Holtz said, "I would buy a ticket because I have no idea what's going to happen with our team."

Notre Dame's recruiting success had developed a deep pool and what the Irish couldn't count on in experience, they could in talent, at least to a degree. There were some exceptional players to build around, such as All-American Chris Zorich at nose tackle and Todd Lyght at cornerback. Bolcar could anchor the middle defensively and offensively, of course, there was Rice, who was 28-3 as a starter in his Notre Dame career.

The Irish built on their success early and the chemistry they may have lacked early kept developing until it became a very close group. There was a different texture to the club's personality than that which seemed to carry the Irish a year earlier. The team was no longer characterized by its characters as in '88 with the "Three Amigos"—defensive end Frank Stams, linebacker Wes Pritchett and Stonebreaker—who got a lot of attention for their pranks and credit for providing leadership.

Players with dominant personalities such as Bolcar were turned off by suggestions that, because those three were gone, the Irish would lack leadership. "We've said all year long this team is much closer than last year's team," he said. "I believe that, even after losing a game, we are closer than we were last year.

"From Tony Rice on down to the last walk-on, we're all equal and we treat everyone with respect. People say, 'Well, what's it like without the "Three Amigos?" Well, we've got 120 "amigos." We don't need a clique or anything like that. That worked for us last year. This year we've got a different personality, but it's working for us. I don't think anybody here stands out in the sense of personality. We're all fun-loving, we all like to play the game, and we all have mutual respect."

It's a good thing because the '89 Irish would spend most of the season leaning on each other.

Game 1
KICKOFF CLASSIC
VIRGINIA
August 31, 1989

Throughout his first couple of years at Notre Dame, Coach Lou Holtz was asked how he felt about playing in the Kickoff Classic. He said Notre Dame would play in it when it had earned a right to play in it. A National Championship seemed like a pretty good credential and the Irish were paired against Virginia, an up-and-coming club from the Atlantic Coast Conference, for the August 31 matchup at the Meadowlands.

There are a number of disadvantages to this game, the most obvious of which is having to report a couple of weeks early to practice. Tacking on two weeks to a season that runs from August to January is no picnic. But the Irish agreed to take their turn and the extra cash in their pocket didn't hurt. For the first time in the history of the Classic, it was sold out.

Virginia looked out of its league. Whether it was first-game jitters or the glare of national lights, the Cavaliers couldn't get out of the starting block—and the Irish were all over them for a 36-13 victory.

Before the game Virginia coach George Welsh admitted, "I've seen it (intimidation factor) happen before. We're not used to games like this, I will admit, but we hope our program has reached the point where we can take the next step and compete at this level." Few thought they had and the Irish were installed as a three-touchdown favorite.

Holtz found that a little hard to believe. "I don't think we're as good as you all think. But we're probably not as bad as I often think. I wish I could tell you what kind of team we have, but we really don't know. I don't think there is a favorite in an opening game, ever." There probably should be if Holtz is coaching. In his four years, the Irish have won three openers and the only loss was by a point when they were an underdog to Michigan.

In the warm August evening, Holtz saw great things from his team and only his early substitutions kept it from becoming an ugly rout. "I think he (Holtz) was nice to us," said Welsh. "It could have been much worse."

On the first play of the game, defensive end Scott Kowalkowski nailed tailback Marcus Wilson for a 2-yard loss and Wilson got only a yard on second down. Then on the third play of the game, quarterback Sean Moore's pass was intercepted by cornerback Todd Lyght, who started his All-American season with two interceptions and a blocked punt. In six plays, the Irish were on the board with Ricky Watters scoring on a pitch from Rice from two yards out. It was the start of a first-half execution in which the Irish scored five times to open up a 33-0 lead.

For his balance, 7-for-11 completions for 147 yards plus 70 rushing yards, quarterback Tony Rice was named the game's Most Valuable Player, and he set a Notre Dame rushing record for quarterbacks that night when he passed Tom Clements in the record books. Rice went over Clements' 1,070 career rushing yards with a nifty 5-yard run in which he set three defenders on their heels with a pump fake, then blew by them for the score.

Rice would have given up the MVP honor to Ricky Watters and he could have built a strong case when Watters carried 12 times for 80 yards, caught two passes for 42 yards, and returned three punts for 67.

Defensively, the Irish first team played superbly and only budged when the staff began to mix in the second and third team. Most impressive was limiting Moore to 10-for-22 with two interceptions and only 85 yards.

Two players particularly on the spot were defensive tackle Bob Dahl, who replaced George Williams, and linebacker Donn Grimm, who stepped in for Michael Stonebreaker. Both gave every indication that they could handle the role.

"I wasn't trying to play like Stoney did or imitate the way Stoney plays," noted Grimm, who had an interception. "I was just playing my kind of football. We miss Stoney—he's a great football player—but I just have to pick up the slack."

"I had no idea how we would play," Holtz said afterwards. "But we covered the spectrum (good and bad)."

Afterward the Irish got a post-game speech from Rev. Jesse Jackson, whose son played for Virginia. "It's unbelievable the people you meet here at Notre Dame," said Anthony Johnson. "That really hits you."

Notre Dame 36, Virginia 13

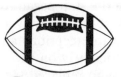

Game 2
MICHIGAN
September 16, 1989

When Colorado coach Bill McCartney was preparing his top ranked club to meet Notre Dame in the Orange Bowl, he had a short chat with his former boss Bo Schembechler. Bo had only a few words of advice: "Don't kick to him."

In his defense, Schembechler's Michigan team wasn't the last to be victimized by Raghib Ismail. But he was the first—in a way that won't soon be forgotten.

With the two college heavyweights slugging it out, the 175-pound Ismail stole the show with a pair of kickoff returns for touchdowns that gave the Irish one final victory, 24–19, over the retiring Schembechler and put another "little guy" in a big spotlight just as placekicker Reggie Ho had been the hero a year earlier.

It was a devastating setback for the Wolverines, some of whom had guaranteed that it would be different this time.

"We really get a charge out of what the other teams say," said fullback Anthony Johnson, who carried 20 times for a team-high 80 yards. "We didn't want to set ourselves up and rely on talk. We just wanted to have a subtle confidence about it."

There was nothing subtle about the contact. The collisions were brutal.

It was the third time in the previous four meetings that the game had been decided by less than a touchdown and the first time a Bo Schembechler-coached team had suffered three straight setbacks.

With the Michigan Stadium artificial surface soaked by rains earlier in the day and occasional light rains falling in the afternoon, Irish head coach Lou Holtz was as conservative as he ever had been in four seasons at Notre Dame and, thanks to Ismail, he could afford to be.

"We didn't throw the ball because we didn't want to open things up and give Michigan anything they didn't earn," Holtz said. "We were never forced to open things up."

The Irish did not have a turnover and quarterback Tony Rice put the ball in the air only two times, one going for a 6-yard touchdown pass to fullback Anthony Johnson in the second quarter. Ironically, the first score of the day followed the only turnover when defensive end Scott Kowalkowski fell on quarterback Michael Taylor's fumble at the 24. With the Wolverines shutting down the perimeter on Tony Rice's option work, the Irish went inside and Johnson did the bulk of the work. In an eight-play drive he carried five times and caught the scoring pass for a 7-0 second-quarter lead.

The Irish accumulated 213 yards on the ground while the Michigan attack was limited to a net 94.

But the Wolverines weren't shut down. First Michael Taylor drew the Wolverines to within a point just before the half when he connected with Chris Calloway on a 9-yard scoring pass to complete a 59-yard drive that was helped by a controversial interference call on free safety Pat Terrell. When J. D. Carlson's kick hit the upright, the half closed with the Irish up, 7-6.

The offense was Ismail in the second half. On the second half kickoff, he found a seam off the block of Ryan

Mihalko and, once in the open, only Corwin Brown had the angle on him. But Ismail blew by him into the end zone for an 88-yard return.

The Irish lead grew to 17-6 late in the third quarter when freshman Craig Hentrich nailed a 30-yard field goal.

But the Wolverines weren't done. Freshman red-shirt quarterback Elvis Grbac came on to replace Taylor after he injured his back in the first series of the second half; the rangy quarterback showed a lot of poise despite the circumstances and engineered a 61-yard drive that got Michigan to within five points at 17–12.

But after the score the Wolverines kicked it to Ismail again and he snapped through three tackles for a 92-yard touchdown run.

Grbac completed eight straight passes in the next drive—he finished 17-for-21 for 134 yards and two touchdowns—and got Michigan in the end zone again. Carlson's kick made it 24-19, but the onside kick failed and the Irish needed only one first down to run out the four minutes on the clock.

The Irish were 2-0 with some good news and bad news ahead—they were coming home, but they had to play host to Michigan State.

Notre Dame 24, Michigan 19

Coach Lou Holtz leads the defending champion Fighting Irish through the tunnel for the home opener against the Spartans of Michigan State. (Photo credit: Bill Leheny.)

Heisman Trophy candidate Tony Rice led the Irish in rushing in his senior year, earning 884 yards and the season MVP award by team vote. (Photo credit: Joe Raymond. Courtesy of the *South Bend Tribune*.)

Sophomore sensation Raghib "Rocket" Ismail was lightning quick all season and cooling his jets, particularly on kickoff and punt returns, was a great challenge for Irish opponents in '89. (Photo credit: Bill Leheny.)

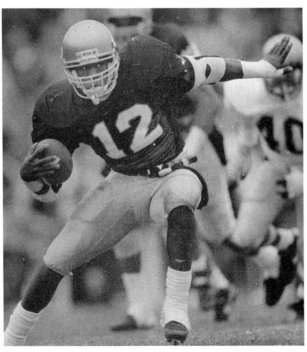

Junior tailback Ricky Watters moved with style and grace, compiling a regular season total of 791 yards rushing and 66 TD points for the Irish. (Photo credit: Ed Ballotts. Courtesy of the *South Bend Tribune*.)

Senior fullback and Irish co-captain Anthony Johnson was class in the clutch, leading the Irish in scoring with 11 touchdowns for 78 points in regular season play. (Photo credit: Joe Raymond. Courtesy of the *South Bend Tribune*.)

Senior linebacker and team co-captain Ned Bolcar was a frequent spokesman for the team in a year when Irish football attracted an even larger share of media hype. (Photo credit: Ian Johanson.)

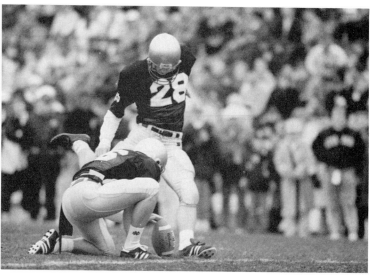

Jim Sexton holds the ball for freshman Craig Hentrich, who played a key role for the Irish as he kicked for a season total of 68 points. (Photo credit: Madeleine Castellini.)

Junior Todd Lyght had an All-American year at cornerback. Here in the third quarter against Michigan State, he makes a key interception, snatching a pass intended for Courtney Hawkins. (Photo credit: Ed Ballotts. Courtesy of the *South Bend Tribune*.)

Strong safety D'Juan Francisco and linebacker Ned Bolcar take down USC's John Jackson. (Photo credit: Joe Raymond. Courtesy of the *South Bend Tribune*.)

Guard Tim Grunhard is all bulk and business as he leads the Irish special teams off the field. (Photo credit: Ed Ballotts. Courtesy of the *South Bend Tribune*.)

Sadness on the sidelines. En route to the heartbreaking loss to Miami, Ricky Watters, Tony Rice, and Dean Brown console each other on the bench. (Photo credit: Ed Ballotts. Courtesy of the *South Bend Tribune*.)

After the loss to Miami, the Irish came back for a decisive win against the then-No. 1 Colorado Buffaloes in the Orange Bowl. Jeff Alm, Ned Bolcar, Scott Kowalkowski, and Chris Zorich believed that the victory had earned them the national crown. (Photo credit: Joe Raymond. Courtesy of the *South Bend Tribune*.)

After his final collegiate game on New Year's Day, Anthony Johnson receives a victorious escort. Four months later he would be an early draft pick of the Indianapolis Colts. (Photo credit: Joe Raymond. Courtesy of the *South Bend Tribune*.)

All-American nose tackle Chris Zorich raises a triumphant fist after the Irish defeated No. 1 Colorado in the Orange Bowl. (Photo credit: Ian Johanson.)

Game 3
MICHIGAN STATE
September 23, 1989

Early season trouble, such as that which they had faced against Michigan State, may have been just what the Irish needed to find out the strength of their ticker.

The fact that the Irish had committed four turnovers — the most since the Cotton Bowl loss to Texas A&M (which happened to be their last loss) — and still survived a strong Michigan State bid gave them more to build on than they probably knew at the time.

A long fourth-quarter drive at gut-check time sewed up a 21–13 victory that both teams remembered for a few weeks.

"It was no place to be for someone who was worried about getting hit," said Spartans coach George Perles. "There were some hits out there that scared me."

The Spartans were hardly intimidated, playing the No.1 Irish in their own backyard, and made a stretch run that had the Irish sweating. With Notre Dame up 21–13, the Spartans drove to the ND 25 before both clubs drew a big breath: Fourth and 1.

Hyland Hickson, who filled in at tailback after Blake Ezor was knocked out in the first quarter, got the call, and tried to slip over right guard. Before he could get to the hole, junior linebacker Donn Grimm split the seam and made the initial contact. A wave, led by strong safety D'Juan Francisco, brought Hickson down. A couple of Irish first downs later, Notre Dame had its 15th straight victory.

At the time, the Spartans were unranked but obviously should have been as they put up just as big a fight the following week at home against Miami. Led by All-American linebacker, Percy Snow, defense took control of the football game in the second half.

The Irish had taken a 14–0 lead on Ricky Watters' touchdown runs of 2 and 53 yards. Both runs were started with pitches from Tony Rice, who in every other way had a less than glowing afternoon. He had two interceptions and accounted for one of two fumbles, but Perles still said the Heisman Trophy candidate was the difference in the game.

"He's one heck of a guy to defend," Perles said. "I've never had to be on a defense where we had such a skilled back at the quarterback position. He really was the big difference."

"Both of my touchdowns should be credited to Tony Rice," Watters said. "The defense tried to shut him down, and when they did, he was able to get me the ball." Sixteen times in all, for 89 yards and two TDs.

The Spartans were keying on him, trying to take away the perimeter, but Rice still rushed for 78 in 14 carries, more yards rushing than the entire Spartans' offense.

Before the half was over, Michigan State capitalized on a pair of Irish turnovers for two John Langeloh field goals, reducing the Irish margin to 14–6 at the half. Energized, Michigan State's defense was a rock at the start of the second half as Notre Dame failed to budge the ball a yard in three straight possessions.

When Dan Enos connected with James Bradley on a 30-yard scoring strike, the Spartans pulled to within one, 14-13. "It was tough and scary at that point," noted fullback Anthony Johnson.

"They had a good defense from the opening," said Hickson, "but I think our defense played a little harder than they did today. To me, we are just as good as Notre Dame."

The Spartans weren't quite good enough in the critical fourth-quarter series in which the Irish pounded away nine times before Johnson went the final yard to cap a 62-yard scoring series with 8:16 to go. The score stood up when Grimm and company made the critical stop on Hickson.

Perles was impressed by the fact that the Irish survived. "You got 'em ranked where they should be," he said. "They made mistakes and still won the game."

Notre Dame 21, Michigan State 13

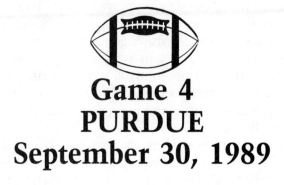

Game 4
PURDUE
September 30, 1989

When your starting inside linebackers combine to participate in only 17 plays, something's amiss. In West Lafayette on October 1, that something was Purdue's offense.

Such easy targets were the Boilermakers at that point in the season that Ned Bolcar was in for only about 10 plays and Donn Grimm for just 17. It was a strange reversal of the previous weeks when both played most of the way, but it was certainly welcome as far as the Irish were concerned. "You don't get as much satisfaction from not playing," Bolcar noted after the 40-7 romp that pushed the Irish record to 4-0, "but it gives us a chance to play some younger people and get our bodies ready for the rest of the season."

After two sub-par weeks Tony Rice resumed his race for the Heisman Trophy with one of the finest performances of his career, though the Boilers offered little resistance. He played little more than a half, but completed 12 of 15 passes for 270 yards while rushing for another 67 and a touchdown. The five first-half touchdowns came under his direction.

"He ran the option well, he threw the ball well, and

he had fun—that's just Tony Rice," Lou Holtz said of his performance that sparked the Irish to 530 yards in offense.

Derek Brown, Notre Dame's 6-7 tight end, finally got into the passing picture with four receptions for 101 yards against Purdue's man-to-man defense. In the previous three games, the sophomore from Florida had only one catch, but Holtz made it clear that Brown never made a fuss about being a blocking tight end.

"The one nice thing about Derek Brown is there is no pressure to get Derek Brown the football," Holtz remarked a couple of days after the game. "Derek is not a moody individual. He doesn't sit around and say, 'I want you to get me the ball.' We knew we had to get the ball to Derek but sometimes the game and the defense dictate that. Many times when we call a pass we have to go to the receiver the coverage takes us to." Against Purdue's man-to-man, Brown was an easy target.

The highlight of the afternoon, considering the ease with which the Irish scored, was the 16-yard interception return by defensive tackle Jeff Alm.

Defensively, there wasn't much more the Irish could have done, accounting for eight turnovers, including three interceptions, while limiting Purdue's passing game to only 11 completions in 28 attempts. One of the interceptions belonged to Todd Lyght, his fourth of the season.

"We worked a lot on dropping our linebackers to cover zones," said Lyght, "and that allowed the defensive backs to lock up on the receiver."

The Boilers, with a week off before meeting the Irish, brought out a new wrinkle with the option, but it just played into the Irish hands as the Boilers managed only 219 yards in total offense. "We're used to playing against the option all the time against our offense," observed free safety Pat Terrell, who also had an interception.

It got embarrassing late in the second half for Purdue when two different reserve quarterbacks fumbled on three straight snaps from center and head coach Fred

Akers had to bring starter Steve Letnich back in just to get the snap.

The victory over Purdue completed a clean sweep against Big Ten teams for the third straight season and was the first leg of a three-game road swing.

Notre Dame 40, Purdue 7

Game 5
STANFORD
October 7, 1989

If you watched Notre Dame file back to its locker room after the game at Stanford and had to guess who won, it probably would have been a wrong guess.

The Irish were low-key and there wasn't much celebrating going on. Senior offensive guard Tim Grunhard looked as if he felt compelled to snap the silence. "Way to go Irish," he yelled. "Way to hang tough." That was about all the Irish did well on October 8.

In any season there are going to be bad days and close games when the opposite is expected, times when reaching one's potential is like reaching the moon. When Notre Dame was winning its national championship, it had that kind of day against Navy when it won, 22-7. In the 1989 season it was in the beautiful setting of Palo Alto, California.

For the first time all year Notre Dame fell behind 6-0 and the Irish struggled to gather their rhythm against a team that had won only one of its first four games. "I wasn't surprised that they (Stanford) played well," Holtz said, ". . . but these (Notre Dame) guys did what they had to do. And each week it gets tougher. I have coached teams before that have lost in this kind of situation. I can't explain it, they just sort of did what they had to do."

"People like to judge how well you play against what the oddsmakers say (Notre Dame was a three-touch-down favorite), but I remember my freshman year," said Grunhard, "when we were 5-6 and all we wanted was to win. Some of the younger guys don't know what that was like. They expect us to blow everybody out. We should expect to be happy with a win."

"There is no way that Notre Dame can leave here feeling that they beat us," Stanford center Chuck Gilling said. "We beat ourselves. They did not come in here and manhandle us."

"If we can't control the line of scrimmage, we can't sustain a running attack," said Holtz, whose club was stopped on fourth down and short from the 5 on one drive. "But we had people open (in the passing game). We should have started throwing much earlier."

Rice did attempt 17 passes, but he connected only seven times for 102 yards.

D'Juan Francisco's interception set up the second TD as the Irish opened up a 14-6 halftime lead.

Stanford came right back after the break, tying the game on a short pass and a 2-point conversion by Tom Vardell, but Raghib Ismail never let momentum set in. He hauled in Hopkins' high floating kickoff at the 18 and slipped by the first wave. Only the speed of Allen Grant and his angle of pursuit prevented another Ismail return for a touchdown. But he carried it to the 16 and in four plays the Irish were in for a 21-14 lead.

First-year Stanford coach Dennis Green felt it was a turning point. "Anytime you have a momentum swing it changes the game," he said. "That's what football is all about."

Ismail's return put him back in the spotlight and suddenly his name was surfacing as a possible Heisman Trophy candidate. He took it all in stride. "For now I think when people mention me as a potential Heisman candidate, they're just trying to break up the monotony of hearing the same names over and over and trying to put some interest into the running. But I don't think any of them mean what they're saying."

If they didn't, they would.

With the odds stacked against the Cardinal doing much harm to Notre Dame running the ball, they simply put it up—play after play—68 times in all by quarterback Steve Smith for a Stanford record and three shy of the NCAA mark. Smith completed 38, but he was intercepted three times and accumulated only 282 yards.

It was just a matter of the offense overloading on mistakes—the Irish had eight penalties for 75 yards compared to Stanford's 1-for-11—that had the Irish struggling all afternoon.

The first six points Stanford put up on the board came by way of some uncharacteristic mistakes. John Hopkins had missed a 47-yard field goal for the Cardinal, but he got a second chance when Francisco was flagged for roughing Hopkins on the play. The second field goal came after punter Craig Hentrich shanked a punt for only 17 yards, giving Stanford the ball at the 32. They didn't move it but got the field goal. "I think we knew Stanford would be up," Grunhard noted. "Before the game, their big thing was that it was a chance of a lifetime. But maybe we didn't expect them to have the defensive intensity they did."

The Stanford lead had lasted only into the second quarter. The Irish went 64 yards in three plays—Rice collecting 38 on an option. Anthony Johnson ran it from the seven for the score and Hentrich's kick put the Irish on top.

That's the kind of day it was offensively. A little feast, but too much famine. The Irish had just one first down in the first quarter against a solid, not great, Stanford front. Tailbacks Rod Culver and Ricky Watters combined for 28 yards in 12 carries. Of Johnson's 75 yards, one-third came in one carry and, of Rice's 71 yards, 54 of it came in two carries.

After Ismail worked his magic, Hentrich added three field goals—two in the fourth quarter—for some cushion and free safety Pat Terrell put it away with an interception in the final minute for a final score of 27-17.

Notre Dame 27, Stanford 17

Game 6
AIR FORCE
October 14, 1989

Excitement in Colorado Springs had reached a new level. Air Force had six straight victories under its belt, a Heisman Trophy candidate at quarterback to showcase, and a dream they could play out on national television.

Scalpers reportedly were getting up to an unheard of $100 for tickets and a record crowd of more than 53,000 turned out. "The stage," Air Force coach Fisher DeBerry said, "was set for us to win."

But it was still Notre Dame's show.

Another first-half blitz of 35 points overwhelmed the Falcons, who fought back gamely, but were knocked back down, 41-27. Air Force's point total and effort were a moral victory while the Irish were left to ponder the degree of trouble they were in with their pass defense.

"We were so far away on some of those passes if the ball was a hand grenade no one would have been hurt," head coach Lou Holtz said.

Air Force was still a long way from stopping the Irish. Some first quarter stats: ND 154 yards, Air Force 11; ND 12:46 possession time, Air Force 2:14; ND nine first downs, Air Force 0; ND 14 points, Air Force 0.

The Irish lead bulged to 21-0 less than a minute into the second quarter when Raghib Ismail returned a punt 56 yards for a touchdown. To go with the punt return, he had another brilliant day, rushing for 92 yards in 10 carries and one TD in his first true test of the season at tailback while also catching three passes for 25 yards. "I could have used a calculator back there to count up all the tackles he broke," said quarterback Tony Rice. "It shows you the little man can do anything, the same thing as anyone else."

Ismail wasn't the only one to prove that.

Pint-sized Air Force quarterback Dee Dowis, who had sparked the Falcons' wishbone to 449 yards a game in offense through the first six games, had to turn to Plan B when Air Force fell behind so quickly. Plan B wasn't bad.

Notre Dame's defense had bottled up the wishbone for 168 yards.

"Notre Dame guessed our option right a bunch," DeBerry noted, but the defense came unglued when Dowis rolled out to pass. Going into the game, Air Force ranked 104th of 106 Division I pass offenses at 77 yards a game. Against the Irish, the Falcons had 306 with two touchdowns and 474 yards overall.

"It's nice to have some success against someone's bread and butter," said defensive end Scott Kowalkowski. "But we were so geared to stopping the run, it (Air Force's passing game) was really tough."

On one 26-yard scoring pass Dowis connected with Steve Senn who had slipped behind cornerback Stan Smagala for a 26-yard TD play.

"For myself, I messed up," Smagala said. "My mind wasn't in the right place, I had no clue.

"We did practice against the run a lot, but we shouldn't have let up on their throwing game."

The Falcons' most costly error came with 2:45 left in the half when Chris Zorich recovered Greg Johnson's fumble at the Falcons' 35. In five plays the Irish were in,

Ismail scoring on a 24-yard end-around. So fooled were the Falcons that Ismail jogged the final 10 yards into the end zone. That gave the Irish a 35-14 lead, just too much ground for Air Force to make up.

The Irish got a couple of Craig Hentrich field goals in the second half while the Falcons came up with two more scores. The first came on a gadget play when Dowis took the snap and dropped the ball between center Paul Walski's legs. Right guard Steve Wilson stumbled by, fell, picked up the ball, and took off to the left side while play action flowed convincingly to the right. He went all the way, 23 yards, while Holtz argued that Wilson was on the ground when he picked up the football. He was, but the officials were fooled as well. It was still too late for the Falcons, who put together one more harmless scoring drive with 3:22 to play.

The worst news for the Irish was that tight end Frank Jacobs was lost for the season when he broke an ankle during the game. That forced Holtz to nix experiments with tight end Rod West at fullback. That luxury was eliminated with the loss of Jacobs, a junior who was a co-starter with Derek Brown.

"We're happy to win, we're happy to be going home," said Holtz, whose club was closing out a three-game road swing and five over six games, including long back-to-back weekend road trips to the West. "I'm not happy we're going home to play Southern Cal and Pitt."

Notre Dame 41, Air Force 27

Game 7
USC
October 21, 1989

When the fallout from another classic clash against Southern Cal had settled, Notre Dame had clearly marked itself as a survivor.

What other way to account for a 28-24 victory against the No. 9-ranked team in the country with the weight of five turnovers on its side?

"I have never seen the ball on the ground that much even in a soccer game," Irish head coach Lou Holtz said of four fumbles. What other way to account for a win despite being outgained by almost 100 yards in offense and yielding 33 pass completions for 222 yards?

It may not have been the Irish at their best, but they were in true form with heroics in the clutch.

Maybe the pre-game scuffle cast a cloud over the start of the game, but the clean, hard-hitting, and marvelous plays on both sides should have blown it all away.

"This is really a truly classic game," said Holtz. From USC coach Larry Smith: "It was a very intense game. I think everyone watching was entertained. It was college football at its best."

And at crunch time, it was Tony Rice stealing the

show. Notre Dame's senior quarterback struggled for three quarters, completing four of 15 passes with an interception, and, unless he was going to come out of it, the Irish weren't.

With nine minutes to play and the Irish trailing, 24-21, Rice marched his club 80 yards and made two big plays along the way. On second and 8 from the 44, he rolled right and waited for flanker Raghib Ismail to shake loose from the man-to-man coverage, then dropped a soft pass into Ismail's hands at the 25. He got it to the 15. On the next play, Rice optioned left, kept it, bounced off one tackle, then dragged cornerback Dwayne Garner into the end zone for the touchdown with 5:18 to play. Craig Hentrich's kick made it 28-24 and the Irish were on their way to their seventh straight victory in the series, but not before they did a little more sweating.

With one pass to John Jackson, quarterback Todd Marinovich moved the Trojans from their own 27 to the Irish 37 and three passes later they were at the 12. On third down, Marinovich hooked up with Larry Wallace in the end zone, but he was a step out of bounds and D'Juan Francisco batted down a fourth-down pass in the end zone.

USC got it back one more time, but on the last play of the game, from the USC 45, all Marinovich could do was step back and chuck it, and it fell incomplete.

"It seemed like we were fighting uphill all day," said Holtz.

Both teams were fighting before it even got underway.

For the third time in two years a scuffle started in the congested tunnel area of Notre Dame Stadium as USC ran through the Irish as they were heading back to the locker room after pre-game drills. Players from both clubs pointed fingers at each other as the perpetrators, but it would have been absurd to call either side blameless.

When Notre Dame runs its final play of practice before returning to the locker room, the reserves routinely line up on the end line. Rather than go around and down the sidelines, some of the Trojans marched through the middle. Who threw the first shot is anybody's guess, but there was a sizeable pileup in the tunnel.

"I sincerely apologize to Southern Cal," Holtz said. "I promise this will never happen again at Notre Dame, regardless of who is at fault."

A letter of apology was sent and Holtz threatened to resign if it happened again. He also altered Notre Dame's pre-game lineup in Notre Dame Stadium, bringing the team over to the sidelines rather than having it line up on the end line.

"It was really low class on their part," said USC wide receiver John Jackson, who caught 14 passes for 200 yards.

Notre Dame's Jeff Alm responded: "I'm not pointing fingers to say who started it. But I saw them giving Rocket (Ismail) a hard time and he's not the biggest guy in the world. I saw USC coaches taunting our band before the game."

Fifth-year captain Ned Bolcar said, "It was just a spontaneous reaction. There was a lot of emotion on the field. We do not care to continue mishaps like that. We want to be a class organization, and I know that USC does, too."

The hardest shot the Irish got came later in the week from Douglas S. Looney's account in *Sports Illustrated*, in which he suggested the Irish were "beyond the control of their own coach."

"As for Notre Dame," he wrote, "it survived, though without style and without much class. Now Holtz has to get the Irish cranked up again this week for a home game against Pitt. Let's hope that while he's doing it, he also teaches the children some tunnel etiquette."

The perception of the Irish being completely to blame for the incident riled Notre Dame, especially given USC's attitude of the day. At halftime, with a 17-7 lead, the Trojans mocked and baited the Irish by singing the Notre Dame Fight Song when they entered the tunnel together.

Notre Dame bit—in the second half. "That was *our* fight song," said Ned Bolcar. "People don't use it against us."

After getting the touchdown run from Ricky Watters to complete a 50-yard dive, Notre Dame went on top when Anthony Johnson broke a fullback dive for a 35-yard touchdown run. The Irish caught USC with their cornerbacks up and ran to the side away from the strong safety. Getting clearing blocks from Dean Brown and Tim Grunhard, Johnson had only to beat free safety Mark Carrier to the end zone.

Some big second half defensive plays, including Todd Lyght's interception in the end zone following a Notre Dame fumble at the USC 20, kept USC in check until 9:01 remained in the game. On first and 10 from the 33, Johnson fumbled it back and Junior Seau recovered. In four plays, the Trojans were in for the score when Marinovich hit Brad Wellman on third down from 15 yards out, putting USC ahead, 24-21. That's when Rice took over and took his team 80 yards for the score and the win. It was Notre Dame's turn to sing the Victory March as USC headed home to the tune of a final score of 28-24.

Notre Dame 28, USC 24

Game 8
PITTSBURGH
October 28, 1989

Pity Pittsburgh. They arrived in South Bend a week after Southern Cal riled up the Irish and only a couple of days after *Sports Illustrated* tweaked the Notre Dame image. The Panthers were left to deal with all the hostility and couldn't. Ranked seventh in the country with a 5-0-1 record coming in, the Panthers were overmatched and taken apart in every manner, 45-7.

"Notre Dame just whipped us in every area," acknowledged Pitt coach Mike Gottfried. "They were a powerful and impressive team."

"Notre Dame is No.1 for a reason," said Pitt defensive back Dan Grossman. "We thought being No.7 meant we could beat them. We have made mistakes before and have come out all right, but our mistakes caught up with us today."

It was the Irish who played catchup, temporarily at least, when the Panthers marched 68 yards in 12 plays with their first possession to grab a 7-0 lead a little more than five minutes into the game.

Not to worry. "We just hadn't fallen into the rhythm yet," said Irish coach Lou Holtz. When they did, Pitt fell with a pronounced thud.

The Panthers had been averaging 31 points a game, but after that first drive, they were limited to 58 yards on the ground in 23 attempts the remainder of the half.

"Unlike last year, their offensive line was a little slower and a little weaker," said nose tackle Chris Zorich, who bulked up his All-American stats with nine tackles. "Basically we just took advantage of that."

"We put together a 60-minute ball game for a change," noted defensive end Jeff Alm. "And it's nice to see the results."

There was one fumble recovery to go with three interceptions, one of which was returned for a touchdown by Pat Terrell from 54 yards out.

Quarterback Alex Van Pelt, who had completed 60 percent of his passes and thrown only five interceptions in 165 attempts coming into the game, was hassled by Notre Dame's front.

"I never dreamed this would happen in my wildest dreams," Holtz said.

So dominant were the Irish on the ground that they barely had to pass the ball. They threw only nine times in all with one completion for 29 yards. They wound up beating the Panthers at their own game. Though Pitt had allowed an average of only 92 yards a game on the ground coming into the game, the Irish rushed for 310 and got a pair of short touchdown runs from Rod Culver, another from Ricky Watters, and TD runs of 13 and 50 yards by Steve Belles and Raghib Ismail, respectively.

It could have been much worse for the visitors had Notre Dame clicked from the start. The Irish started drives at their own 40 and 44, and the 46 and 36 of Pitt. But there were two missed field goals and botched opportunities as the Irish opened up a 17-7 first-half lead, seven coming on Terrell's interception return.

The Irish didn't ease up, obviously reminded of Pitt's rally from a 31-9 deficit to tie West Virginia.

On Pitt's second possession of the second half, Scott Kowalkowski knocked the ball from the hand of quarterback Van Pelt, then fell on it at the 17 and the Irish were off and running. D'Juan Francisco set up the third touchdown of the quarter when he intercepted a Van Pelt pass and returned it 41 yards.

"We were blowing them off the ball," said guard Tim Grunhard. "Primarily it was penalties that were killing us (early in the game). Overall we got the movement we needed inside, and anytime you can do things well, it complements something else. And that's why things opened up outside later."

The victory was the 20th straight and left the Irish one shy of the school record. It also was the eighth straight win over a team ranked in the Top 20, which tied a record set from 1946-50. Holtz was somewhat somber in the post-game press conference, obviously still stinging from the thumping the Irish took for their role in the episode with USC.

"Pitt had an extra week (due to an open week in the schedule) to prepare for us, but we had an advantage there," said Holtz. "The week we had seemed like a month."

Pitt could go one better after it was all over: The Panthers' *day* in South Bend seemed like a month.

Notre Dame 45, Pitt 7

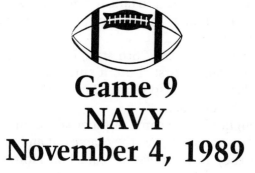

Game 9
NAVY
November 4, 1989

What Notre Dame set out to do on the first Saturday in November was prove that the stumbling around it did against Navy the previous year was just a fluke of fate. The Irish proved that by the end of the first quarter.

With its running game revved up and in rhythm, Notre Dame handed Lou Holtz his 195th career victory with a 41-0 shutout, a victory that tied a school record of 21 in a row.

"Right now we're playing with a lot of togetherness and a lot of love," said tailback Ricky Watters. "Most of our success is due to that. It is not like you are doing it for yourself out there, you are thinking about the team and especially the seniors."

Watters was the standout performer, terrorizing with more speed than the Middies could handle. On the first offensive play of the day, he went off right guard for 43 yards. At halftime, he had 120 yards in six carries, which included a 48-yard touchdown run. But that was about it as he was limited to only three more carries to finish with 134 rushing yards, the first 100-yard rushing performance of the season for the Irish.

It was the kind of day Watters had been waiting for

and it came about one year from the time he asked Lou Holtz if he could return to tailback from flanker. "There's no place like home," he said of playing tailback. "It's something I love . . ."

The victory was the 26th straight in the series and was Notre Dame's first shutout since it blanked Army, 42-0, in '83. It was also Notre Dame's third shutout of Navy in the decade.

"I thought it was a game our football team came out, not fired up or excited, but they came out and they played because they like the game," said Lou Holtz, who offered his usual litany of concerns before the game.

"I'm not trying to insult your intelligence when I tell you I worry about all our opponents. I'm a worrier from day one. It's a sincere worry."

It's sincere because of the way Holtz looks at the picture. First he measures how a team can play, what its potential is when it's at its very best. Then he measures how bad it can get for his own team. If the opposition's very best is good enough to beat Notre Dame at its worst, it's worth worrying about for Holtz.

After the easy victory he admitted, "We had too many athletes for them. We wore them down. But we're not here to embarrass anyone. We want to win and win with class." That's why on a fourth down and 11 late in the game, senior quarterback Pete Graham ran a quarterback sneak.

Keeping in line with his up and down season from the pocket, quarterback Tony Rice completed only one of eight passes, unless the two completed to the Midshipmen are included.

But backup Rick Mirer, one of 14 freshmen who lettered for the Irish in '89, came on to complete eight of 12 passes for 64 yards without an interception and directed two scoring drives. Freshman tailback Dorsey Levens scored on a short run, and senior walk-on fullback Ted "Tank" McNamara scored the first touchdown of his career.

"Once again we really and truly had to play together," said offensive tackle Dean Brown. "We had to show ourselves that no matter who we play, we play hard.

"It wasn't like the Miami game last year (when the crowd was into it). It was truly a game where each person made a commitment to play for their teammates. We happened to do that today."

Notre Dame 41, Navy 0

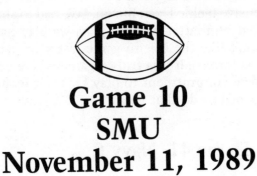

Game 10
SMU
November 11, 1989

For such an easy game there was a considerable "no-win" angle in it for Lou Holtz.

How does one go about holding down the score of a football game? How do you tell your players to turn it off at all costs?

The week leading up to Notre Dame's game against Southern Methodist, which was playing in Notre Dame Stadium in its first season since suffering the two-year death penalty from the NCAA, had its light moments.

One columnist held a contest, soliciting readers to offer their most innovative ideas for holding the score down. All made for a very strange twist.

If the Irish poured it on, they would have been considered merciless; but if they held back, it could be taken as something of a mockery. (One caller to a radio show leveled charges of point-shaving). Well, there was no easy way to hold back, but Notre Dame did and the sellout crowd got their money's worth in anticipation of what trick the Irish would try next in the 56-6 rout.

1) The Irish intentionally drew delay of game penalties to slow down a couple of scoring drives.

2) They handed over an extra possession by kicking off to start off both halves.

3) The starters were watching, for the most part, by the second quarter.

4) And reserve tailback Rusty Setzer made the most difficult decision. Running alone along the sidelines, he intentionally stepped out of bounds at the 8-yard line.

"Coach Holtz told us we could run up and down the field, but he didn't want us to score," Setzer explained. "He told me he was proud of me for doing what I did."

Setzer figures it's better to do what you're told, even if it means giving up six. "If I make Coach mad at me now," he said, "then maybe I won't have any chance (in the future) as I hope."

SMU, with its run and shoot offense, threw 59 passes and completed 30 but for only 206 yards. The Mustangs' rushing total was a negative seven yards.

The Irish totals weren't as outrageous as Houston's 1,000-yard performance against SMU earlier in the season. Notre Dame rushed for 358 and added 214 through the air, averaging 8.4 yards per gain. What the Irish didn't do intentionally was fumble seven times, losing three of them.

Still it was a good way for the seniors to close out their home careers. The victory put the Irish in the record book with 22 straight and Holtz got a couple of touchdowns for two senior reserves. He brought in quarterback Pete Graham to finish off a short touchdown run and he put tight end Rod West in the backfield and gave him the ball two straight times from the 5 so he could score his first touchdown.

"It was a great gesture on Coach Holtz's part," said Graham, a fifth-year senior. "It's something I'll always remember."

"Something like this really helps the closeness of the team," said free safety Pat Terrell. "Everybody's pulling for everybody."

Offensive tackle Dean Brown even figured he'll get in on the scoring act—somewhere down the road. "When I'm about 50 years old—with a bald spot—I'll go over to the Huddle (campus snack bar) and say, 'Yeah, we were the best team, even better than Rockne's and Leahy's (teams).' I'll tell them the old man scored on that last home game, even though I didn't even touch the ball today."

Forrest Gregg, in charge of putting the Mustangs' program back on its feet, appreciated that the Irish went well out of their way, and out of bounds, so they wouldn't run it up.

"That was the honorable thing to do," he said. "They did everything to keep the scoring down. You can't ask kids not to play hard. But I respect 'em for it. It's a credit to them and their coach."

Notre Dame 59, SMU 6

Game 11
PENN STATE
November 18, 1989

I t is often said that there is no substitute for experience. There is a reason.

Early in Notre Dame's 11th game against Penn State,
the offensive line looked over at a defense it hadn't seen
on film, but one that still looked familiar.

"When Penn State went into a defense we hadn't seen
from them, I heard (guard) Tim Grunhard say it was the
same thing Stanford did," related senior tackle Dean
Brown. "And we adjusted."

Oh, did they adjust.

As the wind-chill index hovered around zero in Beaver
Stadium, the Irish ran wild, pounding Penn State for a
record 425 yards on the ground en route to a 34-23 triumph in front of 86,000-plus and a national television
audience.

"They're an outstanding offensive football team," said
Penn State coach Joe Paterno, whose defense had allowed an average of only 104 yards on the ground coming into the game. "(Tony) Rice is a great player. Rice is
the guy we just couldn't handle. They've got a lot of
speed, an outstanding offensive line and they executed
really well—no penalties, nothing foolish. You have to

play great defense to hold them to some degree, much less stop them."

Rice wasn't the only problem, though he led all rushers with 141 yards. Tailback Ricky Watters added 128, giving Notre Dame two 100-yard rushers for the first time since 1983, when Greg Bell and Allen Pinkett did it against Michigan State.

The Irish could have made it three had they given Raghib Ismail a few more carries. He finished with 84 yards in only nine attempts. The four rushing touchdowns gave the Irish 42 for the season, another school record, and the winning streak climbed to a school record 23.

"We executed everything well today," noted Ismail, "and if we do that, we know everything will work out fine. Tony means winning to us. He's just the main man."

The Irish fell twice early in the game, but never for long.

"We answered the challenge a couple of times there," Lou Holtz said. "They scored and they came back. The catalyst is Tony Rice, that's the guy. He just knows the thing to do."

The critical point for the Irish followed Penn State's 79-yard scoring drive midway through the third quarter that cut the margin to 11 at 28-17. On the ensuing kickoff, Ismail fumbled and slipped to his knee while picking it up, forcing the Irish to start at the Notre Dame 11. It put the crowd, which had been sitting on its hands for almost two quarters, back into the game.

But not for long. On first down Rice hit Ismail with a quick out and he dodged one tackle for a 12-yard gain. After eight rushes, Rice hit Pat Eilers for 10 to the Penn State 14. Things finally cooled for the Irish there, but Bill Hackett's 22-yard field goal a couple of minutes into the fourth quarter pumped the lead back to 14 while killing some valuable time. And that about did it for the Lions' shot.

"I never thought it would be an offensive game like

this," said Holtz. "If you would have told me Penn State was going to score 23 points, I'm not certain we would have gotten on the plane."

Penn State's outstanding tailback Blair Thomas caused the usual trouble for the Irish, rushing for 133 yards in 26 carries. The previous back to rush over 100 yards against a Notre Dame defense was Blair Thomas in the same spot two years earlier. His rushing touchdown in the first quarter that gave the Lions a 7-0 lead was the first touchdown the Irish had allowed in 16 quarters.

Holtz and the rest of his staff may have been most concerned by the effect the three previous blowouts would have on his club. The Irish had barely worked up a sweat in the romps over Pittsburgh, Navy, and Southern Methodist and the staff worried most about getting the rhythm back. So practice sessions were intense leading up to the game and only the defense had trouble regaining the feel.

"We came out a little flat," observed defensive end Scott Kowalkowski. "They mashed us around in the first drive (79 yards). They had a lot of second and fours and second and twos so we couldn't dictate . . . We've just got to regroup."

Notre Dame 34, Penn State 23

Game 12
MIAMI
November 25, 1989

A ll season Notre Dame had talked itself into need-
ing to play on an even keel. With too many big
games on a difficult schedule to get "up" for, relying on
emotion could be a little dangerous. Being prepared to
play didn't always mean being emotionally ready to play.

Notre Dame was prepared for Miami. It was not, the
players admitted later, prepared for the emotional peak
of the Hurricanes in the 27-10 defeat.

The situation may have been spelled out by Miami's
tasteless entrance to the Orange Bowl with the finger
pointing and trash talk as the two teams stood a few
yards apart in the middle of the field. Concerned about
a rerun of the incident against USC, the Notre Dame
coaching staff stopped the Irish in their tracks and they
turned around, heading for the sidelines while Miami
relished their first battle won. A year earlier Notre Dame
had stood their ground and shared an equal role in a pre-
game scuffle.

In a game in which the Irish needed to raise their
emotional level a notch, they couldn't find the right buttons to push—and the deafening roar in the Orange Bowl
didn't help calm the Irish. Miami fans wanted blood for

the 31-30 loss inflicted the previous year by Notre Dame
in South Bend, one that prevented another Miami national championship.

And the Hurricanes drew it first. Following a 21-yard
punt by freshman Craig Hentrich, Miami took over on
the 47 and drove to the 12 before settling for a Carlos
Huerta field goal and a 3-0 lead. The next time they
went the distance.

On second and 7 from the Miami 45, Notre Dame
blitzed and Craig Erickson's blockers picked it up. The
Hurricanes' quarterback had enough time for Dale Dawkins to slip behind Greg Davis, who was in man-to-man
coverage, then hit him in stride to complete a 55-yard
play. Miami 10, Notre Dame zip.

The Irish got on the board when Tony Rice directed
an 80 yard drive—he completed two third-down passes
and carried seven times in the march—that resulted in
Bill Hackett's 22-yard field goal. The Irish would have
come up empty had it not been for a controversial call
that went their way. On Anthony Johnson's 11-yard run
to the 4, Charles Pharms got a hand on the ball to knock
it loose, but officials ruled Johnson was already down.
From the replays it appeared to be a fumble.

There weren't too many highlights for the offense
overall as Miami matched the Irish step-for-step in team
speed and was much sharper in its execution. Notre
Dame had been averaging 301 yards on the ground and
was held to 142 while the passing game—Rice's seven
completions in 15 attempts with two interceptions—
accounted for only 106 yards.

"They expected our quickness because everybody knows
how quick our defense is," announced Miami defensive
tackle Russell Maryland. "But expecting our quickness
and doing something about it are two different things.
We used our quickness to our advantage."

So did linebacker Ned Bolcar on one play that had
the Irish hopes soaring. In the second quarter he stepped
in front of an Erickson pass, vaulted over a tackler, and

ran for a touchdown. With Hentrich's PAT the Irish were tied, 10-10.

It was a great game for Bolcar, who finished with 13 tackles, yet another sour taste at the Orange Bowl. "I've got to live with this the rest of my life," he said of the loss. "This was the reason that I came back (for a fifth year), to win another title and beat Miami in its home field. And we didn't even come close."

The Irish were held scoreless in the second half, their only threat being an 87-yard drive that died at the Miami 8 with seven minutes to play.

But it was over by then. Just before the half, linebacker Bernard Clark stepped in front of a Rice pass and took off down the sidelines. He reached the 8 before Derek Brown drove him out of bounds. That set up Stephen McGuire's 5-yard TD run with 24 seconds to go that placed momentum right back in Miami's lap.

"Four or five plays determine the outcome of a game," said Holtz. "Miami had more."

One, in particular, will be forever etched as one of Notre Dame's most embarrassing moments.

Facing a third and 44 from the 7, wide receiver Randall Hill slipped behind cornerback Stan Smagala and Pat Terrell for a 44-yard gain. How did it happen?

"Basically, what happened in the coverage was a lack of communication," said Terrell. "I should have had a better jump on the ball, but he (Erickson) looked me off and I was just a step behind. With their speed a second means a lot."

There were still four third-down conversions (the Hurricanes had 11 of 17, including two for touchdowns) before Miami put it in the end zone and, almost 11 minutes after the drive began, Miami was up 24-10 and well out of Notre Dame's reach.

"That was the longest drive I've ever been associated with," said Erickson. "I've never been around a win like this. It was the greatest win I've ever been associated with. We played well the whole time."

For the Irish it ended the record winning streak at 23 games.

"It's been a while since we lost," Holtz said. "But if we had to lose, it's great to lose to a quality team like Miami."

It's unlikely that Irish fans felt quite the same way.

Miami 27, Notre Dame 10

Game 13
ORANGE BOWL
COLORADO
January 1, 1990

When Notre Dame left for Miami, the Irish probably didn't realize they were leaving for boot camp rather than a holiday at the Orange Bowl.

But so much work was still undone.

"It's almost like spring ball," sighed 290-pound offensive tackle Dean Brown. "There's been no easing back at all. The guys are sore right now."

That was only a couple of days before the No. 4-ranked Irish would try to make one big splash, this time against No.1-ranked Colorado which was playing for its first national title, to try to make up the acres of ground lost with the 27-10 regular-season ending defeat to Miami.

So, Notre Dame saved its best for its last—half—and pushed aside numerous distractions and doubts to wrench the Buffaloes from their dream with a 21-6 victory.

To the great distaste of Irish fans, Notre Dame's victory meant a national title for Miami, which handled Alabama in the Sugar Bowl. And, ironically, a touchdown drive similar in many respects to the 11-minute gem Miami leveled against the Irish, put Colorado away in the final minutes.

Starting at its own 18 with 10:27 to play, Notre Dame's

running game was never better, getting two third-down conversion runs from Rod Culver, a couple more key dashes by Raghib Ismail, and one final 7-yard bolt by Anthony Johnson to snuff Colorado. It took more than eight minutes off the clock.

"We can tie the game if we can stop them and get the ball back but they were too strong and took over the line of scrimmage," said Colorado coach Bill McCartney.

This was not the way it was supposed to end for the Buffaloes. They had battled to live out the dream of their former quarterback, Sal Aunese, who died of cancer on September 23. Darian Hagan, the quarterback who replaced Aunese, said after the heartbreaking defeat, "We're going to be back here next year and he's going to be a legend. That dream is still alive."

Notre Dame was installed as a slight favorite, but Lou Holtz was hard-pressed to understand why.

1) Because of the school calendar, final exams were held from December 17 through the 21st and Holtz released his team to go home for the holidays. He had made that decision earlier in the season. Because of the early start with the Kickoff Classic, he felt it was important for his players to have a chance to get home and away from football for at least a few days.

2) The names of several of his assistant coaches were being linked to head coaching jobs and at least five had been interviewed in December. Defensive line coach John Palermo (Austin Peay), running backs coach Jim Strong (UNLV) and defensive coordinator Barry Alvarez (Wisconsin) took head coaching positions, but stayed on with the Irish through the bowl game. Still, the assistants were forced to miss some practice time.

3) Two starters, defensive tackle Bob Dahl and defensive end Andre Jones, would miss the game. Taking the December practice week off to concentrate on academics, Holtz stuck by his rule of no practice, no play. At the Orange Bowl, he also appeared disgruntled that neither player discussed his status with him before leaving for

the holiday break. Both were allowed to make the trip, joining the team three days before the game, but neither played. On top of that, Raghib Ismail reported tenderness in his shoulder from an injury suffered in the Miami game. With Holtz wanting to use him at tailback, it was particularly frustrating not to have Ismail available for contact work throughout most of the practice sessions. It was one of the reasons Holtz decided to close his practice to the media in South Bend.

4) Add to that the distraction, and fuel for Colorado if you will, of Holtz's taped pep talk by the Denver television station and the concerns for the Irish and things were hardly smooth from the start as they dodged a number of first-half bullets.

For instance:

On its second possession, Eric Bieniemy got loose in Notre Dame's secondary and appeared headed for the score. But when he reached the 20, he tried to switch the ball from one hand to the other and it wound up on the ground, where Pat Terrell recovered.

Late in the first quarter, Colorado started a drive at its 18 and drove to the 5 before Notre Dame's defense stiffened. Ken Culbertson's 22-yard field goal attempt was shanked.

Colorado moved it again in the following possession, 13 plays in all, and got to within inches of the end zone. But two dives into the line and an option to the right were stuffed by the Irish. Culbertson lined up again and this time holder Jeff Campbell faked it and took off to the right. Stan Smagala hit him first, slowing him enough for Troy Ridgley to level him a couple yards shy of the goal line. Ridgley had made the move from nose tackle to tackle to fill in for Dahl and the sophomore performed well in his place.

"I didn't feel we had lost momentum at halftime," said McCartney of the scoreless second half. "I just thought we had lost several opportunities down deep inside. You know when you play a team like this you only have so many chances to capitalize on."

At halftime, Holtz told his club "how we reacted in the second half would go a long way in determining our approach to success the rest of our life."

They put 21 points on the board, starting with the first possession when Johnson capped a 68-yard drive with a 2-yard run. Tony Rice, who completed five of nine for 99 yards, had a 27-yard pass to Tony Smith which, when combined with Johnson's 30-yard run, covered most of the ground.

The Irish went up two touchdowns on the next drive when the Irish caught Colorado pinching its ends. Sending Ismail on an end around, he slipped out of Kanavis McGhee's grasp and bolted down the sidelines for a 35-yard scoring run. Ismail, who finished with 108 yards in 16 carries, was named the game's MVP.

Colorado got back in it before the end of the quarter, when the fleet Hagan broke free down the sidelines, and dodged a couple of tackles for a 39-yard TD run. Culbertson's kick failed again, but the long Irish drive made it a moot point.

After the triumph, Holtz pleaded his case for his club being No.1, but as he entered the press conference on January 2, he got word that Miami had been selected. He knew what his club had gone through, the schedule it had played, and the personnel losses it had overcome.

"All year our motto had been 'Believing in miracles,'" Holtz said.

Finishing second may have been one.

Notre Dame 21, Colorado 6

Into the '90s . . .

For the month leading up to the Orange Bowl, Lou Holtz preferred to distance himself from the great debate.

"Hey, Lou, where does your team belong if you win?" he was asked often.

First things first, Holtz thought. And he would change the subject. There was enough to worry about in top-ranked Colorado.

But once the Buffaloes were disposed of, 21–6, Holtz hit the campaign trail running, starting with the post-game press conference. For the first time all year his true thoughts on the subject came gushing out.

"I can honestly say right now we have the best record (12–1; no other team had 12 victories) and the toughest schedule. I don't know how you can decide on anyone else being No.1—that's my personal opinion—unless you want to say who's the best team on November 25."

If it had been anything but an old fashioned butt-kicking that November 25 night in Miami, maybe it could have been different. Maybe. But it was 27–10 and Notre Dame's offense couldn't even get it across the goal line (Ned Bolcar's interception was the only TD).

Nevertheless, Holtz would give it one last shot. He would make one very strong sales pitch immediately after the convincing victory against top-ranked Colorado.

"We were No. 1 for 11 weeks and the one week we were out of No. 1 we came back to beat the No. 1 team (Colorado) by 15 points," Holtz began. "I know people will say head to head. . . . On that particular day (November 25) you did not see a typical Notre Dame team. But when you play nine bowl teams those things are going to happen. I just believe we have the best record against the toughest schedule. Case rests."

Holtz figured the degree of difficulty in victories over champions of the ACC (Virginia), Big Ten (Michigan), PAC–10 (USC), the Big Eight (Colorado), should have been worth a few votes. It apparently was. Just not enough.

Holtz didn't look like he got much sleep the night after the Orange Bowl victory when he appeared at a press conference at the Omni Hotel in Miami the following morning. It didn't help that he got word of the final Associated Press vote just prior to the start of the conference. Miami No. 1, Notre Dame No. 2.

Twenty-two points, 1,474–1,452, separated the two teams for the second-closest voting in the history of the poll. Holtz's frustration showed, and one can only imagine how he felt when he got word of the United Press International coaches poll—Florida State No. 2, Notre Dame No. 3.

"You can justify why Miami won, what you can't justify is why we didn't," he said that morning. "No way. Nobody played the schedule we did and certainly nobody had one-tenth the adversity this football team had this year. . . . Who accomplished the most in 1989? That's how I look at it. Today sort of sums up this whole year. It's another disappointment but I tell you what, we'll get over it. I'm not bitter. I'm not upset. I'm disappointed."

There was a lot of that for Holtz in '89. In the middle

of the season he dealt with the fall-out from the pre-game fight with USC. He vowed to resign if it happened again.

The trial involving financial irregularities at Minne-sota during his two-year stay was another dark cloud always in the distance, but he didn't talk about it until all was said and done and his name was cleared.

Then toward the end of the season he repeatedly had to deny rumors that had him leaving Notre Dame for a job in the NFL with Atlanta or the Los Angeles Raid-ers or Miami. One radio report before the Orange Bowl had him leaving and Colorado's Bill McCartney coming in.

It worked against Holtz and the Irish during recruit-ing and occasionally Holtz went to great lengths to de-fuse it. In fact, *USA Today*'s defensive player of the year, Oliver Gibson of Romeoville, Illinois, challenged Holtz to vow on the Holy Bible that he would remain at Notre Dame during his career. Gibson reported that Holtz said that he would remain another six or seven years. Holtz indicated only that he would like to stay that long and planned on it. "What if health problems sur-faced," Holtz asked, "like Notre Dame getting sick of me?"

Before the official signing date for all high school players, Holtz and Notre Dame may have had the best recruiting tool ever tossed into his corner. On Monday, February 5, 1990, university officials announced that Notre Dame had signed a five-year contract with NBC to televise all home football games, beginning with In-diana in 1991. No university had ever before entered into such an exclusive agreement with a major net-work, one worth in the neighborhood of $36 million. To put the price in perspective, each game will carry a price tag in excess of some bowl games.

Dick Ebersol, NBC Sports president, expressed his delight over the merger. "The coast-to-coast appeal of Notre Dame football along with Notre Dame's commitment to play college football's most challenging schedule were keys to NBC's regular season pact with Notre Dame," he said.

From Athletic Director Dick Rosenthal: "We are delighted to have this association with NBC. And more particularly we will be able to bring all our home games to our fans all over the country."

For at least the immediate future, it settled a lot of problems for Notre Dame. A stadium considered small (capacity 59,075) by major college football standards should suffice for now and a set game time of 1:30 (in previous years game times ranged from 11:30 a.m. to 8 p.m.) removes a number of headaches. It's ideal for the out of town guests who may want to drive in and drive out; no longer will the portable lights be necessary and community businesses, restaurants, hotels, etc., can prepare for a steady flow of customers at a specific time.

As expected, there was fallout. The move rankled many, particularly the College Football Association, which felt its pockets lighten when the Irish bolted. The contract, shared by 64 teams, lost a big chunk of change when the heavy hitter didn't sign the pact, though that didn't necessarily knock Notre Dame from the CFA. "The involvement with the television package is separated from being involved with the CFA," executive vice-president Rev. E. William Beauchamp stated.

Still, there were few happy CFA campers and those who love to hate the Irish let it be known they considered it an act of greed that showed little concern for other universities. Ironically, none of Notre Dame's opponents have asked to be released from their contract. Mostly because of their share in the pot.

There was a protest from Kansas, which decided the Jayhawks didn't want to play basketball with the Irish. Notre Dame obliged.

Air Force athletic director Col. John Clune was among the most outspoken, though the Falcons are on the schedule for the next two years.

"People are mad," Clune told Tim Mimick of the *Gazette Telegraph* in Colorado Springs. "A lot of ADs think Notre Dame is self-centered and greedy. Penn State and USC may take them to task on it. They can refuse to have the game televised. I don't know who can pass up the money but people are mad about this." Clune essentially said Air Force would not pass up the money.

The Irish probably haven't heard the last of it. The furor died down a short time after the announcement, but it is likely to recur from time to time. It's unprecedented. No one knows yet what will happen down the road. Notre Dame's breaking ground—hard ground.

For now, Notre Dame will grin and bear the heat all the way to the bank. If the Irish program plummets, the Irish still get their money and Saturday prime time.

And if, for a minute, you put yourself in the shoes of the top high school recruit a thousand miles or so away from Notre Dame, you'll understand the recruiting appeal. Mothers and dads won't mind being able to see their children play six times a season. And it won't cost the family a dime in travel expenses.

Recruiting coordinator Vinny Cerrato, who has done a marvelous job in pinpointing the high school talent worth pursuing over the last few years, said the contract came a little late to have much effect on this year's class.

Of course, there was nothing wrong with the 1990 batch the Irish brought in, ranked by experts among the to three in the country.

The Irish got about everything they had put at the top of their wish list. There were three top linebackers, a couple of solid quarterbacks, some speed for wideouts and secondary, and a couple of gifted running backs. There were 23 in all and no apparent gambles in the crop.

"I never get real excited about the recruiting class," said Holtz, who admitted he *was* over this one. "No. 1, they're just good chemistry people, they're easy to get along with—they got along well with our players (while being recruited)—and I think they're coming to Notre Dame for the right reasons. They're intelligent, they're personable and it's a highly-motivated group. I just feel this group might be special."

It won't be easy breaking in immediately. Three consecutive top-flight recruiting classes have put a considerable load of talent in Holtz's lap. When he brought the 1990 group together for its first spring practice in March, he also welcomed back a healthy Michael Stonebreaker. He figures to be a key element, providing he can return to his pre-accident performance level. He gave every indication in spring drills that he was up to it.

"I know my role is to be a leader," he said before practice opened. "I've been through it all. I've been at the top and I've been at the bottom, so I pretty much know what everybody's feeling."

Stonebreaker didn't appear to have too much trouble getting back in sync. Neither did tackle George Williams, back on the field after straightening out academic problems. He was an anchor inside the national championship season and was welcomed back, placed with the first unit by new defensive coordinator Gary Darnell. Darnell was one of four new assistants to join the Irish. The group included Skip Holtz, Lou's son, who signed as a volunteer assistant to work with quarterbacks Rick Mirer and Jake Kelchner, as they seek to replace Tony Rice.

The changes mark a new era, of sorts, for the Irish. Indications are the joyride ought to last for a while.

THE 1989
SEASON STATISTICS

Team Statistics by Game

GAME 1
At the Meadowlands

	ND	VA
1ST DOWNS	24	14
Rushing	16	7
Passing	7	5
Penalty	1	2
RUSHES	59	38
Yardage	303	149
Yardage lost	3	13
RUSHING YDS.	300	136
PASSING YDS.	177	95
Passes	19	25
Completed	9	11
Intercepted	1	3
TTL. PLAYS	78	62
TTL. YDS.	477	231
Average gain	6.1	3.7
PUNTS-avg.	2–36.5	7–38.3
FUMBLES-lost	1–1	2–0
PENALTIES-yds.	6–53	5–32
POSSESSION	33:58	26:02
3RD DOWNS	6–12	4–15

Scoring by Quarter

NOTRE DAME	19	14	0	3–	36
VIRGINIA	0	0	0	13–	13

GAME 2
At Michigan Stadium

	ND	MICH.
1ST DOWNS	13	15
Rushing	12	5
Passing	0	8
Penalty	1	2
RUSHES	54	34
Yardage	220	119
Yardage lost	7	25
RUSHING YDS.	213	94
PASSING YDS.	2	178
Passes	2	28
Completed	1	22
Intercepted	0	0
TTL. PLAYS	56	62
TTL. YDS.	219	272
Average gain	3.9	4.4
PUNTS-avg.	3–37.3	6–33.8
FUMBLES-lost	1–0	1–1
PENALTIES-yds.	5–45	8–70
POSSESSION	30:23	29:37
3RD DOWNS	5–14	4–12

Scoring by Quarter

NOTRE DAME	0	7	10	7–	24
MICHIGAN	0	6	0	13–	19

GAME 3
At Notre Dame Stadium

	ND	MSU
1ST DOWNS	24	21
Rushing	18	10
Passing	6	11
Penalty	0	2
RUSHES	58	40
Yardage	335	182
Yardage lost	3	14
RUSHING YDS.	332	168
PASSING YDS.	123	306
Passes	13	24
Completed	9	15
Intercepted	1	0
TTL. PLAYS	71	64
TTL. YDS.	455	474
Average gain	6.0	7.0
PUNTS-avg.	66.0	38.0
FUMBLES-lost	1–1	5–3
PENALTIES-yds.	4–23	5–35
POSSESSION	29:38	30:22
3RD DOWNS	7–12	6–11

Scoring by Quarter

NOTRE DAME 7 7 0 7–21
MICH. STATE 0 6 7 0–13

GAME 4
At Ross-Ade Stadium

	ND	PU
1ST DOWNS	26	12
Rushing	16	7
Passing	10	4
Penalty	0	1
RUSHES	61	31
Yardage	254	153
Yardage lost	13	23
RUSHING YDS.	241	130
PASSING YDS.	289	89
Passes	21	28
Completed	15	11
Intercepted	0	3
TTL. PLAYS	82	59
TTL. YDS.	530	219
Average gain	6.5	3.7
PUNTS-avg.	3–38.7	5–45.8
FUMBLES-lost	3.2	8.5
PENALTIES-yds.	5–40	1–5
POSSESSION	36:17	23:43
3RD DOWNS	8–14	3–13

Scoring by Quarter

NOTRE DAME 14 20 0 6–40
PURDUE   0   0 0 7– 7

GAME 5
At Stanford Stadium

	ND	SU
1ST DOWNS	16	21
Rushing	12	3
Passing	3	14
Penalty	1	4
RUSHES	52	16
Yardage	206	42
Yardage lost	12	8
RUSHING YDS.	194	34
PASSING YDS.	102	282
Passes	17	68
Completed	7	39
Intercepted	0	3
TTL. PLAYS	69	84
TTL. YDS.	296	316
Average gain	4.2	3.7
PUNTS-avg.	8–43.7	6–40.6
FUMBLES-lost	0–0	1–1
PENALTIES-yds.	8–75	1–11
POSSESSION	31:37	28:29
3RD DOWNS	4–16	7–20

Scoring by Quarter

NOTRE DAME 0 14 7 6–27
STANFORD   6   0 8 3–17

GAME 6
At Falcon Stadium

	ND	AF
1ST DOWNS	24	21
Rushing	1ö	10
Passing	6	11
Penalty	0	0
RUSHES	58	40
Yardage	335	182
Yardage lost	3	14
RUSHING YDS.	332	168
PASSING YDS.	123	306
Passes	13	24
Completed	9	15
Intercepted	1	1
TTL. PLAYS	71	64
TTL. YDS.	455	474
Average gain	6.0	7.0
PUNTS-avg.	1–66.0	2–38.0
FUMBLES-lost	1–1	5–3
PENALTIES-yds.	4–23	5–35
POSSESSION	35:45	24:15
3RD DOWNS	7–12	6–11

Scoring by Quarter

NOTRE DAME 14 21 3 3–41
AIR FORCE   0 14 0 13–27

GAME 7
At Notre Dame Stadium

	ND	USC
1ST DOWNS	20	6
Rushing	16	7
Passing	4	19
Penalty	0	0
RUSHES	49	35
Yardage	278	129
Yardage lost	12	10
RUSHING YDS.	266	119
PASSING YDS.	91	333
Passes	16	55
Completed	5	33
Intercepted	1	3
TTL. PLAYS	65	90
TTL. YDS.	357	452
Average gain	5.5	5.0
PUNTS-avg.	5–48.8	6–34.6
FUMBLES-lost	4–4	0–0
PENALTIES-yds.	2–10	10–75
POSSESSION	24:48	35:12
3RD DOWNS	5–11	8–18

Scoring by Quarter

NOTRE DAME	7	0	7	14–28
USC	14	3	0	7–24

GAME 8
At Notre Dame Stadium

	ND	PITT
1ST DOWNS	18	18
Rushing	6	6
Passing	0	11
Penalty	2	1
RUSHES	57	39
Yardage	316	149
Yardage lost	6	30
RUSHING YDS.	310	119
PASSING YDS.	29	183
Passes	9	35
Completed	1	18
Intercepted	0	3
TTL. PLAYS	66	74
TTL. YDS.	339	302
Average gain	5.1	4.1
PUNTS-avg.	5–46.0	4–44.0
FUMBLES-lost	1–0	2–1
PENALTIES-yds.	5–50	10–81
POSSESSION	30:16	29:44
3RD DOWNS	5–14	6–15

Scoring by Quarter

NOTRE DAME	2	15	21	7–45
PITTSBURGH	7	0	0	0– 7

GAME 9
At Notre Dame Stadium

	ND	NAVY
1ST DOWNS	27	11
Rushing	22	6
Passing	5	5
Penalty	0	0
RUSHES	60	41
Yardage	424	115
Yardage lost	10	48
RUSHING YDS.	414	67
PASSING YDS.	92	99
Passes	20	16
Completed	9	9
Intercepted	2	2
TTL. PLAYS	80	57
TTL. YDS.	506	166
Average gain	6.3	2.9
PUNTS-avg.	1–49.0	6–34.3
FUMBLES-lost	2–1	3–2
PENALTIES-yds.	4–25	1–5
POSSESSION	31:17	28:43
3RD DOWNS	9–14	5–14

Scoring by Quarter

NOTRE DAME	14	10	3	14–41
NAVY	0	0	0	0– 0

GAME 10
At Notre Dame Stadium

	ND	SMU
1ST DOWNS	27	12
Rusing	17	2
Passing	10	9
Penalty	0	1
RUSHES	54	13
Yardage	362	11
Yardage lost	4	18
RUSHING YDS.	358	–7
PASSING YDS.	214	206
Passes	14	59
Completed	11	30
Intercepted	0	3
TTL. PLAYS	68	72
TTL. YDS.	572	199
Average gain	8.4	2.8
PUNTS-avg.	0–0.0	7–38.2
FUMBLES-lost	7–3	3–0
PENALTIES-yds.	10–70	4–25
POSSESSION	30:16	29:44
3RD DOWNS	4–7	5–18

Scoring by Quarter

NOTRE DAME	7	35	10	7–59
SMU	0	6	0	0– 6

GAME 11
At Beaver Stadium

	ND	PSU
1ST DOWNS	29	22
Rushing	25	14
Passing	4	6
Penalty	0	2
RUSHES	71	47
Yardage	448	256
Yardage lost	13	19
RUSHING YDS.	425	237
PASSING YDS.	47	102
Passes	10	20
Completed	5	10
Intercepted	1	0
TTL. PLAYS	81	67
TTL. YDS.	472	339
Average gain	5.8	5.1
PUNTS-avg.	2–30	4–26.5
FUMBLES-lost	4–1	1–1
PENALTIES-yds.	4–39	3–32
POSSESSION	34:08	25:52
3RD DOWNS	9–12	8–13

Scoring by Quarter

NOTRE DAME 7 14 7 6–34
PENN STATE 7 3 7 6–23

GAME 12
At The Orange Bowl

	ND	MIAMI
1ST DOWNS	15	15
Rushing	10	7
Passing	5	8
Penalty	0	0
RUSHES	45	39
Yardage	178	157
Yardage lost	36	62
RUSHING YDS.	142	95
PASSING YDS.	106	210
Passes	16	26
Completed	7	16
Intercepted	2	1
TTL. PLAYS	61	65
TTL. YDS.	248	305
Average gain	4.1	4.7
PUNTS-avg.	3–37.3	4–42
FUMBLES-lost	2–0	2–0
PENALTIES-yds.	3–25	2–20
POSSESSION	29:52	30:08
3RD DOWNS	2–10	11–17

Scoring by Quarter

NOTRE DAME 0 10 0 0–10
MIAMI 10 7 7 3–27

GAME 13
At The Orange Bowl

	ND	UC
1ST DOWNS	18	16
Rushing	14	12
Passing	4	4
Penalty	0	0
RUSHES	52	46
Yardage	295	239
Yardage lost	16	22
RUSHING YDS.	279	217
PASSING YDS.	99	65
Passes	9	13
Completed	5	4
Intercepted	0	2
TTL. PLAYS	71	50
TTL. YDS.	378	282
PUNTS-avg.	5–40.1	3–39.3
FUMBLES-lost	0–0	1–1
PENALTIES-yds.	3–35	1–5
POSSESSION	32:43	27:17
3RD DOWNS	7–12	5–13

Scoring by Quarter

NOTRE DAME 0 0 14 7–21
COLORADO 0 0 6 0– 6

Final Statistics
(Regular Season)

TEAM STATISTICS

	ND	OPP
Total offensive yards	4818	3550
Total plays	845	828
Yards per play	5.7	4.3
Yards per game	401.5	295.8
Rushing yards	3452	1267
Attempts	673	416
Yards per rush	5.1	3.0
Yards per game	287.7	105.6
Passing yards	1366	2283
Attempts	172	412
Completions	87	232
Had intercepted	10	24
Comp. percentage	.502	.563
Touchdown passes	2	18
Yards per attempt	7.9	5.5
Yards per completion	15.7	9.8
Yards per game	113.8	190.3
Punting yards	1548	2351
Number of punts	38	62
Average punt	40.7	37.9
Had blocked	0	3
Punt return yards	317	88
Number of returns	25	12
Average return	12.7	7.3

TEAM STATISTICS (continued)

	ND	OPP
Kickoff return yards	634	1075
Number of returns	30	56
Average return	21.1	19.2
Interception return yards	324	94
Number of interceptions	24	10
Average return	12.7	7.3
Number of penalties	58	54
Penalty yards	483	417
Fumbles (lost)	28	30
Total first downs	257	206
By rushing	193	80
By passing	59	111
By penalty	3	15
Third down conversions	71–151	76–185
Percentage	.470	.411
Possession time	378:06	341:54
Minutes per game	31:36	28:24
Team scoring	406	183
By rushing	42	5
By passing	2	18
By returns	7	0
By recovery	0	0
Field goals (made-att.)	15–23	9–10
Safeties	2	0
PAT-kick	47–49	16–18
PAT-run	1–2	0–2
PAT-pass	0–0	1–3

RUSHING

	TC	Yds	Avg	TD	Lg
T. Rice	174	884	5.1	7	38
R. Watters	118	791	6.7	10	53
A. Johnson	131	515	3.9	11	35
R. Ismail	64	478	7.5	2	50
R. Culver	59	242	4.1	5	15
D. Levens	25	132	5.3	1	30
S. Belles	15	83	5.5	1	13
W. Boyd	9	64	7.1	1	22
R. Setzer	17	59	3.5	1	22
T. Brooks	13	43	3.3	0	11
R. Mihalko	12	44	3.7	0	7

RUSHING (continued)

	TC	Yds	Avg	TD	Lg
R. Mirer	12	32	2.7	0	11
Team					
ND	673	3452	5.1	42	53
OPP	416	1267	3.0	5	36

PASSING

	Att	Com	Pct	Int	Yds	TD
T. Rice	137	68	.496	9	1122	2
R. Mirer	30	15	.500	0	180	0
P. Graham	5	4	.800	0	64	0
ND	172	87	50.6	10	1366	2
OPP	412	232	56.3	24	2283	18

SCORING

	TD	PAT	R-ps	S	Fg	Tp
A. Johnson	13	0–0	11–2	0	0–0	78
C. Hentrich	0	44–45	0–0	0	8–15	68
R. Watters	11	0–0	10–0	1	0–0	66
T. Rice	7	1–2	7–0	0	0–0	44
R. Ismail	5	0–0	2–0	3	0–0	30
R. Culver	5	0–0	5–0	0	0–0	30
B. Hackett	0	3–4	0–0	0	7–7	24
N. Bolcar	1	0–0	0–0	1	0–0	6
P. Graham	1	0–0	1–0	0	0–0	6
W. Boyd	1	0–0	1–0	0	0–0	6
R. Setzer	1	0–0	1–0	0	0–0	6
R. West	1	0–0	1–0	0	0–0	6
J. Alm	1	0–0	1–0	1	0–0	6
S. Belles	1	0–0	1–0	0	0–0	6
D. Levens	1	0–0	1–0	0	0–0	6
D. McNamara	1	0–0	1–0	0	0–0	6
ND	51	48–51	1–r	3	15–23	406
OPP	23	17–23	0	0	9–10	183

SCORING BY QUARTERS

ND	91	167	68	80–406
OPP	44	45	29	65–183

RECEIVING

	PC	Yds	Avg	TD	Lg
R. Ismail	27	535	19.8	0	52
D. Brown	13	204	15.7	0	38
R. Watters	13	197	15.1	0	32
A. Johnson	8	85	10.6	2	27
P. Eilers	5	53	10.6	0	20
W. Pollard	4	117	29.3	0	42
A. Jarrell	4	37	9.3	0	16
S. Belles	3	29	9.7	0	17
D. Levens	3	27	9.0	0	12
R. Mihalko	3	44	14.7	0	33
T. Smith	2	26	12.0	0	18
I. Smith	1	6	6.0	0	6
R. Griggs	1	7	7.0	0	7
ND	87	1366	15.7	2	52
OPP	232	2283	9.8	18	61

PUNTING

	No.	Yds	Avg	Lg
C. Hentrich	26	1159	44.6	66
J. Sexton	12	389	32.4	44
ND	38	1548	40.7	66
OPP	62	2351	37.9	56

PUNT RETURNS

	No.	Yds	Avg	TD	Lg
R. Watters	15	201	13.4	1	97
R. Ismail	7	113	16.1	1	56
P. Eilers	1	3	3.0	0	3
S. Belles	1	0	0.0	0	0
R. Mihalko	1	0	0.0	0	0
ND	25	317	12.7	2	97
OPP	12	88	7.3	0	20

KICKOFF RETURNS

	No.	Yds	Avg	TD	Lg
R. Ismail	20	502	25.1	2	97
D. Francisco	2	57	28.5	0	39
A. Johnson	3	42	14.0	0	27
R. Culver	3	28	9.3	0	11

KICKOFF RETURNS (continued)

	No.	Yds	Avg	TD	Lg
R. Mihalko	1	3	3.0	0	3
S. Belles	1	2	2.0	0	2
ND	30	634	21.1	2	92
OPP	56	1075	19.2	0	42

INTERCEPTIONS

	No.	Yds	Avg	TD	Lg
T. Lyght	8	42	5.3	0	28
P. Terrell	5	96	19.2	1	54
D. Francisco	4	107	26.8	0	46
D. Grimm	2	9	4.5	0	9
N. Bolcar	1	49	49.0	1	49
J. Alm	1	16	16.0	1	16
B. Flannery	1	3	3.0	0	3
D. DiOrio	1	2	2.0	0	2
S. Davis	1	0	0	0	0
ND	24	324	13.5	3	54
OPP	10	94	9.4	0	42

DEFENSE
Tackles

	No.	Fc	Fr
N. Bolcar	109	1	0
D. Grimm	93	0	0
C. Zorich	92	1	2
J. Alm	74	1	0
D. Francisco	66	0	0
B. Dahl	52	0	0
A. Jones	49	1	0
S. Kowalkowski	47	0	2
T. Lyght	47	0	0
S. Smagala	45	0	1
P. Terrell	44	0	1
D. McDonald	34	0	1
T. Ridgley	24	0	3
B. Flannery	23	0	0
G. Davis	23	1	1
R. Smith	14	0	0
S. Smith	13	0	0
E. Simiens	9	0	1

DEFENSE (continued)

	No.	Fc	Fr
M. Smalls	8	0	0
N. Smith	8	0	0
G. Poorman	7	0	0
J. Bryant	7	0	0
D. DuBose	7	0	0
E. Jones	7	0	0
S. Davis	3	0	0
K. McShane	3	0	0
B. Ratigan	3	0	1
M. Crounse	2	0	0
M. deManigold	1	0	0
M. Callan	1	0	0
G. Marshall	1	0	0
J. Bodine	1	0	0
K. McGill	1	0	0
D. DiOrio	1	0	0

PASSES BROKEN UP
Terrell 9, Lyght 6½, Alm 6, Smagala 6, Francisco 5½, Bolcar 3, Grimm 3, Zorich 2, Dahl 2, Kowalkowski 1, McDonald 1, Ridgley 1, Davis 2, R. Smith 1, Poorman 2, E. Jones 3, Ratigan 2.

QUARTERBACK SACKS
McDonald 4–15, Dahl 3½–10, Zorich 3–27, Kowalkowski 3–12, Jones 5–22, Bolcar 2–21, Alm 1–4, Kowalkowski 13–12, McDonald 4–15, Ridgley 1–1, Flannery ½–3, E. Jones 1–23, McShane 1–7.

TACKLES FOR LOSSES
Kowalkowski 6–22, Alm 6–20, Bolcar 6–19, A. Jones 5–22, Zorich 5–12, Dahl 3–9, Grimm 1–8, Lyght 1–1, McDonald 1–5, Ridgley 1–2.

Final 1989 Rankings

Notre Dame Football
Honors and Awards/1989

TONY RICE—senior quarterback
—*Football News* '89 College Player of the Year;
—'89 Heisman Trophy finalist (finished fourth);
Football News All-American (first team);
Gannett News Service All-American (third team);
—United Press International and *The Sporting News* All-American (honorable mention);
—Domino's Pizza "Coaches' Choice" College Football Player of the Year Award Nominee;
—Johnny Unitas Golden Arm Award;
—Notre Dame National Monogram Team MVP;
—MVP in Kickoff Classic;
—ABC Sports/Chevrolet MVP vs. USC;
—Invited to play in Hula Bowl and East-West Shrine All-Star games.

RAGHIB ISMAIL—sophomore flanker
—Associated Press, *The Sporting News*, *Football News*, Writers Association of America (as kick returner), Newspaper Enterprise Association and Gannett News Service All-American (all first team);
—United Press International All-American (second team);
—ABC Sports/Chevrolet MVP, *Sports Illustrated* Special Team Player of the Week, Associated Press Midwest Offensive Player of the Week and *The Sporting News* Offensive Player of the Week vs. Michigan;
—ESPN/VISA Player of the Game vs. Air Force;
—ESPN/VISA Player of the Game vs. Pittsburgh.
CHRIS ZORICH—junior defensive tackle
—Touchdown Club of Washing-

ton, D.C., College Lineman of the Year;

— Associated Press, United Press International, *The Sporting News*, Walter Camp Foundation, Football Writers Association of America and Gannett News Service All-American (all first team);

— Newspaper Enterprise Association All-American (second team);

— Lombardi Award Finalist.

TODD LYGHT — junior cornerback

— Associated Press, United Press Internatoinal, *The Sporting News*, *Football News*, Walter Camp Foundation, American Football Coaches Association (Kodak), Newspaper Enterprise Association and Football Writers Association of America All-American (all first team);

— Gannett News All-American (second team);

— Jim Thorpe Award Finalist.

NED BOLCAR — senior linebacker

— United Press International and *The Sporting News* All-American (second team);

— *Football News* All-American (honorable mention);

— Associated Press Midwest Defensive Player of the Week vs. Michigan;

— CBS Sports/Chevrolet MVP and *The Sporting News* Defensive Player of Week vs. Miami;

— Invited to play in Japan Bowl and East-West Shrine all-star games.

RICKY WATTERS — junior tailback

— *Football News* and *The*

Sporting News All-American (honorable mention);

— CBS Sports/Chevrolet MVP vs. Michigan State.

JEFF ALM — senior defensive tackle

— Associated Press, *Football News* and Gannett News Service All-American (all second team);

— Notre Dame Lineman of the Year, Moose Krause Chapter of National Football Foundation and Hall of Fame.

PAT TERRELL — senior free safety

— Gannett News Service All-American (first team);

— *The Sporting News* All-American (honorable mention);

— Invited to play in East-West Shrine All-Star game.

DEREK BROWN — sophomore tight end

— Gannett News Service All-American (second team);

— United Press International and *Football News* All-American (honorable mention).

TIM GRUNHARD — senior offensive guard

— Newspaper Enterprise Association All-American (second team);

— United Press International, *The Sporting News* and *Football News* All-American (honorable mention);

— Invited to play in Hula Bowl.

MIKE HELDT — junior center

— *The Sporting News* and *Football News* All-American (honorable mention).

STAN SMAGALA — senior cornerback

— United Press International

and *Football News* All-American (honorable mention).

DEAN BROWN—senior defensive tackle

—*The Sporting News* All-American (honorable mention);

—Invited to play in Hula Bowl.

D'JUAN FRANCISCO—senior strong safety

—Invited to play in Hula Bowl.

ANTHONY JOHNSON—senior fullback

—*The Sporting News* All-American (honorable mention);

—Nick Pietrosante Award (by vote of squad to player who best exemplifies the courage, teamwork, loyalty, dedication and pride of the late All-American Irish Fullback);

—Invited to play in Hula Bowl.

DONN GRIMM—junior linebacker

—*The Sporting News* All-American (honorable mention).

TIM RYAN—junior offensive guard

—*The Sporting News* All-American (honorable mention).

SCOTT KOWALKOWSKI—junior defensive end

—*The Sporting News* All-American (honorable mention).

PAT EILERS—senior split end

—Notre Dame Club of St. Joseph Valley Student Athlete Award;

—State Farm Student Athlete of the Year Award;

—Maxwell House Spirit of Notre Dame Award.

CHRIS SHEY—senior linebacker

—Hesburgh/Joyce Hall of Fame Scholarship Award (post-graduate grant for walk-on who has contributed significantly to the football program).

DOUG DiORIO—senior safety

—Hesburgh/Joyce Hall of Fame Scholarship Award.

Afterword

I was glad to read Bill Bilinski's account of this past season because it records so well what this team achieved. I feel very close to the players who are graduating this year. In our first year together, we won five and lost six. In our next two years, we won 24 and suffered only one loss. In those three seasons, we had our share of adversity, but also a lot of very good times. In spite of obstacles, the 1989 team came close to achieving the impossible.

I had a tendency from time to time last year to think that we were judged unfairly, but as I reflect on it, this isn't really true. The fact is that people hold us to a very high standard and we should consider that a compliment.

As I look ahead to the 1990 season and beyond, it is clear that we are counting on a number of our returning players to emerge as leaders on the team. In addition, any time you have coaching changes, it is difficult for the players as well as the new coaches. The fact that four of our coaches accepted head coaching positions could have been a problem. But I am very pleased with how well our four new coaches have blended in and how quickly our players responded to them in spring practice.

That is all the more important because the 1990 schedule is the most difficult one I have ever seen. Faced with such quality opposition, all we want to do is to have a commitment to perfection and to be the very best that we possibly can. We want to make sure that our football team reflects the same qualities that typify this university. People come to Notre Dame not to learn how to do something, but how to be somebody.

I have been asked why I wink when I talk about our incoming freshman class. Maybe I just have something in my eye. It is a good recruiting class, but you can never really evaluate a class until after they arrive on campus. This looks like a very talented group and I hope it is also one that will blend well with our returning players.

We always set individual goals and team goals every year and they are basically pretty much the same from one year to the next. But every season brings with it new experiences, new thrills, as well as new disappointments. How successful we will be depends on how well we handle the adversity that is bound to challenge us. And, of course, let's hope that the luck of the Irish keeps smiling on us.

My advice for our players and fans for the 1990s is really quite simple: be appreciative of what you have and always look for the good things. We have many wonderful things to be grateful for and these far surpass the attitude that asks, "what if this had happened or that had happened?"

It would be a great mistake for anyone to think that we are going to go the whole decade without losing a game or having a single problem. But if we all keep a positive attitude, I think we'll enjoy the successes that our team will experience and, when the lows do come about, continuing that positive attitude will only strengthen our resolve to continue the struggle to the top.

The 1990s will be very, very exciting for Notre Dame and our fans.

Lou Holtz
May 3, 1990

About the Author

Born in 1957, Bill Bilinski was raised in South Bend, Indiana, home of Notre Dame football. He attended St. Joseph High School and majored in English at Indiana's Hanover College. He was active in baseball and football at both schools.

After graduation, Bilinski worked on the sports staff of several Indiana newspapers. Bilinski joined the *South Bend Tribune* in 1983 and is currently that newspaper's assistant sports editor. Except for his wedding day in 1987, Bilinski has covered ND football continuously since 1985. Noting the Irish's 24–0 loss to Miami that day, Bilinski quipped, "I picked a good day to skip a game."

Bilinski has written for *USA Today*, *The Sporting News*, including chapters for its book, *College Football's Twenty-Five Greatest Teams*, as well as articles for the Cotton and Fiesta Bowl programs. *Champions* is his first book.

Bilinski resides in his hometown of South Bend with his wife Jolene and son Nathan.